Teaching the Literature Survey Course

TEACHING AND LEARNING IN HIGHER EDUCATION

James M. Lang, Series Editor

The Spark of Learning: Energizing the College Classroom with the Science of Emotion

Sarah Rose Cavanagh

Teaching the Literature Survey Course

New Strategies for College Faculty

Gwynn Dujardin, James M. Lang, and John A. Staunton

West Virginia University Press
Morgantown 2018

Copyright 2018 West Virginia University Press
All rights reserved
First edition published 2018 by West Virginia University Press
Printed in the United States of America

ISBN:
CL: 978-1-946684-08-0
PB: 978-1-946684-09-7
EPUB: 978-1-946684-10-3
PDF: 978-1-946684-11-0

Library of Congress Cataloging-in-Publication Data is available from the Library of Congress

Cover design by Than Saffel / WVU Press.
Cover image: Bacon, G. W., *Bacon's New Shilling Map of London and Illustrated Guide. With a Large Scale Plan of the City, A Railway Map of the Environs. Street Directory, Cab Fares, & c.*, 1890. This work is in the public domain. Digital image courtesy of Wikimedia Commons.

CONTENTS

INTRODUCTION

The Promises and Perils of the Survey

JAMES M. LANG

When I was an undergraduate in the late 1980s and early 1990s, I took the three literature survey courses that were required of all English majors at my university, and that remain a staple feature of English majors today: two surveys of British literature, divided somewhere between the Restoration and Romantic periods, and one survey of American literature. All proceeded as usual throughout the American and early British surveys, but early in the semester some tragedy befell the professor of the second half of the British literature survey, and the university had to scramble to find a replacement for him to allow the course to continue. The faculty member who took over the course was a political scientist. As an undergraduate, I had no glimpse into whatever internal processes led to this outcome, which now strikes me as exceedingly strange, especially given that this was a moderate-sized research university, which likely had plenty of graduate students and adjuncts on the English Department roster already. Reflecting upon it now, it strikes me as equally strange that this visitor from another department didn't seem to make much difference in the progress or nature of the course. It continued as usual, with the students reading the canonical works of the major authors from our doorstopper anthologies and the professor lecturing to us about the highlights of those works and their historical contexts. I do remember some quirky moments in the class, such as the time when he theatrically mocked Percy Bysshe Shelley for falling on the thorns of life and bleeding, but otherwise I am not sure I could have articulated any real differences between the course as taught by this political scientist and the other surveys I had taken.

This experience seems to me now, in retrospect, as emblematic of the two major pedagogical challenges that literature survey courses pose to us. First, survey courses by their very nature focus on skimming the surface of a large

1

range of course material, which means that you don't need specialized expertise in a particular area to teach them; they lend themselves well to teaching by
generalists—or, in the case of my late-British survey, disciplinary interlopers.
Of course surveys skim surfaces with good intentions, especially if they are
taken at the outset of an English major: they are designed to provide historical
and literary context which will help inform the upper-level courses that students take as they progress into their majors. Against this admirable intention,
however, we must now place the growing body of research in learning which
contrasts *surface* and *deep* learning, and which suggests that surface learning
correlates with short-term and shallow learning. Surface learning occurs when
students focus on memorizing key facts and principles without gaining a more
comprehensive understanding; faculty reinforce surface learning when they
create assessments that reward this approach, such as exams which require
identification of authors or works or events but little analysis, or essays which
require students to parrot back traditional readings in the standard essay format. Deep learning occurs when students see or create connections between
the course material and their own lives and experiences, when they have the
opportunity to take what they are learning and process it in challenging and
creative ways, and when they take active control of their learning and the ways
in which they demonstrate it to their professor.[1] The nature of a survey course,
often taught to large numbers of students in traditional lecture format, does
not encourage these kinds of deep approaches to learning. As a result, I have
always been skeptical of the survey's admirable intentions: a survey course that
spends a few weeks hitting the highlights of Romantic poetry, reading the classic works in the field and then asking students to process them in an essay or
midterm exam, gives students a superficial exposure that seems unlikely to remain with them two years after the conclusion of the course when they are
picking up the material again in an upper-level course.

The second major pedagogical challenge of the survey stems from the fact
that its broad scope of material, covering massive amounts of literary and historical territory, tends to dictate a single pedagogy: the traditional lecture. Because no faculty member earns a PhD in the entirety of American literature, or
in British literature from 1800 to the present, survey teachers are almost always
teaching for much of the semester outside of their traditional areas of expertise—my political science professor, teaching a literature survey course, represented an extreme version of a very common experience for survey teachers.
My experience observing new faculty members, in my role as the director of a
teaching center on my campus, has taught me that when faculty members feel
inexperienced or uneasy with the material, they turn to the lecture, which en-

2

sures that students won't have the opportunity to ask questions or make objections that will reveal the lecturer's lack of expertise. As long as the professor keeps talking, she remains an expert; when a hand goes up, the facade may fall.[2] At the other end of the spectrum, because we place such weight on the survey in terms of its role in the English major, some faculty seem to feel an extra obligation to ensure that the survey covers as much material as possible, and that impulse to "cover" lots of material translates into densely packed lectures stacked upon one another throughout the semester. These faculty members feel that they do students a disservice if they deviate much from the lecture—that giving students the opportunity to discuss it or engage in other forms of active learning detracts from time spent on the essentials. When you have only one day to cover a figure as important and seminal as William Wordsworth, you have to pack in as much poetry and history as possible—how to justify ceding precious class time to students' fumbling interpretations of his greatest poems?

Much has been written in recent years on the problems with lecture as a learning tool, and I won't repeat those arguments here. To some extent I think those arguments have been made too strongly, especially by those who wish to chuck the lecture from the pedagogical toolkit entirely. Deployed for specific purposes, the lecture can promote learning, especially if it can inspire and intrigue students to go further in their learning. Students can also engage in active learning during a lecture, even more so than in other types of classroom activities, as Elizabeth Barkley points out: "Highly skilled listeners who are involved in a lecture by self-questioning, analyzing, and incorporating new information into their existing knowledge are learning more actively than students who are participating in a small group discussion that is off-task, redundant, or superfluous."[3] I wonder how many of us, however, would characterize our students as "highly skilled listeners," and would imagine that this kind of active mental activity occurs in our students throughout a seventy-five-minute lecture. I certainly would not expect it of my students. What we normally think about as active learning strategies—which might comprise everything from discussions to small group work to writing in class or reciting aloud or staging scenes from a play—typically offer more structured opportunities for mental engagement than lectures, even if (as Barkley points out) they can fail us at times as well. At the very least, the evidence strikes me as pretty unassailable that we should vary our teaching methods in almost any classroom context, which means that lecturing should be interspersed with opportunities for students to *do* something, in whatever form that doing might take. The challenge for the survey teacher remains finding the confidence and the class time to allow space for such doing, given everything we expect of these courses.

This volume represents an effort to respond to the dual pedagogical challenges of the literature survey—its tendencies toward surface-level learning and lecture-based teaching—with concrete suggestions from survey teachers who have tried different approaches to the course. The first seeds of the volume were planted during a special session at the 2013 Modern Language Association conference, chaired by two of the editors of this volume, which was advertised in that year's program as "New Approaches to Teaching the Literature Surveys." The Association clearly expected us to draw a modest audience for this teaching-focused panel, and accordingly placed us in a modest-sized room. Much to our surprise, by the time the panel was ready to kick off that afternoon, more than two hundred people were packed into that room, many of them standing in the back and around the edges. It seemed to us afterward that our experience of feeling that something about the survey was not quite working was a shared one, and that many of our colleagues wanted to do something different in their survey courses, but weren't quite sure what that might look like. Later that year we ran another version of the panel at the annual convention of the National Council of Teachers of English to an equally large and interested audience, and began wondering at that point how to open our conversations about survey pedagogy to the discipline as a whole.

The contribution of this volume to that conversation thus emerges from our specific disciplinary questions about the survey, but also appears alongside a growing body of scholarship in the field of teaching and learning in higher education. Recent decades have seen an extraordinary blossoming of new work that documents research on classroom learning, presents new strategies for effective teaching, and invites the profession as a whole to consider new approaches to the enterprise of teaching in higher education. In some cases this research explores wholesale new approaches to course design or classroom practice, such as community service learning or Reacting to the Past (about which you learn more in Chapter 5). In other cases the focus falls on smaller, everyday decisions about how to have more of an impact in the opening or closing minutes of class, how to design an effective multiple-choice exam, or how to help students learn from feedback on papers. The scholarship in this burgeoning field often seeks to uncover general principles of teaching and learning that would affect courses in any discipline, but an equally rich tradition of scholarship in teaching and learning takes the approach we have followed here, and focuses the conversation on teaching within a particular discipline.

We have organized the essays in this volume into three parts, based roughly on the scope of their ambitions in rethinking the literature surveys. Part One, "Pedagogies," presents four approaches to the survey that require reworking it from a design perspective. We begin with Kevin Bourque's essay on taking a spatial approach to the early British survey. Bourque's students consider the texts in the course from a geographical perspective, mapping out the locations of various stories and characters as the semester progresses. This "mapping approach," argues Bourque, "offers the unique opportunity to re-envision the canon as a spatial network, in which texts connect to each other, to present-day locations and to contemporary lived experience." Scott Newstok provides his students with a very different doorway into the canon by orienting his British literature survey courses around the notions of creativity and imitation; his students must take a favorite text and rewrite it in different literary styles throughout the semester. That project imports a clear thematic focus to the survey, one that highlights imitation and achievement as primary drivers of literary history. Desirée Henderson's essay shifts us in two different directions: to the American literature survey, and to the use of team-based learning. Henderson argues that this intriguing approach, widely used in other types of courses in higher education, can help survey teachers "set aside the unreachable goal of comprehensive coverage in favor of other attainable and equally valuable goals including the development of problem-solving skills, the cultivation of interpersonal relationships, and the promotion of the joyful and playful aspects of learning." A spirit of playfulness (and experimentation) marks Aaron Rosenfeld's essay as well, which presents his strategy of orienting the survey around a single, core text. Although this organizing principle has a clear pedagogical function—it helps students "understand the relational nature of literary works"—it ultimately leads Rosenfeld to a reconsideration of the purpose of the survey course, and the role it can play in the lives of students. All four of the essays in Part One are linked by a desire to shift the goal of the survey away from coverage and toward other, deeper objectives.

The scope of the essays in Part Two narrows down somewhat, in that each of them focuses on an assignment or project from a survey course. In all cases, though, that specific project has deep implications for the course as a whole—so it may be more accurate to say that the essays in Part Two, instead of approaching survey innovation from a higher-level design perspective, achieve innovation from the ground up. Joan Varnum Ferretti's essay describes her use of a fast-growing pedagogical technique in higher education, Reacting to the Past, a game-based project in which students take on the roles of historical actors confronting challenges from the past. Instructors who use Reacting to the Past report record levels of engagement from students, which makes it well worth considering for the all-too-often passive pedagogies of survey courses. Chris Walsh solicits that engagement from his students by giving them a voice in the construction of the survey with his use of the "blank syllabus"—or more properly, a syllabus which contains blank spaces that students must fill with the poems they would like to see included in the course. The first assignment of the semester requires students to write in support of their choices, so again we see here how a particular assignment has led to a fascinating new way to encourage student engagement in the course as a whole. Melissa Jones describes how she created new levels of engagement in her course by taking seriously her students' (often hilarious) misreading of canonical texts. Reflecting upon the consequences of their misreadings led her to develop a series of unconventional writing assignments for her students that include talking back to famous literary characters or rewriting survey texts in modern diction. In the final essay of Part Two, Jennifer Page showcases the digital projects of her students, another assignment that helps students create new connections between the canonical texts of the survey and elements outside the course: other works of art, historical contexts, literary places, and artifacts. These multimedia galleries, like all of the creative assignments in this section, move her early British literature surveys well beyond the scope of that one assignment and into new territories of survey design and assessment.

In Part Three, four final essays take up the larger institutional contexts and constraints within which the literature surveys operate. While we can all make shifts to our survey courses in terms of particular pedagogies and projects, truly large-scale changes to the survey run up against constraints dictated by the role that the survey course plays in our departments. Kristin Lucas and Fiona Winters begin their essay by noting the almost impossible burden we put on the survey to accomplish multiple goals. The typical survey course, they explain, "serves as an introduction to the different literary periods, helping to clarify for students their characteristic forms and features; it simultaneously acts as a gateway to the discipline, a tool-box course that helps students to develop the vocabulary, critical acumen, and writing skills that are foundational to English programs." Lucas and Winters sought to clarify the purpose of the survey by shifting its organizing principles from historic to thematic, and their essay describes the various institutional and departmental considerations that played into that revision process. Coeditor Gwynn Dujardin developed her survey pedagogy in response to a department initiative to increase the coverage and number of students in the historical survey course and shift it from an introductory course for all first-year students to a required survey for second-year majors and minors. Students approached this intimidating new course—large in conceptual scope and bodies in the room—with fears and apprehensions that Dujardin learned to leverage for their benefit. Her essay explores the positive role that the anxieties of her students can play in stimulating new learning. Tim Rosendale's essay considers how constraints become opportunities in the wake of his decision to cram the multi-course British-literature survey content into a single semester. The most fascinating result of that decision was that the survey course became a powerful and effective training ground for the graduate students in the department, who became active participants in the challenging process of determining what earns a coveted spot on the survey syllabus and, more generally, how to help students learn in survey courses. The final essay in the volume, provided by coeditor John Staunton, begins with his explanation of "transmediations," a specific pedagogical strategy that he has used with his survey students and with future survey teachers. It concludes in a more reflective place, considering how the process of creating transmediations—in which students and teachers combine image, text, and music in creative new forms—may lead us to think in new directions about the survey. These final four essays can help all of us see pathways toward new roles that the survey might play in the education of our majors and in the ongoing development of the English major within higher education.

All of the essays in the volume have been supplemented with one or more course documents that we asked the authors to provide, and which you will find at the end of each essay. These take different forms: many of our authors contributed the syllabi for their survey courses, while others chose to include assignment sheets or descriptions from the projects they assigned to their students. If you are like the three editors of this volume, you are always curious to see what other people are doing in their survey courses, and we thought this final section of course documents would give you a handy place to view some other ways in which survey teachers frame their courses and describe them for their students. Although teaching is in some ways a highly social activity, in that we are always in the room with lots of other human beings, it can also seem like a very lonely activity, in that none of those other human beings in the room are our fellow teachers. We also tend to limit our conversations about teaching to quick hallway or social media exchanges, and hence don't have the time to settle in and consider how another teacher might approach the same course that we are teaching, and re-see our own courses in the light of these other possibilities. You will find among the documents possibilities from every one of the major literature surveys. We hope that, in addition to ideas that might emerge from your reading of the essays, others might arise from your perusal of the course documents.

That hopeful sentiment brings us to the ultimate goal of these essays: to provide teachers of literature surveys with new ideas that will help them create significant learning experiences for their students. You can feel confident in the educational grounding of those ideas; the essays that we selected for inclusion in this volume all present approaches that reflect well what we know about how students learn. The pathways they offer to innovation in survey courses are well-grounded in research on teaching and learning in higher education. But new approaches to the survey have the potential to benefit not just the students. A few consecutive years of teaching the survey can lead all of us into well-traveled ruts that grind away at our own passion for the literatures and histories we offer to our students. Faculty need fresh injections of energy and inspiration as much as students, and nothing livens up a teaching career like launching a major new pedagogical strategy or reconceptualizing a course around a major new project. We hope you will find essays or documents in here that provide a blueprint for exploring new territories of survey pedagogy, beginning next semester and in the years to come.

NOTES

1. Ken Bain provides an overview of deep vs. surface learning in *What the Best College Students Do*. Ken Bain, *What the Best College Students Do* (Cambridge: Harvard University Press, 2012), 34–39.

2. See Therese Huston's *Teaching What You Don't Know* for an excellent analysis of this special challenge, and suggestions for how faculty can teach effectively outside of their specialties. Therese Huston, *Teaching What You Don't Know* (Cambridge: Harvard University Press, 2012).

3. Elizabeth Barkley, *Student Engagement Techniques: A Handbook for College Faculty* (San Francisco: Jossey-Bass, 2010), 17.

BIBLIOGRAPHY

Bain, Ken. *What the Best College Students Do*. Cambridge: Harvard University Press, 2012.

Barkley, Elizabeth. *Student Engagement Techniques: A Handbook for College Faculty*. San Francisco: Jossey-Bass, 2010.

Huston, Therese. *Teaching What You Don't Know*. Cambridge: Harvard University Press, 2012.

_____

PART ONE

Pedagogies

Mapping the Literature Survey

Locating London in British Literature I

KEVIN BOURQUE, ELON UNIVERSITY[1]

Geoffrey Chaucer's *Canterbury Tales* begins in London, and so do we. In the first meeting of British Literature I, a single location is marked on our course map: the present-day site of the Tabard Inn, where Chaucer's pilgrims prepare to wend "to Canterbury with ful devout corage."[2] Click and drag to Google Street View, and we stand where Chaucer stood; indeed, swivel about ninety degrees to the right, and we can read the modern-day plaque that commemorates the site. The map expands as we move through the *Tales*: an additional location for the "Miller's Tale," close enough to the Inn that the speaker is still drunk on "the ale of Southwark,"[3] and another for the Manciple, who tells his story in the village of Harbledown, just a half-hour walk from Canterbury Cathedral. *Piers Plowman* finds us swarming over London Bridge to the Tower of London, taken by the Peasant's Revolt in 1381. We pick up again at that same Tower two centuries later, and trace Elizabeth I's coronation procession to Westminster Abbey, passing by Falstaff's Eastcheap tavern in *Henry IV, Part 1*, Thorowgood's place of business in *The London Merchant*, and St. Margaret's Church, the site of Olaudah Equiano's baptism in *The Interesting Narrative*. For the semester we spend mapping the changing shape of British literature, we also map the contours of England's capital (see Figure 1)—connecting key sites in the texts not only to each other, but also to the present-day contours of a living, breathing city.

This chapter positions geographic space as the unifying element for a literature survey, and argues that mapping meets the traditional needs of such a course, even as it prompts us to reimagine the survey in fresh ways. Cartography helps communicate course content: historical maps, readily available through digital databases, can elucidate the broad historical arc of a national

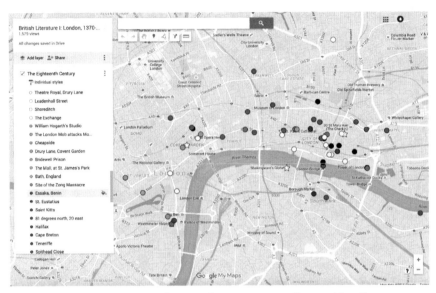

Figure 1. Google course map for *British Literature I*, Fall 2016 (detail).

literature, while mapping the movements of characters generates new ways for students to connect to individual texts. Even more powerfully, a mapping approach offers the unique opportunity to re-envision the canon as a spatial network, in which texts connect to each other, to present-day locations, and to contemporary lived experience. Rather than island-hopping from luminary to luminary, or masterwork to masterwork, students revisit the same location again and again, continually painting new layers of meaning on their existing knowledge—just as our course map, from that single location at our first meeting, progressively accrues more locations through the term. Mapping the literature survey—in our case, locating London in British Literature I—emphasizes continuity and change over time, a time that extends through centuries of literary history to the present-day classroom.

Mapping Literary Space

Though the pedagogical possibilities of literary space remain underexplored, a burgeoning body of work applies mapping to literary criticism. Franco Moretti articulates the radical potential of literary mapping in *Atlas of the European Novel, 1800–1900*, a bellwether of the so-termed "spatial turn." Moretti construes geography as neither "an inert container" nor "a box where cultural history 'happens,'" but as "an active force, that pervades the literary field and shapes it in depth. Making the connection between geography and literature explicit, then—mapping it: because a map is precisely that, a connection made visible—will allow us to see some significant relationships that have so far escaped us."[4] Digital platforms offer new ways to make these connections visible, and recent years have seen the launch of multiple online projects intended to uncover the "significant relationships" Moretti's phrasing promises.[5] A wealth of material now available online, including archives and databases of historical maps, Google Maps and Street View, and sites devoted to recreating physical space through history, make it newly possible to adapt Moretti's critical apparatus for the survey classroom.

British Literature I centers on London, due both to that city's significance in British literature, and because a wealth of online resources recreate the British capital at distinct moments in its history. For Daniel Defoe, London took pride of place as the "great center of England,"[6] and culturally speaking, London's thrum and bustle have been at the center of the English experience for millennia. That centrality extends to the written word. The literature of London, writes Peter Ackroyd, "also represents the literature of England; few novelists, poets or dramatists have not been touched or moved by London."[7] City life, then, offers a transhistorical approach, suitable for a broad survey— potentially spanning from Londinium's founding by the Romans, c. 43 AD, to the present day.[8] Course lectures, interactive activities, and assignments draw on the many digital archives devoted to London's history. The British Library's fantastic online exhibition *London: A Life in Maps* charts the changing shape of London "by looking at maps of it through the ages,"[9] supplementing a broad historical approach with the Library's considerable collections—from a sketch of Caesar's camp at what would later be St. Pancras, through early modern and Enlightenment panorama of the city, to maps from the Industrial Revolution and Victorian London. Many such maps can be overlaid on the modern-day capital, using the British Library's online georeferencer tool. Other resources recreate the city during specific epochs: *The Map of Early Modern London* adapts the *Civitas Londinium* (1561) to "map the spatial imaginary of Shakespeare's city,"[10] while *Locating London's Past* and *The Grub Street Project* refigure London during the eighteenth century. In recreating the city through history, these digital resources offer ways to resituate the literary survey in historical context. Finally, because they offer pedagogical partnerships (as with *The Map of Early Modern London*) or encourage outside submissions (*The Grub Street Project*), they afford students possibilities for real-world research and writing assignments with lasting online presence.

"London &c. Actually Survey'd": Teaching Period

Mapping lends itself extraordinarily well to the teaching of literary period in our course, particularly as regards shifts in power and influence—from the Medieval emphasis of the Church, to the Renaissance privileging of the court, to the Enlightenment rise of the city. Each major literary period begins with a map of London at that historical moment, and lectures use cartography to reveal the selfsame broad historical trends evident in the texts. Our work on the Middle Ages is punctuated with Medieval maps that figure London in spiritual terms: church spires stand in for the city in the 1480 *Poésies* of the Duc d'Orléans, and Matthew Paris's *Historia Anglorum* and George Lily's map of Britain reduce London to the towering steeple of St. Paul's (see Figure 2). "In medieval times," writes D. K. Smith, the primary function of maps "was not to measure space, but to impose on the template of the physical world a constant reminder and organizational outline of the events of Christian history. They provided little more of the world than was needed to contemplate heaven."[11] Similarly, although London takes central importance in *Piers Plowman*—the text begins in the Malvern Hills, looking east toward the city—it warrants representation only insofar as it relates to Christian devotion. In the "Prologue," priests and parsons request "license and leave to live in London, / And sing Masses there for simony, for silver is sweet."[12] Later, Lady Mede "convinces London's mayor, in return for a bribe, to ignore the law."[13] Medieval maps of London prepare students to understand the representation of London in the texts, as well as the broader characteristics of the historical period.

The Medieval preeminence of the Church has its Renaissance counterpart in the court, and early modern cartography showcases monarchical splendor. "Lanes and courts and alleys," demonstrates Cynthia Wall, "were loftily overlooked by the Renaissance bird's-eye-views—they didn't 'fit' topographically or conceptually with the concern to present a rich, spacious, coherent sense of a national capital."[14] Instead, maps like *The Coronation Procession of Edward VI* (1547), or John Norden's 1593 map "showing the aristocratic riverside houses" facing the Thames present not so much a navigable scheme of the city than a "rich, spacious, coherent"[15] performance of noble power—the selfsame kind of monarchy endorsed by Shakespeare's *Henry IV, Part 1*, or enacted by the coronation procession of Elizabeth I. Preeminence begins to shift from the Crown to the city during the Restoration. Just as *Annus Mirabilis* construes national identity as equal parts Crown and city, describing the two as "a pair of matchless lovers,"[16] seventeenth-century maps seem equally interested in representing

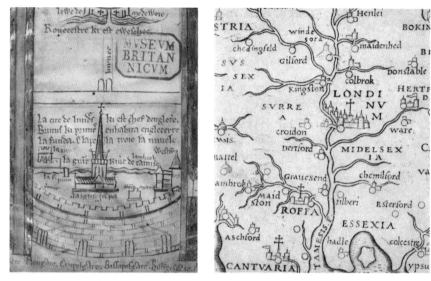

Figure 2. Depictions of London in Matthew Paris's *Historia Anglorum, Chronica majora* (1250-59) and in George Lily's map of Great Britain (1546). From the Collections of the British Library.

the monarch's power and the city itself. William Morgan's 1682 *London &c. Actually Survey'd*, for example, decorates an overhead scheme of London with images of Charles I and Charles II, along with "views of the Royal Exchange, Guildhall and Mercers' Hall."[17] Both *Annus Mirabilis* and Morgan's map depict London through equal parts city and court.

The Enlightenment marks the confident emergence of the city, and London becomes a consumer capital, buoyed by the transcendent pleasures of urban entertainment, mass-market celebrity, and shopping districts—a city, as writes Laura Rosenthal, defined by "its traders, stock market, shops, lawyers, fashions, imports, and exports."[18] In maps, the city's newfound sense of itself as a mercantile paradise can be traced in the expansion of London's West End, still the seat of many of the city's tourist attractions, theaters, gardens, shops, and entertainment venues. Jan Kip's *Veue et Perspective de la Ville de Londre* (1720) reorients London in favor of the West End, St. James's Square, and the Mall, "the epicentre of fashion," where "well-dressed ladies and gentlemen parade"[19]—indeed, members of London's smart set can be seen front and center, strolling in the latest fashions. Similarly, the capital students glimpse in *Fantomina* or *Memoirs of a Woman of Pleasure* shimmers with *arriviste* distractions and choice baubles: London's "fine sights," such as "the Tombs, the Lions, the King, the Royal Family, the fine Plays and Operies," its satin gowns, "taudry ribbons, and shoes belaced with silver!"[20] The heady sway of consumer culture, as evident in literature as in cartography, altered even the physical medium of maps, which took shape as ladies' fans.[21] For those who could afford it, cartography itself could be reduced to fashion.

British Literature I ends with the very beginnings of Romanticism, characterized in our course by a turn away from the city. While the titles of poems in the *Lyrical Ballads* "all refer, with extreme specificity, to time and place, especially place,"[22] none of those places are urban. Mapping Wordsworth requires plotting points near Tintern Abbey or Esthwaite Water, not Covent Garden or Fleet Street. Blake's London, comprised of "charter'd streets / Near where the charter'd Thames does flow,"[23] suffocates and misleads, and Wordsworth locates true genius not in the city, but in "low and rustic life."[24] As with earlier eras, the sense of London students gain from Romantic texts characterizes the spirit of the age. The priorities and preconceptions of each major literary period manifest both in maps of the city and in the literature itself.

"Connections Made Visible": Mapping the Literary Text

These separate maps of London through history are supplemented by our course Google Map. Just as we can turn to read the blue plaque commemorating Chaucer's Canterbury pilgrimage, Google Maps offers perpetual ways to link historical moments to the present-day shape of the city, reminding students that texts relate not to some undefined long-ago-and-far-away, but to real places with real social meanings. Working in groups, students plot locations in the texts on our collaborative map. Their work reveals new meanings in class discussion—those "significant relationships," to use Moretti's term, that might otherwise escape us. In the case of Chaucer, mapping the pilgrimage to Canterbury elucidates the overall structure of the *Tales*. As the narratives progress and the pilgrims approach Canterbury Cathedral, the content turns heavenward, becoming progressively more religious in tenor.[25] In this case geography neatly parallels a governing metaphor of *The Canterbury Tales*. The pilgrimage at hand, like the Christian's journey through life, ends with thoughts of God, and with accounting for the misdeeds of youth—the selfsame kind of penitent reflection performed by the Manciple, the Parson, and Chaucer's Retraction, all found toward the end of the text. It matters, too, that the pilgrimage begins in Southwark, "home to taverns, theatres and brothels,"[26] which lay "outside the jurisdiction of the city" and could thus develop "a freewheeling character of its own."[27] Southwark furnishes the kind of carnivalesque setting that might blend the myriad estates, professions, and sensibilities that make *The Canterbury Tales* a panoramic picture of medieval life.[28]

Just as mapping Chaucer's route offers students new approaches to *The Canterbury Tales*, a Google Map of the coronation procession of Elizabeth I (or, alternately, the excellent procession map available through *The Map of Early Modern London*)[29] foregrounds important themes in the early modern canon. Elizabeth's procession through the city began at the Tower of London, then went through Cornhill, Cheapside, and Fleet Street to Westminster Abbey, passing through Eastcheap on the way[30]—the precise district where Falstaff and Prince Hal drink, plot, and parody monarchical trappings. (The actual tavern is popularly associated with the sixteenth-century Boar's Head Inn, whose present-day building features boars' heads on its external facade—also visible through Google Street View.) In *Henry IV, Part 1*, as asserts James Bulman, "kingship depends for its authority not on God, but on performance."[31] It shares much in common, then, with Elizabeth's coronation procession: "the City of London," wrote a contemporary observer, became "a stage wherein was showed the wonderful spectacle of a noble-hearted princess toward her most loving people."[32] The very structure of *Henry IV, Part 1*, which alternates scenes at the royal palace with scenes in an Eastcheap tavern, calls for a monarch who tempers birthright with popular appeal. Map Elizabeth's procession, and you note that she also balanced Westminster and Eastcheap, royal patrimony and urban celebrity. The ostentatious, performative display endorsed by Shakespeare, who sanctions a monarch that dazzles the public "like a comet,"[33] pervades Elizabeth's speeches and inspires deep ambivalence in Edmund Spenser's *The Faerie Queene*.[34] In turn, the "Speech to the Troops at Tilbury" resonates far more powerfully when students understand Tilbury's precise location, on the estuary of the Thames and therefore between the Armada's approach and London itself; and the route of Elizabeth's coronation matters far more knowing her imprisonment ended precisely where her coronation began, at the Tower of London.

We pay scrupulous attention to locations mentioned in John Dryden's *Annus Mirabilis* and Daniel Defoe's *Journal of the Plague Year*, and working in groups, students map the origin and direction of the Fire of London in Dryden (see Figure 3) and the spread of plague in Defoe (see Figure 4). *Annus Mirabilis*—which is in fact dedicated to London—evokes the actual spread and devastation of the 1666 fire, as evinced by John Leake's *Exact Survey* of 1677 (see Figure 5). It also articulates national identity, poising the reborn city, and the remade nation, atop the three equal pillars of trade, history, and Crown:

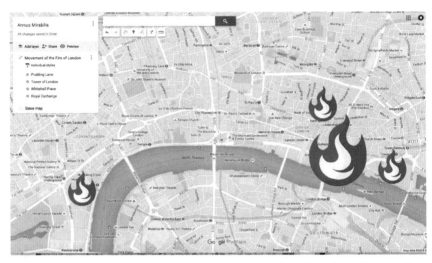

Figure 3. Google Map: outbreak point and targets of the fire of London in John Dryden's *Annus Mirabilis.*

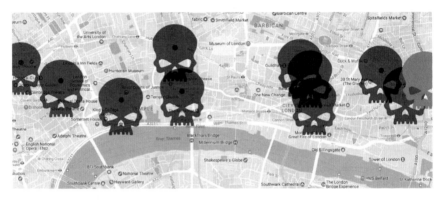

Figure 4. Google Map: outbreaks of plague in Daniel Defoe's *Journal of the Plague Year,* with residence of the narrator at far right.

Figure 5. John Leake, *An Exact Surveigh of the Streets Lanes and Churches Contained within the Ruines of the City of London* (1677). Courtesy of the New York Public Library.

One mighty squadron, with a side wind sped,
Through narrow lanes his cumbered fire does haste,
By powerful charms of gold and silver led
The Lombard bankers and the Change to waste.

Another backward to the Tower would go,
And slowly eats his way against the wind;
But the main body of the marching foe
Against th'imperial palace is designed.[35]

Divided into three menacing regiments, the fire—conflated throughout with the "ghosts" of Cromwell's Commonwealth, and England's current rival, the Dutch—targets the Change, the Tower, and Whitehall Palace. These three sites, the seats of English finance, English history, and English rule, together constitute national identity. Mapping *Annus Mirabilis* reveals not only the damage wrought by the conflagration, but a new sense of London, defined equally by trade as by king. This emergent sense of the capital culminates with the poem's ending, "a glorious Virgilian vision of London rising from the fire as a phoenix from the ashes, becoming itself the major artery of world trade," the "entrepôt and 'famed emporium' of the world."[36]

A Journal of the Plague Year itself maps London compulsively; the narrator mentions nearly two hundred distinct geographic locations, according to Cynthia Wall, and "much of the Journal's plot (and all of its allusions) depend on an intimate knowledge of the London streets."[37] In mapping *The Plague Year*, we perform the same actions as the narrator, constantly charting and recharting the city, in attempts to make sense of the devastation, understand the plague, and ultimately survive. Mapping Defoe also helps students make sense of the oppressive dread that the narrator, in his constant wanderings through the city, seems to be trying to shake. We learn, relatively early on, that the narrator lives in Whitechapel, "about mid-way between Aldgate Church and White-Chappel-Bars."[38] Chart the progress of the plague in relation to his home (see Figure 4), and you find that death slowly but ineluctably creeps nearer and nearer—from its first appearance "at the other End of the Town,"[39] to the City of London, to Tokenhouse Yard, a three-minute walk from the Bank of England. Soon after the narrator visits the plague pit at Aldgate, where the dead-carts unceremoniously dump bodies "together into the common Grave of Mankind."[40] Map Aldgate in relation to his residence, and you find he confronts death quite literally on his doorstep, a scant block or two from his own home. By Google Mapping the progress of the plague, students saw that while the plague circles London, seeming to strike randomly and unpredictably, its circling closes in on an inevitable target: the narrator himself.

For *The Interesting Narrative of Olaudah Equiano*, students plotted nearly a hundred of Equiano's destinations (see Figure 6), paying attention to their order and to the narrator's self-conception. Like *A Journal of the Plague Year*, Equiano's *Narrative* is rich with locations, although his are much farther flung; he moves three thousand miles, from St. George's Hospital in London to St. George, Halifax, in three scant pages.[41] Even while Equiano's scope is transatlantic, London serves as the fixed center of our map, and as a kind of lodestar for Equiano: his heart is "fixed on London,"[42] he writes, or his eyes long for the city.[43] Through the map, students noted that London serves as the beginning and end point of most of Equiano's major voyages. Along those lines, the capital also functions as a transformative space, making possible multiple versions of self—a locale that both reconciles Equiano's several identities and holds the promise of a future, perpetually deferred Englishness. In London, Equiano the free man metamorphoses into Equiano the sailor; in London, a sea change remakes the sailor into Equiano the Christian; and in London, the Christian

Figure 6. Google Map: destinations of Olaudah Equiano in *The Interesting Narrative of Olaudah Equiano.*

becomes the full-fledged Englishman. Furthermore, as Equiano becomes more English, each return to London involves locations deeper within the capital: from Deptford, five miles outside the city, to Cherry Garden, then St. Paul's, where his spiritual makeover manifests as literal whiteface.[44] The narrative finishes with a letter to the Queen, which Equiano the British subject signs with his ultimate address: fashionable Baldwin's Gardens, in modern-day Camden. Mapping the *Interesting Narrative* plots London at the center of the colonial project and at the center of Equiano's Romantic selfhood—just as maps helped us survey Chaucer's overarching structure, Elizabeth's performative authority, Dryden's idea of nation, and Defoe's narrative technique.

Apart from accentuating the meanings of individual texts, common locations generate overarching narratives for the course. St. Paul's Cathedral, which "dominated the medieval landscape for centuries,"[45] burns vividly in *Annus Mirabilis*, then reemerges in *The Interesting Narrative*. That same "high dome of Pauls" makes a final appearance in Blake's "Holy Thursday."[46] Dryden's vision that trade will make "one city of the universe"[47] is realized a century later with Equiano, when our map expands and London becomes the center of a global empire. Students engage with the material in sustained ways—not only thematically (say, the gender politics of "The Knight's Tale," *Henry IV, Part 1*, and *Fantomina*), but geographically (the route of the Canterbury pilgrims passes through Gad's Hill, where Prince Hal robs Falstaff, and Tilbury, where Elizabeth's forces defeated Spain). Perhaps most importantly, those narratives also extend to today, and assignments can further encourage students to connect historical space with the present. In our course, groups of students linked location, history, and literature in an audio podcast assignment, in which teams of students created "walking tours" of London at particular moments in history: among others, Westminster Abbey during the Middle Ages, the Globe Theatre during Shakespeare's heyday, St. Paul's Cathedral at the Restoration, and Covent Garden during the eighteenth century. Future sections of the course may be travel-embedded; a semester on the literature of London might end with a week in that same city, where students visit the locations we've studied all term, conducting research for final projects "on the ground." Even without visiting the city firsthand, however, a geographic approach bridges past and present in generative, exciting ways. Thanks to Google Maps, we can still stand where Chaucer's pilgrims did.

Mapping the Literature Survey

Even while the information revolution has compelled us to rethink how and what we teach, the Internet has ushered in new possibilities: novel ways for students to visualize literary content, to make connections within and among literary texts, and to relate literature to the present. Mapping the literature survey makes smart use of a wealth of digital resources, and applies twenty-first-century methods to the enduring purpose and needs of the survey course. Mapping also mitigates an especial challenge of the survey: that the material might seem dated, static, and completely removed from modern-day life. When I locate the Tabard Inn on our first day, then drop us into a 360-degree view of its modern-day location, students respond with delight—not merely delight in the digital environment, or in whiz-bang technology for technology's sake, but delight in connecting the past and present. More than anything, a common central location joins all the texts together, and relates the literature of the past to the space of the present. We move through time, but we remain, for the entire course, in the same space.

We live in exciting times: scholars have only begun to explore the capacity of digital platforms to reimagine literary space. Even at this early juncture, however, ample resources exist to approach the literature survey spatially. Online projects such as *The Map of Early Modern London* or *London: A Life in Maps* can shape course content, and lectures can be supplemented by digital collections, including those of the British Museum. Google Maps has a remarkable capacity to translate historical space into modern-day terms. Maps, writes Moretti, are "connections made visible,"[48] and mapping the literature survey helps students visualize new connections: ways to assess the meaning of texts, to understand historical and literary periods, and to frame the past by way of lived experience. "When a man is tired of London, he is tired of life," said Samuel Johnson in 1777, "for there is in London all that life can afford."[48] This aspect of London, its remarkable capacity to reflect so many facets of human experience, breathes fresh life into the literature survey—as does a spatial approach more broadly.

NOTES

1. The author would like to thank the members of *British Literature 1* (Fall 2015), particularly Nicole Galante, Charles Hawes, Spencer Hodges, Rebecca Murphy, and Liz Sellers-Bruch, for their sustained engagement, willingness to experiment, and good humor.

2. Geoffrey Chaucer, "General Prologue," in *The Norton Anthology of English Literature*, eds. Stephen Greenblatt, et al. (New York and London: W. W. Norton & Company, 2012), 1.244.

3. "The Miller's Tale," 1.265.

4. Franco Moretti, *Atlas of the European Novel, 1800–1900* (London and New York: Verso, 1998), 3.

5. Among others, see Paul Youngman's *Mapping the Literary Railway*, Meredith Goldsmith's *Mapping Literary Visions*, Melissa Dinsman's *Reading Modernist Cities*, and Google Lit Trips and Literary Location Field Trips. Paul Youngman, *Mapping the Literary Railway*, http://literaryrailway.academic.wlu.edu/. Meredith Goldsmith, *Mapping Literary Visions* http://www.meredithgoldsmith.com/. Melissa Dinsman, "About," Reading Modernist Cities. http://modernism.gistemp.com/omeka/about. GLT Global Ed, *Google Lit Trips*, http://www.googlelittrips.org/. GLT Global Ed, "Literary Locations," *Google Lit Trips*, http://www.googlelittrips.org/litTripLibrary/literaryLocations.php.

6. Daniel Defoe, *A Tour through the Whole Island of Great Britain*, ed. P. N. Furbank and W. R. Owens (New Haven and London: Yale University Press, 1991), 133.

7. Peter Ackroyd, *London: The Biography* (New York: Anchor Books, 2000), 763.

8. Because the course centers on London, we begin with Chaucer rather than *Beowulf*, but there are reasons beyond geography to do so: "literature in English was performed orally and written throughout the Middle Ages, but the awareness of and pride in a uniquely English literature did not actually exist before the late fourteenth century." James Simpson and Alfred David, "The Middle Ages to ca. 1485," in *The Norton Anthology of English Literature*, 3 vols., ed. Stephen Greenblatt et al. (New York and London: W. W. Norton & Company, 2012), 1.4–5.

9. The British Library Board, *London: A Life in Maps*, http://www.bl.uk/onlinegallery/features/londoninmaps/exhibition.html.

10. Janelle Jenstad and MoEML Team, "Mission Statement," *The Map of Early Modern London*, https://mapoflondon.uvic.ca/mission_statement.htm.

11. D. K. Smith, *The Cartographic Imagination in Early Modern England* (Aldershot: Ashgate Publishing, 2008), 2–3.

12. William Langland, "The Vision of Piers Plowman," in Greenblatt et al., *The Norton Anthology of English Literature*, 1.375.

13. Ralph Hanna, "Images of London in Medieval English Literature," in *The Cambridge Companion to the Literature of London*, ed. Laurence Manley (Cambridge: Cambridge University Press, 2011), 30.

14. Cynthia Wall, *The Literary and Cultural Spaces of Restoration London* (Cambridge: Cambridge University Press, 2006), 117.

15. Peter Whitfield, *London: A Life in Maps* (London: The British Library, 2006), 10.

16. John Dryden, *Selected Poems*, ed. Paul Hammond and David Hopkins (Harlow: Pearson Longman, 2007), 36.

17. Peter Barber, *London: A History in Maps* (London: The London Topographical Society, 2013), 60.

18. Laura J. Rosenthal, "Staging London in the Restoration and Eighteenth Century," in Manley, *The Cambridge Companion to the Literature of London*, 86.

19. Barber, *London: A History in Maps*, 66.

20. John Cleland, *Memoirs of a Woman of Pleasure*, ed. Peter Sabor (Oxford: Oxford World Classics, 2008), 3.

21. See, for example, Thomas Balster's "Ladies Travelling Fann," which mapped England and Wales, including all "Principal Roads, Rivers, Market & Post Towns; with their distances from London." In the British Museum's online collections, Museum Number 1891, 0713.451.

22. Ralph Pite, "Wordsworth and the Natural World," in *The Cambridge Companion to Wordsworth*, ed. Stephen Gill (Cambridge: Cambridge University Press, 2003), 181.

23. William Blake, *Songs of Innocence and of Experience*, ed. Sir Geoffrey Keynes (Oxford: Oxford University Press, 1967), n.p.

24. William Wordsworth, *Lyrical Ballads*, ed. Michael Gamer and Dahlia Porter (Peterborough, ON: Broadview Press, 2008), 174.

25. A fascinating map of the pilgrimage can be found in Larry Benson, ed., *The Canterbury Tales Complete*. Titled "The Pilgrims' Way from London to Canterbury," the map relates quotations from the *Tales* to locations on the journey: St. Thomas Watering, Deptford, Greenwich, Dartford, Sittingbourne, Ospringe, Boughton-upon-Bleane, and Harbledown.

26. Whitfield, *London: A Life in Maps*, 8.

27. Laurence Manley, "Introduction," in Manley, *The Cambridge Companion to the Literature of London*, 11.

28. Our course also thematically linked passages to areas of the city. "The Prioress's Tale," for instance, might be used to introduce Old Jewry and the history of London's Jews, just as a discussion of the Peasant's Revolt, in relation to *Piers Plowman*, would likely touch on Smithfield, where Richard II confronted rebels in June 1381.

29. See "The Queen's Majesty's Passage," at *The Map of Early Modern London*, http://mapoflondon.uvic.ca/QMPS1.htm/.

30. "The parade route from Fenchurch to Eastcheap," writes Ilona Bell, "was lined by guildsmen wearing their livery hoods, rich furs, and red silk ordered by the queen herself. The streets were thronged with shouting, jostling, cheering crowds," while "platforms erected along the route presented historical and biblical scenes containing lessons for the new queen and her subjects." Ilona Bell, *Elizabeth I: The Voice of a Monarch* (New York: Palgrave Macmillan, 2010), 32.

31. James Bulman, "Henry IV, Parts 1 and 2," in *The Cambridge Companion to Shakespeare's History Plays*, ed. Michael Hattaway (Cambridge: Cambridge University Press, 2002), 162.

32. Richard Mulcaster, "The Passage of Our Most Dread Sovereign Lady Queen Elizabeth through the City of London to Westminster on the Day before Her Coronation," in Greenblatt et al., *The Norton Anthology of English Literature*, 2.751.

33. William Shakespeare, *Henry IV, Part 1*, ed. Barbara A. Mowat and Paul Werstine (New York: Simon and Schuster, 1994), 133.

34. As in Spenser's depiction of Lucifera, a "mayden Queene" whose "bright blazing beautie did assay / To dim the brightnesse of her glorious throne, / As envying her selfe, that too exceeding shone." Edmund Spenser, *The Faerie Queene*, in Greenblatt et al., *The Norton Anthology of English Literature*, 2.819.

35. Dryden, *Annus Mirabilis*, in *Selected Poems*, 108.

36. Brean Hammond, "London and Poetry to 1750," in Manley, *The Cambridge Companion to the Literature of London*, 72.

37. Wall, "Introduction," xx.

38. Daniel Defoe, *A Journal of the Plague Year*, ed. Cynthia Wall (London: Penguin Books, 2003), 9.

39. Ibid., 109.

40. Ibid., 62.

41. Olaudah Equiano, *The Interesting Narrative and Other Writings*, ed. Vincent Carretta (London: Penguin Books, 2003), 71–73.

42. Ibid., 138.

43. Ibid., 164.

44. At "St. Paul's Church yard," writes Equiano, "I whitened my face, that they might not know me, and this had the desired effect." Ibid., 180.

45. James Simpson, "Religious Forms and Institutions in *Piers Plowman*," in *The Cambridge Companion to Piers Plowman*, ed. Andrew Cole and Andrew Galloway (Cambridge: Cambridge University Press, 2014), 101.

46. William Blake, *Songs of Innocence and of Experience*, ed. Sir Geoffrey Keynes (Oxford: Oxford University Press, 1967), n.p.

47. Dryden, *Selected Poems*, 92.

48. Moretti, *Atlas of the European Novel, 1800–1900*, 3.

49. James Boswell, *The Life of Johnson*, ed. R. W. Chapman (Oxford: Oxford University Press, 1998), 859.

BIBLIOGRAPHY

Ackroyd, Peter. *London: The Biography*. New York: Anchor Books, 2000.

Balster, Thomas. "Ladies Travelling Fann." British Museum's online collections, Museum Number 1891,0713.451.

Barber, Peter. *London: A History in Maps*. London: The London Topographical Society, 2013.

Bell, Ilona. *Elizabeth I: The Voice of a Monarch*. New York: Palgrave Macmillan, 2010.

Benson, Larry, ed. *The Canterbury Tales Complete*. Boston and New York: Houghton Mifflin Company, 2000.

Blake, William. *Songs of Innocence and of Experience*. Edited by Sir Geoffrey Keynes. Oxford: Oxford University Press, 1967.

Boswell, James. *The Life of Johnson*. Edited by R. W. Chapman. Oxford: Oxford University Press, 1998.

The British Library Board. "Georeferencing." http://www.bl.uk/georeferencer/.

———. *London: A Life in Maps*. http://www.bl.uk/londoninmaps.

Bulman, James. "Henry IV, Parts 1 and 2." In Hattaway, *The Cambridge Companion to Shakespeare's History Plays*, 158–76.

Chaucer, Geoffrey. *The Canterbury Tales Complete*. Edited by Larry D. Benson. Boston and New York: Houghton Mifflin Company, 2000.

———. "The General Prologue." In Greenblatt et al., *The Norton Anthology of English Literature*, 1.241–64.

———. "The Miller's Tale." In Greenblatt et al., *The Norton Anthology of English Literature*, 1.264–80.

Cleland, John. *Memoirs of a Woman of Pleasure*. Edited by Peter Sabor. Oxford: Oxford World's Classics, 2008.

Defoe, Daniel. *A Journal of the Plague Year*. Edited by Cynthia Wall. London: Penguin Books, 2003.

———. *A Tour through the Whole Island of Great Britain*. Edited by P. N. Furbank and W. R. Owens. New Haven and London: Yale University Press, 1991.

Dinsman, Melissa. "About." *Reading Modernist Cities*. http://modernism.gistemp.com/omeka/about.

Dryden, John. *Selected Poems*. Edited by Paul Hammond and David Hopkins. Harlow: Pearson Longman, 2007.

Equiano, Olaudah. *The Interesting Narrative and Other Writings*. Edited by Vincent Carretta. London: Penguin Books, 2003.

GLT Global Ed. *Google Lit Trips*. http://www.googlelittrips.org/.

———. "Literary Locations." *Google Lit Trips*. http://www.googlelittrips.org/litTrip Library/literaryLocations.php.

Goldsmith, Meredith. *Mapping Literary Visions*. http://www.meredithgoldsmith.com/.

Greenblatt, Stephen, et al., eds. *The Norton Anthology of English Literature*. 3 vols. New York and London: W. W. Norton & Company, 2012.

Hammond, Brean. "London and Poetry to 1750." In Manley, *The Cambridge Companion to the Literature of London*, 67–84.

Hanna, Ralph. "Images of London in Medieval English Literature." In Manley, *The Cambridge Companion to the Literature of London*, 19–33.

Hattaway, Michael, ed. *The Cambridge Companion to Shakespeare's History Plays*. Cambridge: Cambridge University Press, 2002.

Langland, William. "The Vision of Piers Plowman." In Greenblatt et al., *The Norton Anthology of English Literature*, 1.373–408.

Manley, Laurence, ed. *The Cambridge Companion to the Literature of London.* Cambridge: Cambridge University Press, 2011.

———. "Introduction." In Manley, *The Cambridge Companion to the Literature of London*, 1–18.

Jenstad, Janelle, and MoEML Team. "Mission Statement." *The Map of Early Modern London.* https://mapoflondon.uvic.ca/mission_statement.htm.

Moretti, Franco. *Atlas of the European Novel, 1800–1900.* London and New York: Verso, 1998.

Mulcaster, Richard. "The Passage of Our Most Dread Sovereign Lady Queen Elizabeth through the City of London to Westminster on the Day before Her Coronation." In Greenblatt et al., *The Norton Anthology of English Literature*, 2.751–53.

Pepys, Samuel. *The Diary of Samuel Pepys: Selected Passages.* Edited by Richard Le Gallienne. Mineola, NY: Dover, 2004.

Pite, Ralph. "Wordsworth and the Natural World." In *The Cambridge Companion to Wordsworth*, edited by Stephen Gill, 180–95. Cambridge: Cambridge University Press, 2003.

"The Queen's Majesty's Passage." *The Map of Early Modern London.* http://mapoflondon.uvic.ca/QMPS1.htm/.

Rosenthal, Laura J. "Staging London in the Restoration and Eighteenth Century." In Manley, *The Cambridge Companion to the Literature of London*, 85–101.

Shakespeare, William. *Henry IV, Part 1.* Edited by Barbara A. Mowat and Paul Werstine. New York: Simon and Schuster, 1994.

Simpson, James. "Religious Forms and Institutions in *Piers Plowman*." In *The Cambridge Companion to Piers Plowman*, edited by Andrew Cole and Andrew Galloway, 97–114. Cambridge: Cambridge University Press, 2014.

Simpson, James, and Alfred David. "The Middle Ages to ca. 1485." In Greenblatt et al., *The Norton Anthology of English Literature*, 1.3–25.

Smith, D. K. *The Cartographic Imagination in Early Modern England.* Aldershot: Ashgate Publishing, 2008.

Spenser, Edmund. *The Faerie Queene.* In Greenblatt et al., *The Norton Anthology of English Literature*, 2.775–984.

Wall, Cynthia. "Introduction." In *A Journal of the Plague Year* by Daniel Defoe. London: Penguin Books, 2003.

———. *The Literary and Cultural Spaces of Restoration London.* Cambridge: Cambridge University Press, 2006.

Whitfield, Peter. *London: A Life in Maps.* London: The British Library, 2006.

Wordsworth, William. *Lyrical Ballads.* Edited by Michael Gamer and Dahlia Porter. Peterborough, ON: Broadview Press, 2008.

Youngman, Paul. *Mapping the Literary Railway.* http://literaryrailway.academic.wlu.edu/.

COURSE DOCUMENT: BOURQUE

Audio Walking Tours

Each of you, in groups of four to five students, will be designing, scripting and recording an audio "walking tour" of a specific location in London. Your goal is to connect your assigned location with a specific moment in history, and to bridge its present-day appearance with the sights and sounds of historical London. In the process, you should also make connections with literary texts, historical figures and concepts we've talked about this semester. (It's a good idea to quote the text[s], if you can.) Your "director's cut" must be uploaded to the class Moodle site before class on Monday, November 30. I expect them to be roughly five to ten minutes long. We will listen to them together and discuss them in class, and questions taken from them will likely appear on the final exam.

Your assigned locations and historical dates are:

Westminster Abbey during the Middle Ages; the Globe Theatre between 1599 and 1644; St. Paul's Cathedral between the fire of London and its consecration, in 1697; Covent Garden during the 1720s; 'Change Alley during the mid-to-late eighteenth century; and the East India House c. 1800

Pretend your listener is actually *at* the modern-day location. Pay attention to how the place appears right now using, for example, Google Maps, YouTube, and similar online resources. Do your best to link the present day with the past, and compare the modern appearance with the historical one. I'll be emailing each group individually, suggesting potential books and websites for research on these locations, but you may also want to research daily life in London for your assigned period.

You are free to depart from your precise assigned date, to give the listener a sense of the overall history of the location. I do, however, want you to do your best to recreate the "look and feel" of the location for your assigned historical moment. What was city life like then? What would someone hear, see, smell, and feel at that moment in time? Think about what you might hear if you sat at the fountain at Alamance with your eyes closed, or in Belk Library, or at the Oak House, and how that reflects the way the space is used. Contrast that to what you might hear at Target in Burlington, for example.

How can you recapture that kind of experience—the way a location feels unique—in your audio tour?

Consider ways you might layer voice, music, and sound effects for particular effect. You might use voice to tell a story; to describe the present-day listener's surroundings; to recreate the space in the past; or to interview an authority - or a historical figure, an author, or a character, because why the heck not? Use music to add emotion, or to "call back" to the period (Medieval music is, of course, different from Renaissance music, or the music of the Romantic era). Add sound effects to convey a sense of realism to the scene.

Remember to make connections with the course. Mention historical figures and ideas that have come up in lecture. I also expect you to make direct connections to the literature: the Westminster Abbey group should show off their knowledge of *The Canterbury Tales*; the Globe group, Shakespeare and *Henry IV, Part 1*; St. Paul's, Pepys and Dryden; Covent Garden, Hogarth and Cleland; 'Change Alley, *The London Merchant*; and the East India House, Olaudah Equiano.

Teaching and Learning Technologies will be joining us on November 6 for GarageBand instruction, and to walk us through online resources for music and sound effects. You're welcome to bring your laptops to class on that date. There are also student technology leaders at the front desk of Belk from 8 a.m. to 11 p.m., who can help you if questions about the software crop up.

I will be emailing the members of each group, both to share your email addresses with each other and to provide you with a list of possible sources on the location. Please make sure that you find a way to actively contribute to your group; I will be asking you to evaluate one another, just to make sure all members of the group have taken part. I recommend that you start your planning and preparation early—well before the deadline. Remember that I am at your disposal. Good luck, and by all means HAVE FUN.

Audio Tour Rubric

CREATIVITY (20 points)

The tour is scripted well, and effectively engages the audience. Music is used to convey emotion; voice, to tell a story; and sound effects, to add realism. The three are effectively layered and overlapped. Elements of the tour are surprising, engaging, amusing, and/or fun. I enjoyed listening.

INFORMATION TRANSFER (20)

The tour made sense; ideas flow logically. The information is well structured. The location has clearly been researched, and difficult concepts are made transparent for the audience. Any historical information is correct.

ENGAGEMENT WITH COURSE (20 points)

The tour makes reference to concepts, historical figures, London locations, and/or literary works we've discussed in class.

CONNECTING PAST TO PRESENT (20 points)

The students have paid attention to the modern-day look, feel, and appearance of London, and have recreated that same space in history. The tour evokes the look, smells, and sounds of the past. Students have paid close attention to the appearance of the space in the present, using online resources such as Google Maps. Ideally, the group moves seamlessly back and forth between the present tense and the assigned historical period.

AUDIO QUALITY (10)

Audio is clear. Voices are easily heard and make sense. Transitions are smooth. Music and sound effects enhance rather than distract.

TEAMWORK (10 points)

The student found ways to contribute to the group project, and was an asset to his or her team members.

Creative Imitation

The Survey as an Occasion for Emulating Style

SCOTT L. NEWSTOK, RHODES COLLEGE

The four-decade decline of the mandatory survey of literary history has been well documented, and is part of the occasion of this volume. Less often noted, I sense, is this decline's coincidence with the institutional rise of creative writing over that same span of time. While correlation need not imply causation, I would nonetheless suggest that this simultaneous decline and rise might be mutually constitutive, both in fantasy and in practice.

In the minds of many students (and, with distressingly increasing frequency, some faculty), the historical survey and the creative writing workshop would seem to be inverted images of each other, as if the former were the aging portrait of Dorian Gray, anxiously sequestered by the latter in a hidden room. Whereas the survey seems to embody all the historical antecedents we seem only too embarrassed to overcome, the workshop presents itself as the venue for vivacity, currency, and diversity, in the accessible prose of the present. Much is demonstrably false about this imagined opposition. But it's not difficult to understand why the workshop seems, howsoever fantastically, to overcome the perceived oppressions of the survey.

To be clear: the survey vs. workshop opposition is a false one. Indeed, I propose that incorporating creative exercises within the literary historical survey helps students better appreciate meter, form, and genre. They thereby recognize writers as practitioners rather than monuments who make us marble with too much conceiving. In the spirit of Thomas Greene,[1] I call these exercises "creative imitations," a phrase invoked to unsettle and reconcile the (only apparent) contradiction in its terms. While students might initially concur with the Romantic Emerson of "Self Reliance," who enjoins us to "insist on yourself; never imitate," the Emerson of "Quotation and Originality" later acknowledges that in literature "the debt is immense to past thought. None escapes it. The originals are not original. There is imitation, model, and suggestion, to the very archangels, *if we knew their history*" (emphasis added).[2]

These creative imitations have been a central component of my British Literature survey for over a decade, across multiple institutions. While I believe I deploy such exercises more extensively than other teachers have done,[3] they are certainly not novel. In fact, in assigning them I am emulating my own professor of British Literature at Grinnell College, Peter Connelly, who required his students to write a Spenserian stanza and then "translate" it into a Shakespearean sonnet. Such exercises used to be standard in the English curriculum: John C. Briggs notes that throughout the twentieth-century English classroom, "Judiciously chosen literary texts . . . serve[d] as models for emulative and creative imitation," citing "generations of textbooks" that featured "a mimetic and creative approach to literary models."[4] Nor is this a model unique to the last century: in his *Autobiography*, Benjamin Franklin recounts how he taught himself to become a better writer by scrupulously imitating Addison and Steele's style from "The Spectator."

But most strikingly, such emulative exercises *were the very genesis of academic "creative writing" itself.* As D. G. Myers relentlessly insists in his polemical study *The Elephants Teach: Creative Writing Since 1880*, the initial goal of creative writing *exercises* (not *programs*) over one hundred years ago was not to produce professional *writers*, but rather to produce better *readers*:

> Originally the teaching of writing in American universities ("creative" or otherwise) was an experiment in education. . . . The goal—an educational one—was to reform and redefine the academic study of literature, establishing a means for approaching it "creatively," that is, by some other means than it had been approached before that time, which was historically and linguistically. . . . it was an effort on their part to bring the teaching of literature more closely in line with the ways in which (they believed) literature is genuinely created. . . . They sought to impart the *understanding* of literature through the *use* of it.[5]

Myers avers that creative writing swerved from its purpose when it became preoccupied with professional self-reproduction.[6]

While the practice of creative imitation is far from an exclusively Western phenomenon, and applies to artistic media beyond writing (most notably, music and the visual arts), the ongoing praxis of creative imitation was first thoroughly articulated by the Romans' defense of their adoption of Greek culture, as per Horace: "Captive Greece overcame her barbarous conqueror and brought civilization to the wild Latins."[7] With respect to writing in particular,

Quintilian devotes an entire chapter of his *Institutio Oratoria* to imitation, asserting that it is from

> authors worthy of our study that we must draw our stock of words, the variety of our figures and our methods of composition, while we must form our minds on the model of every excellence. For there can be no doubt that in art no small portion of our task lies in imitation.[8]

Seneca popularized the apiary metaphor of imitation, analogizing the writer's process of creation to the bees' gathering of nectar from flowers. In a handout (see the end of this essay) for my students, I anthologize some of the many bee metaphors, including passages from Plato, Sappho, Lucretius, Horace, Plutarch, Macrobius, Petrarch, Castiglione, and Erasmus, concluding with Montaigne:

> The bees steal from this flower and that, but afterwards turn their pilferings into honey, which is their own; it is thyme and marjoram no longer. So the pupil will transform and fuse together the passages that he borrows from others, to make of them something entirely his own; that is to say, his own judgment.[9]

This handout quickly conveys not only how long-standing this intellectual preoccupation has been, but also how *fraught* it has been. Is imitation merely the busy assemblage of the work of others, or does it produce something new, "modified in the guts of the living"?[10] Does imitation convey respect for antecedents, or does it rather enact a competitive violence upon the source? Such an anthology, I hope, helps make manifest the genuine ambivalence that every writer feels about engaging with predecessors, and thereby encourages students to reflect upon their own status as interpreters of, and contributors to, literary history.

I thus begin the semester by thematizing *imitatio* as crucial to early modern poesis. Without appreciating the constitutive role of imitation in the Renaissance, much of the era's literary preoccupations—with genre, with authority, with voice, with satire, with allusion[11]—are perplexing to the point of incomprehensible for contemporary students. Foregrounding humanist pedagogy, in particular, opens up the intellectual practices of the premodern era, and helps situate their own creative imitations within the context of the course. On the one hand, the era valued an imitation so pure that it resembled nothing other than the source itself, as in Ascham's famed "double translation"[12] from *The Schoolmaster* (1570). On the other hand, the era valued imitation so extravagant that it threatened to dissolve into verbal profusion, as per Erasmus's *de Copia*, ringing the changes on the phrase *tuae litterae me magnopere delectarunt*. Robert Greene's famous Aesopian scorn of Shakespeare as "an upstart crow beautified with our feathers" aptly captures the tensions inherent in dressing in borrowed plumage.

On the very first day of the semester, I distribute examples of student portfolios of imitations (and their associated explications) from prior semesters. When I first explain the process to them, many students express concerns: they haven't previously written poetry; they don't know "old" literature. These examples from their peers help reassure them that while the task is daunting, it's achievable—and indeed fun. To help them further apprehend what we are seeking to produce, in the first weeks of seminar I continue to circulate excerpts from Raymond Queneau's *Exercises in Style*, ninety-nine variations on a banal anecdote about riding the bus; John Hollander's *Rhyme's Reason*, a series of meta-poetic pastiches (e.g., sonnets on sonnets, couplets on couplets); Pope's juvenile imitations of Chaucer, Swift, and others; and further examples of student portfolios of imitation and explications from prior semesters. If we had world enough and time, I would also have them read the "Oxen of the Sun" episode from *Ulysses*, where James Joyce "raided several other prose anthologies to construct his parodies."[13] I keep insisting upon the truism: writers read other writers, and learn to write in part by emulating their predecessors.

For the second class session, students submit a "source" passage from a favorite contemporary book. This source will provide the narrative core for them to return to repeatedly throughout the semester, as they revise that same paragraph into various verse and prose forms. Prose passages are preferable to lyrics for sources. There's the temptation, with a lyric source, merely to borrow lines and import them directly into their form, rather than aggressively recomposing the source material into an entirely different imitation. The source passage should guide the imitations; ideally, after a few imitations, students begin to recognize how radically the same material can be reshaped in different forms. Thus I encourage students to stick comparatively close to their source for their own benefit. They thereby develop a deep familiarity with these (largely poetic) forms, making them better able to compare, cumulatively, the same source "material" across different genres. *Pippi Longstocking, The Bluest Eye, The Suicide Diaries, The Hunger Games, Pride and Prejudice, The Great Gatsby*—all have been used as sources, with terrific results.

After choosing a favorite prose passage (a paragraph or two in length) as their source, students commence "translating" this source on a weekly basis, in imitation of some of the major texts we are reading. These include: *ballad*

34

stanzas, Beowulfian epic, Chaucerian couplets, Skeltonics, Spenserian stanza, Shakespearean sonnet, Bacon essay, Herbert shape poem, Miltonic blank verse, and Pope couplet. This insistence upon formal imitation constantly forces us to read closely: What precisely do we mean by "Spenserian" (and what did later Spenserians think they meant when they were imitating Spenser)? What "counts" as sufficient imitation of Baconian equipoise? How on earth can one compress so much (*multum in parvo*) into a mere two rhyming lines? The process is salutary for both instructor and student, as I am constantly isolating and identifying key stylistic details for the class, and they are attending to them with real scrutiny: a particular meter, or rhyme scheme; a characteristic syntactical structure, or rhetorical trope; a typical subject addressed, avoided, etc. The only downside of this approach is that some students want to read with a kind of checklist in mind: What are the dozen things I have to do to sound like Milton? This can make for some rather flat imitations and explications. Early in the term, I do two things to prevent this checklist approach: first, I make summative responses to everyone's assignments, noting common problems across the class. Second, I make copies of everyone's first assignment (the ballad form), and distribute this to the class. In the best circumstances, outstanding submissions help encourage some less inspired students to improve their writing in order to match the level of their peers.

The creative imitation need not be long (a verse paragraph of approximately twenty lines) in order to instantiate many of the conventions. The accompanying explication (roughly five hundred words) forces students to articulate precisely what they did, with key quotations from their imitative model to justify their practice. The imitations help them internalize the mechanics of the texts we are reading; the explications allow them to demonstrate their critical familiarity with the conventions of these texts. The explication—an *unfolding*—doesn't involve a simple paraphrase of the imitation (since we already know the source). Rather, students need to justify what they have done. Perhaps there is a long list of adjectives in their imitation; can they explain why they wrote this way? Perhaps they resort to monosyllabic words in one section before returning to polysyllabic words in another; can they cite a precedent for why this is effective? Why would a sonneteer include an epigrammatic couplet at the close? I offer many opportunities for drafting and revision: circulating imitations-in-progress in class, for peer feedback; marking (but not grading) imitations and explications with suggestions for rewriting; and requiring a final, revised portfolio at the close of the term. All of this is fairly anodyne pedagogy derived from the creative writing workshop, but I believe it's unusual to be found in a survey of literary history.

To foreground the complexity of imitation, and in particular the nostalgia that it often entails, I open the survey with a discussion of the eighteenth-century ballad revival. This immediately introduces students to the yearning for origins that literary history entails, so much so that such yearning often produces self-projecting origins. (Wordsworth: "I have proposed to myself to imitate, and, as far as is possible, to adopt the very language of men."[14]) The old chestnut of "Western Wind" provides the occasion to begin addressing ballad meter, as well as to introduce students to editorial history (earlier editions of the *Norton Anthology* used to include such "ballad" poems at the front of the volume, before chronologically demoting them to later pages).[15] Marlowe's "Passionate Shepherd" offers an instance of a deceptively simple ballad that exposes its own fictive fantasy; Bob Dylan's "Boots of Spanish Leather" provides an example of a more recent ballad revival; and Dudley Randall's 1968 "Ballad of Birmingham" reveals how the genre can be reconfigured for contemporary social protest.

I conclude with an example a former student's imitation and explication of a passage from Ian McEwan's novel *Atonement* in the style of *Beowulf*. Tara Loftus was an English major at Gustavus Adolphus in 2004 when she took my course; a dozen years out of college, she now works at a professional Web development firm. As you can see in the following, some aspects of form are more conducive to imitation than others, and I always encourage students to note what they were unsuccessful in incorporating—in fact, sometimes that's just as instructive as what they were able to incorporate. Since I'm convinced that students pay ever less attention to the texture of reading in their secondary school courses, I believe that such fine-grain emulation is more needful than ever. The process of imitation requires a kind of "slow reading in a hurried age," to invoke David Mikics's book of the same title.[16] This is admittedly hard work. But I can attest that it's immensely rewarding, not only for those students who plan to be creative writing majors, but also for those concentrating in literary history as well as those simply taking the course for general education credit. Often the students who have the most fun with the imitations are those who I would otherwise anticipate would be quite bored with a typical survey of British Literature. An eminently imitable achievement.

• • •

O I heard say that entombed in this temple lies
Nicholaf, warrior of the risen reef, begotten of
Nichologar and his good wife.
For him, feats of fiend were no light thing; for he was

505   the most fearsome fighter these insels ever saw.
From this lofty height did his funeral fire burn,
flickering and raw on the faces of his gloomy[17] kinsmen.
But now all the life cinders are gone, whisked away
by the howling wind; an epoch has gone since then,
510   his name bore only on the breath of seers and sages
whose whispers haunt the gullet of his tomb.
And yet the wind wheezes and whines
through the cracking oaks, harassing the cold and
crumbling walls of the island temple that marks his earthbed.

Explication:

In my imitation of *Beowulf*, I tried to replicate the genre in many ways, perhaps the most prominently, on first glance, by numbering the lines in the five hundreds. I did this so my imitation would appear as an excerpt of a lengthy archaic epic. I started the first line with an intrusion by the narrator, to set up the omniscient narrator that surfaces periodically and strategically during the narrative progression of Beowulf's story ("I never heard before of a ship so well furbished with battle-tackle, bladed weapons . . . [lines 8–9]). Lacking a hero from my original passage, I created the character of Nicholaf. (The name was inspired by a certain Nicholas Revett who appears in my original passage; I added the suffix *-laf*—as in Wiglaf—to indicate the patronymic naming system used in Beowulf's era.) I continued the ancestry theme by providing Nicholaf's heritage, as Beowulf's lineage is given in his tale ("'His father before him was called Ecgtheow. Hrethel the Geat gave Ecgtheow his daughter in marriage. The man is their son, here to follow up an old friendship'" (lines 373–76). I gave his father a similar-sounding name, and then, in keeping with the feminine emptiness[18] of *Beowulf*, I referred to his mother as simply her husband's "good wife." Interestingly, because the setting of my passage is an island temple, my imitation echoes the mystique of Avalon and the venerated King Arthur.

Beowulf is also known for its use of epithets, and so, right away in line 502 I imposed "warrior of the risen reef" on the hero Nicholaf in hopes that it was strong enough to stand in place of his actual name. With "risen reef," I attempted to use kenning, but I probably succeeded better in line 508 with "life cinders" and in the last line with "earthbed." (Not quite as eloquent as "whaleroad," I admit!) I also employed the device of litotes in deeming Nicholaf's bouts with evil antagonists as "no light thing" in line 504. This egregious use of understatement emerges many times in *Beowulf*.

Formally, I tried to echo the abrasive sound of *Beowulf* by using monosyllabic, consonantal German/Anglo-Saxon words like "feat," "fiend," "fire," "tomb," "breath," "gullet," "cracking oaks," and "cold." Finding the word "island" too soft and Latinate, I used the German word, *insel*, instead (line 505). The *f* sound is especially predominant in my imitation; while it may appear I was trying to weave in the alliterative revival of *Sir Gawain and the Green Knight*, I promise I only used it so profusely because I liked the effect of its harsh sound. I wanted to convey the hard earthiness characteristic of *Beowulf* and Seamus Heaney's "Digging." Heaney's poem also inspired my use of onomatopoeia in "whisked away by the howling wind" and "cracking oaks" in lines 508 and 513 respectively.

For the content of my imitation, I chose to describe the grave (site of funeral fire) of my hero. I viewed this somber event from the past so as to capture the dark, serious tone of *Beowulf* and its characters' nostalgia for days gone by ("Then his warriors laid him in the middle of [the pyre], mourning a lord far-famed and beloved" [lines 3141–42]). By using the pathetic fallacy and manipulating the wind, I tried to invoke an aura of doom and destruction that would signal only tragedy and melancholy for the future of Nicholaf's descendants. I wanted this to echo the ominous foreshadowing in Beowulf: "but his fate that night was due to change, his days of ravening had come to and end" (lines 733–35).

There are many Beowulfian elements that I didn't use, including the implementation of the supernatural, pairings of binary forms, and extending my imitation to include the *fitts* that punctuate the prose of Beowulf. I used the elements I could to promote the epic grandeur, earthy sounds, and dark tone that is signature of *Beowulf*.

NOTES

1. See the Festschrift edited by Quint et al. in honor of Greene's pathbreaking *The Light in Troy*, on the legacy of humanist imitation; see also West and Woodman, eds., *Creative Imitation and Latin Literature*. David Quint, Margaret Ferguson, G. W. Pigman III, and Wayne Rebhorn, eds., *Creative Imitation: New Essays on Renaissance Literature in Honor of Thomas M. Greene* (Binghamton: Medieval and Renaissance Texts and Studies, 1992); David West and Tony Woodman, eds., *Creative Imitation and Latin Literature* (Cambridge: Cambridge University Press, 1979). As to the word *creative* itself, Williams's *Keywords* explains its belated (eighteenth-century) emergence: "Since the word evidently denotes a faculty, it had to wait on general acceptance of *create* and *creation* as human actions, without necessary reference to a past divine event." Raymond Williams, "Creative," in *Keywords: A Vocabulary of Culture and Society*, rev. ed. (New York: Oxford, 1983), 84.

2. Ralph Waldo Emerson, "Self-Reliance," *Essays: First Series* (Boston, J. Munroe and Company, 1841): 68; Ralph Waldo Emerson, "Quotation and Originality," *Letters and Social Aims* (Boston: James R. Osgood, 1876): 159. See also Dryden's Preface to his translation of *The Ae-*

neid: "Who then can pass for an inventor, if Homer, as well as Virgil, must be depriv'd of that glory? Is Versailles the less a new building, because the architect of that palace hath imitated others which were built before it? . . . The poet who borrows nothing from others is yet to be born." John Dryden, Dedication to the *Aeneid* (London: Jacob Tonson, 1697), 32.

3. Brinkman recounts similar, if less regularly assigned, creative imitations in his literature courses. Weinsheimer argues for a return to the virtues of imitation as espoused in eigthteenth-century rhetoric. Bartholomew Brinkman, "Imitations, Manipulations and Interpretations: Creative Writing in the Critical Classroom," *Iowa Journal of Cultural Studies* 12/13 (Spring/Fall 2010): 158–62; Joel Weinsheimer, *Imitation* (Boston: Routledge & Kegan Paul, 1984).

4. John C. Briggs, "Writing Without Reading: The Decline of Literature in the Composition Classroom," *Forum: A Publication of the Association of Literary Scholars, Critics, and Writers* 1 (Winter 2004): 22. Briggs catalogs many such textbooks (n. 39). Williams's too-laconic-to-be-satirical campus novel *Stoner* includes a late scene where the contrarian eponymous professor devotes his freshman composition class to "examples of medieval verse and prose." John Williams, *Stoner* (1965; New York: New York Review of Books, 2003), 223. Stoner's idiosyncratic seminar produces a small triumph: his students go on to earn the highest score in their junior English exams (230).

5. D. G. Myers, *The Elephants Teach: Creative Writing Since 1880* (Chicago: University of Chicago Press, 1996), 4, 8.

6. Ibid., 168. For a less jaded view, see Louis Menand, "Show or Tell: Should Creative Writing be Taught?" *New Yorker*, June 8, 2009, 106–12. Rhodes, in his coyly titled chapter "Did Shakespeare Study Creative Writing?" concurs with Myers, who suggests that "The most promising way in which [Raymond] Williams' programme for English could be adapted for the present day is through a recombining of the active, performative arts of writing and speaking with the more passive, interpretative, and analytical arts of reading." Neil Rhodes, "Did Shakespeare Study Creative Writing?" *Shakespeare and the Origins of English* (Oxford: Oxford University Press, 2004), 229.

7. Epistle 2.1.156. On non-European imitative practices, see Lucken and Reiss; on imitation in the non-verbal arts, see Ackerman, Brown, and Gombrich; on imitation in antiquity, see Clark, Conte, Fiske, and McKeon; on imitation in the Renaissance, see Bjørnsted, Galbraith, Mack, Pigman, Steadman, and White; for a general overview of imitation, Edwards's encyclopedia entry is the best place to start. I thank my classicist colleague Susan Satterfield for sharing with me her knowledge of Roman *imitatio*. Michael Lucken, *Imitation and Creativity in Japanese Arts: From Kishida Ryusei to Miyazki Hayao* (New York: Columbia University Press, 2016); James S. Ackerman, *Origins, Imitations, Conventions: Representation in the Visual Arts* (Cambridge, MA: MIT Press, 2002); Howard Mayer Brown, "Emulation, Competition, and Homage: Imitation and Theories of Imitation in the Renaissance," *Journal of the American Musicological Society* 35, no. 1 (Spring 1982): 1–48; E. H. Gombrich, *Art and Illusion: A Study in the Psychology of Pictorial Representation*, 2nd ed. (New York: Pantheon, 1961); Donald Lemen Clark, "Imitation: Theory and Practice in Roman Rhetoric," *Quarterly Journal of Speech* 37, no. 1 (1951): 11–22; Gian Biagio Conte, *The Rhetoric of Imitation: Genre and Poetic Memory in Virgil and Other Latin Poets*, trans. Charles Segal (Ithaca, NY: Cornell University Press, 1986); George C. Fiske, *Lucilius and Horace: A Study in the Classical Theory of Imitation*, University of Wisconsin Studies in Language and Literature 7 (Hildesheim: Georg Olms Verlagbuchhandlung, 1966); Richard McKeon, "Literary Criticism and the Concept of Imitation in Antiquity," *Modern Philology* 34, no. 1 (August 1936): 1–35; Hall Bjørnsted, ed., *Borrowed Feathers: Plagiarism and the Limits of Imitation in Early Modern Europe* (Oslo: Academic Press, 2008), 21–38; David Galbraith, *Architectonics of Imitation in Spenser, Daniel, and Drayton* (Toronto: University of Toronto Press, 2000); Robert Mack, *The Genius of Parody: Imitation and Originality in Seventeenth- and Eighteenth-Century English Literature* (New York:

Palgrave, 2007); G. W. Pigman, "Versions of Imitation in the Renaissance," *Renaissance Quarterly* 33, no. 1 (1980): 1–32; John M. Steadman, *The Lamb and the Elephant: Ideal Imitation and the Context of Renaissance Allegory* (San Marino: The Huntington Library, 1974); Harold Ogden White, *Plagiarism and Imitation During the English Renaissance: A Study in Critical Distinctions* (Cambridge, MA: Harvard University Press, 1935).

8. Quintilian, *The Institutio Oratoria*, 4 vols. (New York: G. P. Putnam's Sons, 1922), 4:74–75. Passannante notes that Gabriel Harvey's copy of Quintilian's *Institutes* includes the following marginalia: "The best imitation," he says, "is required of the best authors, and indeed with the most strenuous rivalry. But cunningly with secret ambition." Gerard Passannante, "The Art of Reading Earthquakes: On Harvey's Wit, Ramus's Method, and the Renaissance of Lucretius," *Renaissance Quarterly* 61, no. 3 (2008): 807.

9. Michel de Montaigne, "On the Education of Children," in *Essays*, trans. John M. Cohen (New York: Penguin, 1993), 108.

10. W. H. Auden, "In Memory of W. B. Yeats," *Collected Poems* (1939; New York: Random House, 2007), 245.

11. Following Guillory's *Cultural Capital*, I devote our class session on Gray's "Elegy" to a discussion of commonplacing and borrowing in the eighteenth century, placing in parallel passages from Gray's poem with excerpts from Dryden, Addison, Gray, Young, and others whose phrases he lifted. John Guillory, "Mute Inglorious Miltons: Gray, Wordsworth, and the Vernacular Canon," *Cultural Capital* (Chicago: University of Chicago Press, 1993), 85–133.

12. As Rhodes notes: "The school exercise that is really at the heart of the Tudor schoolboy's exposure to creative writing is the practice of double translation. This was in fact sometimes called 'imitation' by Elizabethan schoolmasters, and it is this that really confirms the transferability of writing skills between Latin and the vernacular in the Renaissance." Rhodes, "Did Shakespeare Study Creative Writing?" 68. See also Lynn Enterline's more recent study of *Shakespeare's Schoolroom: Rhetoric, Discipline, Emotion* (Philadelphia: University of Pennsylvania Press, 2011).

13. Sarah Davison, "Joyce's Incorporation of Literary Sources in 'Oxen of the Sun,'" *Genetic Joyce Studies* 9 (Spring 2009): n.p., http://www.geneticjoycestudies.org/GJS9/GJS9_SarahDavisonOxen.htm.

14. William Wordsworth, "Preface," *Lyrical Ballads* (London: T.N. Longman and O. Rees, 1802): xviii. Apposite here is Sir Walter Scott's later "Essay on Imitations of the Ancient Ballad" (1830). For more on the Victorian reception of the ballad, see also Meredith Martin, "'Imperfectly Civilized': Ballads, Nations, and Histories of Form," *ELH* 82, no. 2 (Summer 2015): 345–63.

15. Mary Ellen Brown has written insightfully on the vicissitudes of the ballad's chronological placement (namely: Medieval vs. eighteenth century) in successive editions of the *Norton Anthology of English Literature*.

16. David Mikics, *Slow Reading in a Hurried Age* (Cambridge: Harvard University Press, 2013).

17. [Loftus note:] I replaced "disconsolate" with the harsher, more Germanic-sounding "gloomy" here; however, when I originally used "disconsolate" I lifted it right from Heaney's translation: "They were *disconsolate* and wailed aloud for their lord's decease" (lines 3148–49).

18. [Loftus note:] Female characters are limited to the mothers of warriors or "great men" in *Beowulf*; they are simply named and never developed. There is no love and/or romance element like that of Guinevere in the Arthur stories.

BIBLIOGRAPHY

Ackerman, James S. *Origins, Imitations, Conventions: Representation in the Visual Arts.* Cambridge, MA: MIT Press, 2002.

Ascham, Roger. "Of Imitation." In *The Schoolemaster.* 1570. *Elizabethan Critical Essays,* edited by G. Gregory Smith, 1–45. Oxford: The Clarendon Press, 1904.

Auden, W. H. "In Memory of W. B. Yeats." *Collected Poems.* 1939. Reprint, New York: Random House, 2007.

Bjørnsted, Hall, ed. *Borrowed Feathers: Plagiarism and the Limits of Imitation in Early Modern Europe.* Oslo: Academic Press, 2008.

Briggs, John C. "Writing Without Reading: The Decline of Literature in the Composition Classroom." *Forum: A Publication of the Association of Literary Scholars, Critics, and Writers* 1 (Winter 2004): 1–27.

Brinkman, Bartholomew. "Imitations, Manipulations and Interpretations: Creative Writing in the Critical Classroom." *Iowa Journal of Cultural Studies* 12/13 (Spring/Fall 2010): 158–62.

Brown, Howard Mayer. "Emulation, Competition, and Homage: Imitation and Theories of Imitation in the Renaissance." *Journal of the American Musicological Society* 35, no. 1 (Spring 1982): 1–48.

Brown, Mary Ellen. "Placed, Replaced, or Misplaced? The Ballads' Progress." *The Eighteenth Century* 47, no. 2 (Summer 2006): 115–29.

Clark, Donald Lemen. "Imitation: Theory and Practice in Roman Rhetoric." *Quarterly Journal of Speech* 37, no. 1 (1951): 11–22.

Connelly, Peter. "Traditions of English Literature I." Grinnell College, Spring 1992.

Conte, Gian Biagio. *The Rhetoric of Imitation: Genre and Poetic Memory in Virgil and Other Latin Poets.* Translated by Charles Segal. Ithaca, NY: Cornell University Press, 1986.

Cook, Trevor James Neilson. "Plagiarism and Proprietary Authorship in Early Modern England, 1590–1640." PhD diss., University of Toronto, 2011.

Davison, Richard Allan. "Hemingway's *A Farewell to Arms.*" *The Explicator* 29, no. 6 (1971): 89–91.

Davison, Sarah. "Joyce's Incorporation of Literary Sources in 'Oxen of the Sun.'" *Genetic Joyce Studies* 9 (Spring 2009): n.p. http://www.geneticjoycestudies.org/GJS9/GJS9_Sarah DavisonOxen.htm.

Dryden, John. Dedication to *The Aeneid.* London: Jacob Tonson, 1697.

Edwards, R. R. "Imitation." In *Princeton Encyclopedia of Poetry and Poetics,* 4th ed., edited by Roland Greene et al., 675–80. Princeton: Princeton University Press, 2012.

Emerson, Ralph Waldo. "Quotation and Originality." In *Letters and Social Aims,* 157–81. Boston: James R. Osgood, 1876.

———. "Self-Reliance." In *Essays: First Series.* Boston: J. Munroe and Company, 1841.

Enterline, Lynn. *Shakespeare's Schoolroom: Rhetoric, Discipline, Emotion.* Philadelphia: University of Pennsylvania Press, 2011.

Erasmus, Desiderius. *De Copia*. Paris: Badius, 1512.

Esterly, David. *The Lost Carving: A Journey to the Heart of Making*. New York: Penguin, 2013.

Fiske, George C. *Lucilius and Horace: A Study in the Classical Theory of Imitation*. University of Wisconsin Studies in Language and Literature 7. Hildesheim: Georg Olms Verlagbuchhandlung, 1966.

Franklin, Benjamin. *The Autobiography*. London: J. Parsons, 1793.

Frey, Charles. "Interpreting 'Western Wind.'" *ELH* 43, no. 3 (Autumn 1976): 259–78.

Galbraith, David. *Architectonics of Imitation in Spenser, Daniel, and Drayton*. Toronto: University of Toronto Press, 2000.

Gombrich, E. H. *Art and Illusion: A Study in the Psychology of Pictorial Representation*. 2nd. ed. New York: Pantheon, 1961.

Greene, Thomas. *The Light in Troy: Imitation and Discovery in Renaissance Poetry*. The Elizabethan Club Series 7. New Haven: Yale University Press, 1982.

Guillory, John. "Discipline and Knowledge Base: The Uses of the Historical Survey Course." https://ade-adfl.commons.mla.org/files/2016/03/John-Guillorys-Discipline-and-Knowledge-Base.pdf.

————. "Mute Inglorious Miltons: Gray, Wordsworth, and the Vernacular Canon." *Cultural Capital*, 85–133. Chicago: University of Chicago Press, 1993.

Hemingway, Ernest. *A Farewell to Arms*. 1929. New York: Macmillan, 1957.

Hollander, John. *Rhyme's Reason: A Guide to English Verse*. 4th ed. New Haven: Yale University Press, 2014.

Horowitz, Maryanne Cline. *Seeds of Virtue and Knowledge*. Princeton: Princeton University Press, 1998.

Lucken, Michael. *Imitation and Creativity in Japanese Arts: From Kishida Ryusei to Miyazki Hayao*. New York: Columbia University Press, 2016.

Mack, Robert. *The Genius of Parody: Imitation and Originality in Seventeenth- and Eighteenth-Century English Literature*. New York: Palgrave, 2007.

MacLeish, Archibald. "Public Speech and Private Speech in Poetry." *Yale Review* 27 (March 1938): 536–47.

Martin, Meredith. "'Imperfectly Civilized': Ballads, Nations, and Histories of Form." *ELH* 82, no. 2 (Summer 2015): 345–63.

McKeon, Richard. "Literary Criticism and the Concept of Imitation in Antiquity." *Modern Philology* 34, no. 1 (August 1936): 1–35.

Menand, Louis. "Show or Tell: Should Creative Writing be Taught?" *New Yorker*, June 8, 2009, 106–12.

Mikics, David. *Slow Reading in a Hurried Age*. Cambridge, MA: Harvard University Press, 2013.

Miller, William. "Double Translation in English Humanistic Education." *Studies in the Renaissance* 10 (1963): 163–74.

Montaigne, Michel de. "On the Education of Children." In *Essays*, translated by John M. Cohen, 49–85. New York: Penguin, 1993.

Myers, D. G. *The Elephants Teach: Creative Writing Since 1880*. Chicago: University of Chicago Press, 1996.

Ong, Walter J. "Oral Residue in Tudor Prose Style." *PMLA* 80, no. 3 (June 1965): 145–54.

Passannante, Gerard. "The Art of Reading Earthquakes: On Harvey's Wit, Ramus's Method, and the Renaissance of Lucretius." *Renaissance Quarterly* 61, no. 3 (2008): 792–832.

Pigman, G. W. "Versions of Imitation in the Renaissance." *Renaissance Quarterly* 33, no. 1 (1980): 1–32.

Puttenham, George. *The Arte of English Poesie*. London: Richard Field, 1589.

Queneau, Raymond. *Exercises in Style*. 1947. New York: New Directions, 2013.

Quint, David, Margaret Ferguson, G. W. Pigman III, and Wayne Rebhorn, eds. *Creative Imitation: New Essays on Renaissance Literature in Honor of Thomas M. Greene*. Binghamton: Center for Medieval and Early Renaissance Studies, 1992.

Quintilian. *The Institutio Oratoria*. Translated by H. E. Butler. 4 vols. New York: G. P. Putnam's Sons, 1922.

Reiss, Timothy J. *Against Autonomy: Global Dialectics of Cultural Exchange*. Palo Alto, CA: Stanford University Press, 2002.

Rhodes, Neil. "Did Shakespeare Study Creative Writing?" In *Shakespeare and the Origins of English*, 45–84. Oxford: Oxford University Press, 2004.

Robinson, Peter. *Poetry, Poets, Readers: Making Things Happen*. Oxford: Oxford University Press, 2002.

Steadman, John M. *The Lamb and the Elephant: Ideal Imitation and the Context of Renaissance Allegory*. San Marino: The Huntington Library, 1974.

Weinsheimer, Joel. *Imitation*. Boston: Routledge & Kegan Paul, 1984.

West, David, and Tony Woodman, eds. *Creative Imitation and Latin Literature*. Cambridge: Cambridge University Press, 1979.

White, Harold Ogden. *Plagiarism and Imitation During the English Renaissance: A Study in Critical Distinctions*. Cambridge, MA: Harvard University Press, 1935.

Williams, John. *Stoner*. 1965. New York: New York Review of Books, 2003.

Williams, Raymond. "Creative." In *Keywords: A Vocabulary of Culture and Society*, 82–84. Rev. ed. New York: Oxford University Press, 1983.

Wordsworth, William. "Preface." In *Lyrical Ballads*. London: T. N. Longman and O. Rees, 1802.

COURSE DOCUMENT: NEWSTOK

"No Bees, No Honey" (Sappho I.vi.62)
"Ancient analyses of bees and flowers are at the bedrock of
humanist theory of *imitatio.*"

—Horowitz, *Seeds of Virtue and Knowledge*, 114

Homeric Hymn to Hermes (c. seventh to sixth century BCE)
From there flying now here, now there, they feed on honeycomb and *bring
each thing to pass. And after that they eat the yellow honey, they are seized
with manic frenzy and are eager to speak the truth.* But if they are robbed of
the sweet food of the gods, then they do buzz about in confusion and lie.
(558–63; Reiss, *Against Autonomy*)

Plato, *Ion* (c. 380 BCE)
Poets tell us that they bring songs from honeyed fountains, culling them
out of the gardens and dells of the Muses; they, like the bees, winging their
way from flower to flower. And this is true. For the poet is a light and
winged and holy thing, and there is no invention in him until he has been
inspired and is out of his senses, and the mind is no longer in him: when he
has not attained to this state, he is powerless and is unable to utter his
oracles.

Lucretius (99–55 BCE), *De rerum natura* 3.10–12
From your pages, as bees in flowery glades sip every blossom, *so do I crop
all your golden sayings.*

**Vergil (70–19 BCE), *Aeneid*, 1.432ff [Aeneas marveling at
Carthage's industriousness]**
Just as bees in early summer carry out their tasks among the flowery
fields, in the sun, when they lead out the adolescent young of their race,
or *cram the cells with liquid honey, and swell them with sweet nectar,* or
receive the incoming burdens, or forming lines drive the lazy herd of
drones from their hives:

Horace (65–27 BCE), *Carmina* **4.2.27–32**
I, after the way and manner of the Matinian bee, *that gathers the pleasant thyme with repeated labor* around the groves and banks of well-watered Tibur, I, a humble bard, *fashion my verses with incessant toil.*

Seneca (54–39 BC), *Epistulae morales* **84, letter to Lucilius**
We should follow, men say, the example of the bees, who flit about and cull the flowers that are suitable for producing honey, and then arrange and assort in their cells all that they have brought in; these bees, as our Vergil says, *pack close the flowing honey, And swell their cells with nectar sweet.*
It is not certain whether the juice which they obtain from the flowers forms at once into honey, or whether they change that which they have gathered into this delicious object by blending something therewith and by a certain property of their breath. . . .

But I must not be led astray into another subject than that which we are discussing. We also, I say, ought to copy these bees, and sift whatever we have gathered from a varied course of reading, for such things are better preserved if they are kept separate; then, by applying the supervising care with which our nature has endowed us,—in other words, our natural gifts,— we should so blend those several flavors into one delicious compound that, even though it betrays its origin, yet it nevertheless is clearly a different thing from that whence it came. This is what we see nature doing in our own bodies without any labor on our part; the food we have eaten, as long as it retains its original quality and floats in our stomachs as an undiluted mass, is a burden; but it passes into tissue and blood only when it has been changed from its original form. So it is with the food which nourishes our higher nature,— we should see to it that whatever we have absorbed should not be allowed to remain unchanged, or it will be no part of us. We must digest it; otherwise it will merely enter the memory and not the reasoning power. Let us loyally welcome such foods and make them our own, so that something that is one may be formed out of many elements, just as one number is formed of several elements whenever, by our reckoning, lesser sums, each different from the others, are brought together. This is what our mind should do: it should hide away all the materials by which it has been aided, and bring to light only what it has made of them. Even if there shall appear in you a likeness to him who, by reason of your admiration, has left a deep impress upon you, I would have you resemble him as a child resembles his father, and not as a picture resembles its original; for a picture is a lifeless thing.

Quintilian (c. 35–c. 100), *Institutio Oratoria*

We know that these are composed of ingredients which produce many and sometimes contrary effects, but mixed together they make a single compound resembling no one of its component parts, but deriving its peculiar properties from all: *so too dumb insects produce honey, whose taste is beyond the skill of man to imitate, from different kinds of flowers and juices.* Shall we marvel then, if oratory, the highest gift of providence to man, needs the assistance of many arts, which, although they do not reveal or intrude themselves in actual speaking, supply hidden forces and make their silent presence felt?

Plutarch (46–120)

The bee by nature finds the smoothest and the best honey in the most bitter flowers and sharpest thornes; so children, if they are properly educated in poetry, will learn somehow to extract something useful and helpful even from works which are suspected of being immoral and inappropriate.

Macrobius (395–423), *Saturnalia* (preface, from Loeb translation)

5. We ought to imitate bees, if I can put it that way: wandering about, sampling the flowers, they arrange whatever they've gathered, distributing it among the honeycomb's cells, and by blending in the peculiar quality of their own spirit they transform the diverse kinds of nectar into a single taste . . . blending the varied samples so that we experience a single flavor: even if some item's source should be clear, it still seems different from that evident source.

Peter of Blois (c. 1130–c. 1211), *Epistles* 92

Why should that be accounted envy which fuses into a single study of virtue and exercise of prudence all that I have taken from my wide reading and digested with keen ardor? For as we read in the *Saturnalia* and in Seneca's epistles to Lucilius, *we must imitate those bees gathering flowers whose various nectars are turned to honey and are mingled to create a single savor.*

Petrarch (1304–74), *Rerum Familiarum*, 1.8
"Letter to Tommaso da Messina"

[I]n this matter I cannot give much more than a single piece of advice. . . . In short I want you to realize that [Seneca] is the source of this advice. *His loftiest advice about invention is to imitate the bees which through an astonishing process produce wax and honey from the flowers they leave behind.* Macrobius in his Saturnalia reported not only the sense but the very words of Seneca so that to me at the very time *he seemed to be following this advice in his reading and writing, he seemed to be disapproving of it by what he did. For he did not try to produce honey from the flowers culled from Seneca but instead produced them whole and in the very form in which he had found them on the stems.* . . . These are the things I thought I should say about imitating the bees. From their example, select and conceal the better ones in the beehive of your heart and hold on to them with the greatest diligence and preserve them steadfastly, lest anything should possibly perish. And be careful not to let any of those things that you have plucked remain with you too long, *for the bees would enjoy no glory if they did not transform those things they found into something else which was better.*

Petrarch, Letter 23, to Boccaccio

An imitator must take care to write something similar yet not identical to the original, and that similarity must not be like the image to its original in painting where the greater the similarity the greater the praise for the artist, but rather like *that of a son to his father* . . . Seeing the son's face, we are reminded of the father's although if it came to measurement, the features would all be different. . . . It may all be summarized *by saying with Seneca, and Horace before him, that we must write as the bees make honey, not gathering flowers but turning them into honeycombs, thereby blending them into a oneness that is unlike them all, and better.* ["Petrarch fathers his text by ingesting Seneca's writing and concocting it into his own literary offspring."

Aeneas Sylvius Piccolomini, *De liberorum educatione* (1450, rpt. 1551)

A master thus qualified will be competent to fulfill his duty, which is to fence in the growing mind with wise and noble precept and example, as a careful gardener hedges round a newly-planted tree. For in right training of the boy lies the secret of the integrity of the man . . . Other creatures enjoy the colour, or the scent, of the flower; they, however, *are wise to extract its lurking sweetness.* Thus they choose where they will settle, and are content that with just that fruition of their choice which serves their end . . . Herein is laid down an *admirable principle by which we may be guided in reading all authors of antiquity.*

Baldassare Castiglione, *The Book of the Courtier* (1528; English trans. 1561)

And even as in green meadows *the bee flits about among the grasses robbing the flowers, so our Courtier must steal this grace* from those who seem to him to have it, taking from each the part that seems most worthy of praise.

Erasmus, *Ciceronianus* (1528)

They fashion a liquid with their organs, and after it is made their own, they give that forth in which you do not recognize the taste or odor of flower or shrub but a product mingled in due proportion from them all.

Montaigne, *Essays* (1570–92)

The bees steal from this flower and that, but *afterwards turn their pilferings into honey, which is their own*; it is thyme and marjoram no longer. So *the pupil will transform and fuse together the passages that he borrows from others,* to make of them something entirely his own; that is to say, *his own judgment.*

Robert Burton, *The Anatomy of Melancholy* (1621)

As a good housewife out of divers fleeces weaves one piece of cloth, *a bee gathers wax and honey out of many flowers, and makes a new bundle of all, Floriferis ut apes in saltibus omnia libant* [as bees in flowerly glades sip from all—Lucretius], I have laboriously collected this cento out of divers writers . . . The matters is theirs most part, and yet mine, *apparaet unde sumptum sit* [it is plain whence it is taken] (*which Seneca approves*), *aliud tamen quam unde sumptum sit apparet* [yet it becomes different from whence it is taken]; which nature doth with the aliment of our bodies, incorporate, digest, assimilate, I do *conquoquere quod hausi* [digest what I have swallowed], dispose of what I take.

Jonathan Swift (1667–1745), *The Battel of the Books* (1704)

[the bee] by an universal Range, *with long Search, much Study, true Judgment*, and Distinction of Things, *brings home Honey and Wax.* [the bee's] infinite *Labour, and search,* and ranging thro' every Corner of Nature [provide] the two Noblest of Things, which are *Sweetness and Light.*

Bingo Pedagogy

Team-Based Learning and the Literature Survey[1]

DESIRÉE HENDERSON, UNIVERSITY OF TEXAS ARLINGTON

At the university where I teach, the survey of American literature is offered as a one-semester course that is intended to cover the entire history of American literature from the beginning to the present in fifteen weeks. The typical challenges encountered by every teacher of survey courses are maximized in this course. Like others, I aspire to achieve coverage while knowing that the limited time frame makes the task impossible. I wrestle with the question of which authors and texts to include and exclude, and with the political stakes of each choice. And I struggle to make my teaching in this recurring service class fresh, engaged, and impactful for my students. For the past several years, I have employed the pedagogical method known as Team-Based Learning as the foundational structure for this survey course. Team-Based Learning is, as the name suggests, an instructional strategy that privileges collaborative learning and critical thinking through activities and assignments that are completed by teams of students. In this essay, I introduce Team-Based Learning (or TBL), describe how I apply its methods in my literature survey, and make the case that TBL is particularly suited to addressing some of the central challenges of teaching survey courses. I show that implementing a modified TBL pedagogy enables faculty to set aside the unreachable goal of comprehensive coverage in favor of other attainable and equally valuable goals, including the development of problem-solving skills, the cultivation of interpersonal relationships, and the promotion of the joyful and playful aspects of learning.

In addition, I suggest that the communal nature of TBL has a particularly appropriate place within a survey of American literature. The tensions between individualism and community that run throughout American literary history take on new resonance in a class structured around collective learning activities. Students are likely to think differently about both the ringing endorsements and scathing critiques of individuality they encounter in their reading, including such famous quotes as Ralph Waldo Emerson's "Trust thyself: every heart vibrates to that iron string" and Claude McKay's "O kinsmen! we must meet the common foe! / Though far outnumbered let us show us brave."[2] The questions about self and other at the core of such texts are concretely manifest in students' relationships with and dependence upon each other within a TBL class. Furthermore, many American literary texts that grapple with the themes of individual and community are situated within educational environments. Stories of learning are central to American literature, including those that explore the consequences of authoritarian pedagogical practices. I propose that the TBL method allows pedagogy itself to become a site of inquiry within an American literature survey, enabling students to think critically about how their own educations relate to the processes of nationalism, assimilation, revolution, and liberation represented in the works they read.

> "I obliged [my students] to Study their Books, and to help one another."
> —Samsom Occom, *A Short Narrative of My Life* (c. 1760)

Team-Based Learning was originally developed by Larry Michaelsen in the late 1970s and has now become an influential pedagogical method, widely adopted across university campuses.[3] While TBL remains more common in medical, science, and social science fields than in the humanities, the system has much to offer to the literature classroom. TBL has four constituent elements:

1. Permanent and strategically formed teams;
2. Pre-testing at the beginning of each unit;
3. Problem-solving activities that involve the application of knowledge;
4. Peer evaluations to enhance accountability between team members.[4]

As I describe it to my students at the start of the semester, TBL courses require students to work in teams and to have at least a portion of their final grades be determined by teamwork, including graded evaluations by fellow students. Early in the semester, students are sorted into teams in such a way as to spread strengths and resources across the teams; students will work in the same teams throughout the semester, which cultivates relationships and accountability. The teams encourage peer-to-peer teaching, incentivize out-of-class preparation, and make mutual support an integral part of the learning process. There is an extensive body of scholarship on TBL and particularly on the best methods for forming TBL teams, developing a fair and functional peer evaluation process, and managing team conflict.[5] My remarks primarily focus on the use of pre-tests and problem-based team activities and what these contribute to literature survey courses. I begin by addressing what I see as some of the main challenges that students face in a literature survey.

One central challenge presented by survey courses is that the large number of texts covered in the semester can quickly become an undifferentiated mass to students. Particularly if you employ an anthology as I do in my survey of American literature, the number of short works and excerpts from longer works blur together. I teach as many as seventy texts by thirty-five different authors in my survey of American literature and students find it difficult to locate individual texts within a specific historical moment. In the past, I struggled to provide students with effective conceptual scaffolding, even though I employ a fairly straightforward chronological order, but TBL has equipped me to address this issue. TBL follows a structure of activities and assessments that is repeated with every unit of the course (see Table 1).

Table 1. **Team-Based Learning Unit Sequence**

Advance Preparation	Readiness Assurance Process (pre-test) (1 class period)	Application Activities (1-4 class periods)	Post-test
Students complete a substantial reading assignment outside of class.	Students are tested on their reading, following the RAT sequence: 1. iRAT 2. tRAT 3. Appeals 4. Instructor feedback: discussion or mini-lecture.	Teams work together to solve problems, following the 4-S activity format.	Students individually complete a second form of assessment to evaluate how their knowledge has been deepened or refined through the TBL process.

First, students complete a substantial reading assignment and are tested with a pretest method known as Readiness Assessment Tests or RATs (which I discuss in more detail below). After students have completed the RATs, the faculty member may step in to provide whatever instruction remains necessary to answer students' questions or clarify their knowledge. Second, several course days are devoted to team activities that privilege problem solving and the application of knowledge. Last, students are assessed again on their understanding of the material or issues covered in the unit. My American literature survey is organized around six units that follow this structure; for instance, a unit on the nineteenth century begins with a pretest on Douglass's *Narrative of the Life*, proceeds through several application exercises related to authors such as Dickinson, Jacobs, Melville, and Whitman, and concludes with a short writing assignment on the themes of individualism and community. Repeating this sequence of activities and assessments in each unit has clear pedagogical benefits by allowing students to gain familiarity and confidence as they do similar tasks over again, and to learn from their mistakes along the way. In addition, it segments a large body of information into comprehensible parts, overlaying the course material with a grid that helps to orient students. I have seen that the clear landmarks established by the TBL sequence enhance students' ability to recall, recognize, and evaluate the material we have covered.

Although the challenge of student preparedness is not an obstacle specific to survey courses—as any faculty member can attest—it can have a particularly negative impact upon student success in a survey course. RATs are an effective tool for encouraging students to read before arriving to class. Each unit of the class commences with an extensive out-of-class reading assignment upon which students are tested before they have received instruction from faculty. Similar to the logic of the "flipped" classroom, this aspect of TBL places the burden upon students to familiarize themselves with basic information or foundational materials on their own, freeing up class time for more advanced critical engagement. However, the TBL pretest system follows a unique sequence: in a single class session at the beginning of the unit, students take a multiple-choice pretest as individuals (iRAT) and then immediately retake the identical test as a team (tRAT). The tRAT format is what gives rise to the title of my essay; tRATs are taken using scratch-off test forms, which my students familiarly call "bingo cards"[6] (see Figure 7). This testing mechanism encourages students' advance preparation and assesses their retention and comprehension of information, but it is also a core component of team building. The experience of working with classmates to come to consensus on test questions and the immediate feedback provided by the scratch-off cards is gratifying, as well

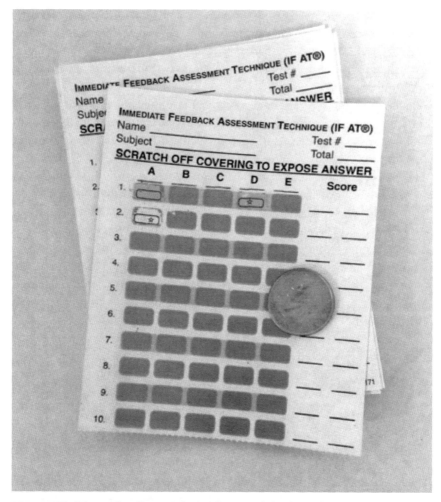

Figure 7. IF-AT scratch-off testing form. Photograph by the author.

as fostering peer-to-peer instruction, vocal encouragement, and a great deal of laughter. The scratch-off cards allow teams to make repeated attempts to arrive at the correct answer (following an "answer-until-correct" format, with diminishing points for each attempt), a process that requires discussion, negotiation, and reconsideration. While RATs are primarily designed to jump-start each new unit, they establish a classroom culture that encourages and rewards preparedness, while also providing a concrete measure of teamwork. Students are graded for both their individual and team RATs but the tRATs are more heavily weighted; as my students quickly discover, every tRAT score is higher than any iRAT score, concretely demonstrating that working together and building upon each team member's strengths benefits them all.[7] In my observation, students begin to look forward to RAT days on the syllabus, rather than dreading the testing process.

Yet another problem specific to the literature survey has to do with the fact that, for the most part, students register for survey courses out of obligation, not interest. Surveys are often required courses and are perceived by students as something to get out of the way so that they can move on to upper-division electives on specialized topics. It can be difficult for teachers of survey courses to overcome students' preconceptions and to spark their curiosity about the material, no matter how much enthusiasm we may have for it. I find that the TBL method introduces an element of fun into my survey classes, greatly improving students' attitudes toward both the class and the material it covers. While fun is sometimes derided as a pedagogical goal, it is central to TBL. For instance, the use of scratch-off cards to complete tRATs makes test taking resemble playing a game. In an era when so many games are played alone or virtually, the RAT method harkens back to a retro tabletop game. I watch my students huddled in their teams, debating possible responses, holding their breath as one student scratches off their selected answer, and then cheering out loud when they see they have identified the correct answer—or groaning in disappointment when they discover they did not. A similar kind of excitement, humor, and interpersonal connection is fostered by the application activities that occur during the third part of the TBL sequence, and which I introduce below. Together, these two constituent elements of TBL pedagogy break down the conventional structure of the classroom and enliven students' curiosity and interest.

A final challenge of the survey has little to do with specific course content and everything to do with institutional culture, yet it is one of the most significant obstacles that the students at my university face. My students are preponderantly nontraditional: almost all have jobs off-campus, many have spouses and children, many are returning students, and most commute to campus. These factors result in a highly disconnected student body. While students generally do not perceive that their lack of connectedness has an impact upon their scholastic success, interpersonal relationships can play a considerable role in determining whether, how quickly, and how well students complete their degrees. As Daniel Chambliss and Christopher Takacs declare in *How College Works*, "satisfactory personal relationships are a *prerequisite* for learning."[8] I have employed a variety of methods in my classes to create the opportunity for such relationships to develop, from group work to service learning. But I have found TBL to be one of the most effective mechanisms for fostering interpersonal relationships because TBL makes face-to-face interaction a core component of the course.[9] Students are obligated to interact, but because the interaction takes the form of play and occurs repeatedly across the semester, the stakes are altered and almost all discover that they can contribute to the success of the team. Ideally, the experience of working together in teams will lead to friendships that last beyond the end of the semester.

I have described how these team benefits arise through the scratch-off testing method, but they are equally reliant upon the application exercises that form the third component of the TBL sequence. While each unit of the course begins with an iRAT/tRAT pair, it is followed by several class days in which teams work together on problem-based activities or "application activities" that follow four basic criteria:

1. Significant problem
2. Specific choice
3. Same problem
4. Simultaneous reporting[10]

This 4-S structure invites faculty to develop activities that center on a problem, question, or case study that has significant implications within the discipline. Teams are presented both with the problem and with a set of possible choices (answers, actions, interpretations, etc.) from which they must choose. All teams work on the same problem, consider the same set of choices, and—key to the TBL format—reveal their choices at the same time. Simultaneous reporting cuts down on the scenario in which, after hearing another answer, a team of students might waver in their confidence in their own answer, change their answer altogether, or make the weak claim, "That's what we were going to say." Instead, by revealing their answers concurrently, teams commit to defending their choices. Within the 4-S structure, application activities take many forms: some exercises are completed as gallery walks; others involve concept mapping or other visual mapping activities, or any number of digital applications such as wikis or social media polls. I frequently make use of voting cards printed with the letters A, B, C, and D in large, visible font; I call upon each team to vote for their chosen answer by holding up a card for everyone in the class to see. In the moment of simultaneous revelation, the range of possible responses becomes immediately apparent to us all.

One of the application activities that I have developed and used successfully in my survey of American literature follows a deceptively simple "Agree or Disagree" format: I present a series of interpretive claims about an assigned text on the classroom projector screen and the teams must decide whether or not they agree or disagree with each claim. After a brief discussion, they must choose to hold up A) Agree or B) Disagree voting cards, and then defend their choice with evidence from the text. I deliberately write bold and provocative claims that require students to take a strong stance. For instance, regarding Frederick Douglass's *Narrative of the Life*: "Douglass advocates violent resistance as a necessary step in eradicating slavery from the United States." Or, with regard to Sarah Orne Jewett's "The White Heron": "Sylvia's attachment to the tree and white heron symbolizes a rejection of her feminine identity." One of my goals is to encourage students to consider the rhetorical advantage of making emphatic interpretive claims, instead of the safe, middle-of-the-ground arguments common in student writing. For the same reason, I do not give teams the option to choose a "somewhat agree, somewhat disagree" position during this exercise. I take the opportunity to talk about how making affirmative claims can result in better and more effective analytical essays. However, I modify the 4-S structure insofar as all the provided claims can be both supported and challenged by the text; in keeping with the disciplinary goals of literary studies, this exercise demonstrates that textual analysis is designed to produce persuasive and well-supported claims, not to uncover a singular truth. The exercise works best when both A and B cards are held up, and teams make counterarguments that capture the complexity of the text under consideration.

> "I want you to hear this story . . . [about] a terrible question which
> men here have gone mad and died trying to answer."
> —Rebecca Harding Davis, *Life in the Iron Mills* (1861)

Although I have thus far focused on the many positive benefits TBL has made to my survey of American literature, here I would like to address some of my early reservations and how I came to think differently about TBL. When I first learned about TBL I thought that its emphasis upon pretesting was incompatible with the study of literature.[11] The idea that students are tested on their comprehension and recall of a substantial out-of-class reading appeared to me to favor more information-based, as compared to analysis-based, disciplines. Additionally, while I considered myself a practitioner of the progressive and student-centered pedagogy advocated by Paulo Freire in *Pedagogy of the Oppressed*, I had to admit to myself how strongly I held onto the idea that my students needed me in order to fully engage with a literary text. By relying upon their out-of-class reading to provide them with all the knowledge they needed to progress, I instead had to place faith in my students that—given the right materials and the incentive to read them deeply—they could learn on their own. The literature survey has turned out to be the right course for this approach in part because the anthology I assign, the *Bedford Anthology of American Literature* (Shorter Edition), has excellent introductory essays on historical periods and literary movements, and headnotes before every primary text. While I previously chafed at the limitations imposed by a preset anthology, I have learned to appreciate the anthology as a resource that, if used well, can facilitate independent learning.

By incorporating the pretesting method, I also had to accept that whatever texts were assigned on RAT days were going to receive more focused attention than other texts in the semester. Survey courses as a rule have a flat structure: no single text or author is favored over the others, providing students with a bird's-eye view of the literary tradition. By its nature, TBL raises certain texts to prominence, namely those readings that appear at the start of each unit. Yet, I have found this to yield a number of surprising benefits within my survey course, including reinforcing the organizational structure of the class. I describe the primary texts that kick off each of the six units in my course as "key texts" that exemplify prominent questions, issues, or stylistic developments for the period under consideration. In the most recent version of this course I offered, these key texts were Mary Rowlandson's captivity narrative, Benjamin Franklin's autobiography, Douglass's *Narrative of the Life*, Charles Chesnutt's "The Passing of Grandison," Ernest Hemingway's "Big Two Hearted River," and Donald Barthelme's "The School." The emphasis placed upon these texts enables my students to gain a sense of mastery because they are tested on them (and relevant contextual essays from the anthology) at the start of each unit through the RAT tests and then will write about these texts again in posttests. The arc of learning that occurs between their first and second encounters with the key texts reinforces the value of returning to and reconsidering previous conclusions, particularly when the introduction of additional voices, perspectives, and opinions may result in new insights.[12]

The other major reservation I had about the implementation of TBL had to do with the applicability of problem-based learning to literary studies. My initial reaction was that some disciplines are more obviously organized around urgent problems that can be solved by arriving at specific, informed solutions. I was unaccustomed to thinking of the study of literature in this way. My change in perspective was influenced by the course design method known as "backwards design." In *Understanding by Design*, Grant Wiggins and Jay McTighe call upon teachers to organize their classes around "essential questions," which they describe in part as "important questions that recur throughout all our lives" and which reflect "core ideas and inquiries within a discipline."[13] Identifying such questions reveals the deep, underlying, but often poorly artic- ulated reasons for why we do what we do in the classroom. These questions are the problems around which our disciplines cohere but they also transcend dis- ciplinary-specific concerns and enable us to engage with much larger issues. Importantly, as Wiggins and McTighe explain it, essential questions provoke a range of responses, which is why they remain alive and engaging. Essential questions should generate debate, discussion, and reconsideration and, for this reason, the answers will be complex and multifaceted—offering no easy solutions.

One of the essential questions I identified as central to my conception of the American literature survey can be summed up as: What can we learn from his- torical works of literature about the issues that continue to spark debate and controversy in our contemporary era? To enable students to engage with this question, I constructed a set of written assignments that ask students to exam- ine a contemporary problem through the lens of an earlier body of writing. One such assignment prompts students to consider the question: Is religious pluralism possible in the United States? This assignment functions as the posttest for an early unit in the semester. After reading a selection of works from the colonial period, anchored by the key text of Mary Rowlandson's cap- tivity narrative, students conclude by demonstrating their ability to interpret literary texts through standard analytical methods. But, they do so in order to establish links between the past and the present, and to grapple with a question that remains urgent and unresolved in our present day. Ultimately, as assign- ments like this demonstrate, the conceptual work of backwards design enabled me to better articulate what essential questions were at the heart of the class. As a result, I have come to embrace problem-based learning like TBL as entirely appropriate to literature courses and, in fact, as bringing to the forefront the stakes of literary analysis.

Moreover, a problem-based approach draws attention to the fact that a great deal of American literature is itself problem-based, that is, grappling directly with specific social or political problems: slavery, gender inequality, immigrant rights, poverty, war, and so forth. Among the problems that American authors have explored is education itself—namely, how the promises of liberation and self-improvement offered by education are often negated by the limitations and violence inherent within many of its institutional forms. As I suggested at the beginning of this essay, approaching the study of American literature through a TBL format provides a unique opportunity to make learning itself an object of study. Students encounter perspectives on education in texts as diverse as

Franklin's autobiography, Antin's *The Promised Land*, Ellison's *Invisible Man*, and Barthelme's "The School," to name a few. For instance, a work like Zitkála-Šá's *The School Days of an Indian Girl* portrays education as a tool for forced assimilation. My students are alert to the damage inflicted by the oppressive pedagogical regime of the missionary school Zitkála-Šá attends, as well as to the strategies that she employs to succeed despite the racism she encounters. It takes little prodding for students to offer up their own stories of educational environments meant to produce docile conformity instead of critical thinking. Moments like these provide an opportunity to talk about the objectives behind collaborative learning methods like TBL and how they can be seen to run parallel to the arguments made by American authors regarding the value of building relationships across our differences, and the dire consequences when we fail to do so. Acknowledging that a team-based learning method is designed to address entrenched structural problems within higher education invites students to recognize that the pedagogical form of an American literature survey course may grow directly out of the struggle for rights and representation depicted in the texts assigned within it.

> "I wander the streets with a regular crew, my teammates, my defenders, and my posse . . . We matter to one another if we don't matter to anybody else."
> —Sherman Alexie, "What You Pawn I will Redeem" (2003)

In this essay, I have identified what I see as the primary ways in which Team-Based Learning improves students' experiences and outcomes within the American literature survey. I will conclude by briefly describing why TBL is also good for faculty members. It will be obvious that TBL decenters the classroom, allowing faculty to step away from their perch as experts and privileging the process of collaboration and decision-making between peers. The rewards for students are significant in terms of the fun they have, the relationships they build, and the mastery they develop. But, the excitement, energy, and goodwill generated by team activities extend to faculty, as well. In my experience, the fact that TBL breaks down conventional academic hierarchies results in students being more willing to approach me as a resource rather than to perceive me as a judge or evaluator. Although my primary goal is for students to establish meaningful connections with each other, I have been rewarded with many opportunities for meaningful interactions with my students as well.

However, to arrive at these benefits requires a great deal of work. It can be challenging to plan a TBL course, particularly if the faculty member engages in the backwards design methodology. To do so necessitates a significant amount of advance preparation, organization, and development of materials before the first day of class. While I have argued that the payoff is substantial, I am also convinced that it is only worthwhile to develop a TBL course if that course will be repeated often. It is for this reason that TBL is particularly well suited for teachers of literature survey courses. Survey courses are often offered frequently over many semesters and sometimes in multiple sections in a single semester. The time invested in developing a TBL survey course will, under such circumstances, be returned in full measure. In my experience, redesigning my American literature survey course with Team-Based Learning transformed it from a necessary obligation and into one of my favorite courses to teach.

NOTES

1. I am thankful to my ENGL 3340: History of American Literature students for their patience and encouragement over the past few years as I adapted the course to Team-Based Learning.

2. All quotes from literary texts, including epigraphs, are taken from the anthology I assign in my survey course, Susan Belasco and Linck Johnson, eds., *Bedford Anthology of American Literature, Shorter Second Edition* (Boston: Bedford/St. Martin's, 2014). Ibid., 557, 1661.

3. TBL is such a distinctive system that it has been trademarked to distinguish it from other group-based or flipped teaching methods. The term "modified TBL" or MTBL has sprung up to reflect the fact that many faculty adopt some, but not all, elements of TBL. My survey course would be most properly labeled "modified TBL" because I find a combination of more conventional discussion-based classes and TBL problem-solving classes works best for my students.

4. There are many books and essays on TBL that provide more detailed introductions to these elements than I can provide here. I have primarily relied upon Michaelsen, Knight, and Fink; and Sweet and Michaelsen. Larry K. Michaelsen, Arletta Bauman Knight, and L. Dee Fink, eds., *Team-Based Learning: A Transformative Use of Small Groups* (Westport, CT: Praeger, 2002). Michael Sweet and Larry K. Michaelsen, eds., *Team-Based Learning in the Social Sciences and Humanities: Group Work that Works to Generate Critical Thinking and Engagement* (Sterling, VA: Stylus, 2012). See also the *Team-Based Learning Collaborative*, http://www.teambasedlearning.org/. Scholarly publications on the use of TBL in literature or writing courses remains rare; in addition to the sources cited elsewhere in this essay, see Harde and Thomas. Roxanne Harde, "'The Union of Theory and Practice': Using Team-Based Learning in the Feminist Literary Theory Classroom," *Feminist Teacher* 22, no. 1 (2013): 60–75. Theda Ann Thomas, "Developing Team Skills Through a Collaborative Writing Assignment," *Assessment & Evaluation in Higher Education* 39, no. 4 (2014): 479–95.

5. On team-formation, peer evaluations, and dealing with problem teams, see Peter Balan, Michele Clark, and Gregory Restall, "Preparing Students for Flipped or Team-Based Learning Methods," *Education + Training* 57, no. 6 (2015): 639–57; and L. Dee. Fink, "Beyond Small Groups: Harnessing the Extraordinary Power of Learning Teams," in Michaelsen, Knight, and Fink, *Team-Based Learning*, 3–25.

6. The scratch-off testing cards or IF-AT (immediate feedback assessment technique) cards are available for purchase from Epstein Educational Enterprises, http://www.epsteineducation.com/. Digital alternatives are available, but my preference remains for the material experience provided by the scratch-off cards.

7.   Teams are also provided with a mechanism for appealing RAT questions. Appeals are another way for students to engage in critical thinking and argumentative rhetoric, and they empower students to claim their expertise over the material under review.

8.   Daniel F. Chambliss and Christopher G. Takacs, *How College Works* (Cambridge: Harvard University Press, 2014), 4; italics in original.

9.   For more on the benefits of TBL for nontraditional student populations, see Patricia Goodson, "Working with Nontraditional and Underprepared Students in Health Education," in Michaelsen, Knight, and Fink, *Team-Based Learning*, 119–27; and Vanessa Hunn, "African American Students, Retention, and Team-Based Learning: A Review of the Literature and Recommendations for Retention at Predominately White Institutions," *Journal of Black Studies* 45, no. 4 (2014): 301–14.

10.   It is important to note that within the TBL system, team activities take place during regularly scheduled class time. This avoids the problem of students being obliged to find a time they can meet outside of class and means that all team activities are actively supervised by the faculty member, thereby addressing some of the conflicts that commonly emerge during graded group work. Equally, this practice emphasizes that that teamwork is a central and valued component of the class.

11.   My initial hesitance was colored by the skepticism that pervades literary studies regarding multiple-choice testing. See Bill Roberson and Christine Reimers, "Team-Based Learning for Critical Reading and Thinking in Literature and Great Books Courses," in Sweet and Michaelsen, *Team-Based Learning in the Social Sciences and Humanities*, 129–41.

12.   Here I refer to one of the most significant ways in which I modify TBL. Whereas the conventional structure of a TBL unit has students complete all their out-of-class reading before the unit begins, I continue to assign reading throughout each unit. This is more consistent with the structure of literature classes and allows me to cover a wider range of primary material.

13.   Grant Wiggins and Jay McTighe, *Understanding by Design*, 2nd ed. (Upper Saddle River, NJ: Pearson, 2005), 108–9.

BIBLIOGRAPHY

Balan, Peter, Michele Clark, and Gregory Restall. "Preparing Students for Flipped or Team-Based Learning Methods." *Education + Training* 57, no. 6 (2015): 639–57.

Belasco, Susan, and Linck Johnson, eds. *The Bedford Anthology of American Literature: Shorter Second Edition*. Boston: Bedford/St. Martins, 2014.

Chambliss, Daniel F., and Christopher G. Takacs. *How College Works*. Cambridge: Harvard University Press, 2014.

Emerson, Ralph Waldo. "Self-Reliance." In Belasco and Johnson, *Bedford Anthology*, 555–74.

Fink, L. Dee. "Beyond Small Groups: Harnessing the Extraordinary Power of Learning Teams." In Michaelsen, Knight, and Fink, *Team-Based Learning*, 3–25.

Freire, Paulo. *Pedagogy of the Oppressed*. Translated by Myra Bergman Ramos. New York: Continuum, 2011.

Goodson, Patricia. "Working with Nontraditional and Underprepared Students in Health Education." In Michaelsen, Knight, and Fink, *Team-Based Learning*, 119–27.

Harde, Roxanne. "'The Union of Theory and Practice': Using Team-Based Learning in the Feminist Literary Theory Classroom." *Feminist Teacher* 22, no. 1 (2013): 60–75.

Hunn, Vanessa. "African American Students, Retention, and Team-Based Learning: A Review of the Literature and Recommendations for Retention at Predominately White Institutions." *Journal of Black Studies* 45, no. 4 (2014): 301–14.

McKay, Claude. "If We Must Die." In Belasco and Johnson, *Bedford Anthology*, 1661.

Michaelsen, Larry K., Arletta Bauman Knight, and L. Dee Fink, eds. *Team-Based Learning: A Transformative Use of Small Groups.* Westport, CT: Praeger, 2002.

Roberson, Bill, and Christine Reimers. "Team-Based Learning for Critical Reading and Thinking in Literature and Great Books Courses." In Sweet and Michaelsen, *Team-Based Learning in the Social Sciences and Humanities*, 129–41.

Sweet, Michael, and Larry K. Michaelsen, eds. *Team-Based Learning in the Social Sciences and Humanities: Group Work that Works to Generate Critical Thinking and Engagement.* Sterling, VA: Stylus, 2012.

"Team-Based Learning Collaborative." *Team-Based Learning Collaborative.* http://www.teambasedlearning.org/.

Thomas, Theda Ann. "Developing Team Skills Through a Collaborative Writing Assignment." *Assessment & Evaluation in Higher Education* 39, no. 4 (2014): 479–95.

Wiggins, Grant, and Jay McTighe. *Understanding by Design.* 2nd ed. Upper Saddle River, NJ: Pearson, 2005.

A Sample Team-Based Learning + Literature Survey Syllabus

This syllabus is based on the survey of American Literature I taught in Spring 2015. Although I generally preserve the chronological structure indicated here, I vary the assigned reading every semester so other iterations of this course may appear different, particularly if I select alternate texts to serve as the "key texts" upon which students will be tested using the iRAT/tRAT method. However, this sample syllabus provides an overview of the pacing of each unit and the forms of assessment I employ.

It is important for students to be informed about the team-based learning format early on. My students take ungraded practice RATs on the first day of the semester to familiarize themselves with the method, and I schedule the first official RATs in the second week. Because 15 percent of their course grades will be based on teamwork, I want students to quickly gain an understanding of how they are being assessed—and to see how working in teams provides measurable benefits.

ENGL 3340: History of American Literature

Professor: Dr. Desirée Henderson

Course Description: This class provides students with a broad introduction to American literature from the seventeenth century to the present. Students will be exposed to major texts, authors, and movements from American literary history. They will read a variety of literary genres, including political documents, essays, autobiographies, poetry, and short fiction. The breadth of the course and the variety of the reading allow students to gain an understanding of the role that literature played in both constructing and reflecting the development of the nation.

Required Book: Susan Belasco and Linck Johnson, eds., *The Bedford Anthology of American Literature, Shorter Second Edition*. Boston: Bedford/St. Martin's, 2014. ISBN: 978-0-312-59713-9.

Assignments:

iRATs (6) = 5%

tRATs (6) = 10%

Peer Evaluations (2) = 5%

Theater Assignment = 5%

Problem Papers (3) = 15%

Test 1 = 15%

Test 2 = 20%

Final Exam = 25%

Team-Based Learning: This course implements a team-based learning pedagogy. The specific nature of this course design (and the meaning of the assignments listed above) will be explained in class, but students should be prepared for the fact that they will be working in teams throughout the semester, and that part of their grade will be based on their contributions to their teams.

ENGL 3340 Reading and Assignment Schedule

All reading is from the *Bedford Anthology of American Literature*, Shorter Edition, unless otherwise indicated. Students should always read the introductions to each assigned text.

I. Colonial Period

Day 1: Introduction to Team-Based Learning

Day 2: "Literature to 1750"; Columbus "Letter"; Equiano, "Interesting Narrative"

Day 3: iRAT and tRAT 1

"Colonial Settlements"; Rowlandson, *Sovereignty and Goodness of God*

Day 4: Rowlandson (cont.)

Day 5: Winthrop, "Modell of Christian Charity"

Day 6: Bradstreet, all poems; "Bradstreet Through a Modern Lens"

Day 7: Hawthorne, "Young Goodman Brown"

Day 8: Problem Paper 1 due

Colonial period wrap-up

II. Early National Period

Day 9: iRAT and tRAT 2

"American Literature, 1750–1830"; "Writing American Lives"; Franklin, *Autobiography*

Day 10: Franklin (cont.)

Day 11: Jefferson, "Declaration of Independence"; Wheatley, all poems

Day 12: "Amelia or the Faithless Briton" (online): http://www.common-place.org/justteachone/?page_id=81

Day 13: Hawthorne, "My Kinsman, Major Molineux"

Day 14: Test 1

III. The Nineteenth Century

Day 15: iRAT and tRAT 3

"American Literature, 1830–1865"; Douglass, *Narrative of the Life*; "Douglass through a Modern Lens"

Day 16: Douglass (cont.)

Day 17: Emerson, "Self Reliance"

Day 18: Mid-semester Peer Reviews due

Day 19: Melville, "Bartleby the Scrivener"

Day 20: Jacobs, *Incidents in the Life of a Slave Girl*

Day 21: Whitman, "Song of Myself"; "Whitman through a Modern Lens"

Day 22: Dickinson, poems 67, 241, 252, 258, 303, 324, 465, 709, 754, 986; "Dickinson through a Modern Lens"

Day 23: Lincoln, "Gettysburg Address"; Whitman, "Beat! Beat! Drums," "Vigil Strange," and "When Lilacs Last"; Dickinson, poems 409, 444

Day 24: Problem Paper 2 due

Nineteenth-century literature wrap-up

IV. Turn of the Century

Day 25: iRAT and tRAT 4

"American Literature, 1865–1914"; "Realism, Regionalism, and Naturalism: Introduction"; Chesnutt, "The Passing of Grandison"

Day 26: Chesnutt (cont.)

Day 27: Drieser, "Butcher Rogaum's Door"

Day 28: Jewett, "A White Heron"

Day 29:Zitkála-Šá, "School Days"

Day 30: Test 2

V. Literary Modernisms

Day 31: iRAT and tRAT 5

"American Literature, 1914–1945"; Hemingway, "Big Two Hearted River"

Day 32: Hemingway (cont.)

Day 33: Faulkner, "That Evening Sun"; "Toni Morrison on Faulkner" (1869)

Day 34: Hurston, "Gilded Six-Bits"; "Alice Walker on Zora Neale Hurston"

Day 35: "Modernisms in American Poetry"; Stevens, "Anecdote of the Jar," "Thirteen Ways of Looking at a Blackbird," and "Of Modern Poetry"; Moore, "Poetry" (both versions)

Day 36: Lowell, "Aubade"; Williams, "Red Wheelbarrow" and "This Is Just"; Pound, "In a Station of the Metro"; cummings, "[in Just]" and "[Buffalo Bill's]"

Day 37: Eliot, "Love Song of J. Alfred Prufrock"

Day 38: McKay, "If We Must Die" and "The Lynching"; Hughes, "Negro Speaks of Rivers" and "I, Too"

Day 39: Problem Paper 3 due

Modernist poetry wrap-up

VI. Literary Postmodernisms

Day 40: iRAT and tRAT 6

"American Literature since 1945"; "From Modernism to Postmodernism"; Barthelme, "The School"

Day 42: Ginsberg, "Howl"

Day 43: DeLillo, "Videotape"

Day 44: Bachelder, "Deep Wells, USA" (handout)

Day 45: Alexie, "What You Pawn I Will Redeem"

Day 46: End-of-Semester Peer Review due

Literary postmodernisms wrap-up and final exam review

Final Exam

Extended Engagement

In Praise of Breadth

AARON ROSENFELD, IONA COLLEGE

Going Off-Read

Several years ago, I began "Part II" of our college's general education literature survey class, which typically surveys literature from 1800 to the present, with T. S. Eliot's "The Love Song of J. Alfred Prufrock." The poem was the overture in a syllabus torturously constructed to negotiate a treacherous path between breadth and depth. My classroom was wired with Internet access and a projector, so I literally had the world at my fingertips. As we discussed what Eliot might have meant by calling this a love song—since, as a student sagely observed, there is no love in it—I began calling up and posting other love poems on the screen. These included works Eliot's poem alludes to, like Marvell's "To His Coy Mistress," and Gerard de Nerval's "El Desdichado," and those Eliot's poem does not, like Wyatt's "Whoso List to Hunt" and Herrick's "Upon Julia's Breasts." From there, we bounced around until we finally ended the class on music videos of Leonard Cohen's "Hallelujah" and Led Zeppelin's "Whole Lotta Love."

Though we had yet to venture beyond the title of "Prufrock," it was a powerful discussion of the varieties of love song: love songs that treat love as heavenly sacrament and those that treat it as bodily indulgence; those that celebrate the beloved and those that celebrate the lover; those that woo and those that lament the impossibility of human love. All told, the class provided a thorough answer to the student's observation. We saw the love poem tradition Eliot conspicuously defaces alongside more contemporary swerves away from Eliot's ethos of hesitation.

I resolved to try this approach a second day, and plotted out a few coordinates, which I prepared in an electronic document and posted for the students to read for the next class.[1] I did not want what had originally been intended as a historical survey to focus on only a single theme, so I let the first lines of Eliot's poem suggest a new focus. "Let us go then, you and I / When the evening is spread out against the sky / Like a patient etherized upon a table" led to the land "like the century's corpse outleant" in Thomas Hardy's "The Darkling Thrush" and then on to a discussion of the sky as modern trope, moving from Paul Fussell's commentary on the sky viewed from the trenches in World War I to the skywriting passage from Virginia Woolf's *Mrs. Dalloway*, originally scheduled for later in the semester.[2] I opened the next class with the line, "Let us go, through certain half-deserted streets," and shifted the thematic focus again, to the walk of self-discovery. We began with William Wordsworth's "Tintern Abbey," then continued on to Robert Frost's "The Road Not Taken" and Hawthorne's short story "Young Goodman Brown."[3] And so on. By the end of the second week, we still had not gotten very far in "Prufrock," though we had covered vast swaths of literary territory. I scrapped the regularly scheduled syllabus, and vowed to spend the entire semester reading "Prufrock."

The plan was to cover a survey course's worth of material while at the same time extending students' engagement with a single text. In lower-level survey courses that emphasize breadth, the opportunity to apply extensive knowledge to individual works is either postponed to later author or topic courses that students may never take, or lost within a framework that emphasizes coverage or skills at the expense of the works themselves. Here, I wanted students to have a sense of the interplay of motifs, themes, and images that constitute Eliot's poem, and to stage for them what it feels like to read with a library of literary works close at hand. Eliot's ironies become far more accessible when anchored in the texts he ironizes and in texts that, intentionally or incidentally, reread his work.

Fifteen weeks of poems, novels, plays, and short stories later, the semester ended with a discussion of how the voices from the sea in Walt Whitman's "Out of the Cradle Endlessly Rocking," Elizabeth Bishop's "The Fish," and Wallace Stevens's "The Idea of Order at Key West" compared to those that close "Prufrock." By the end, the students were casually and learnedly citing other poets and novelists as they talked about the texts we were reading. For example, a discussion of Cormac McCarthy's novel *The Road* generated comments about distinctions between McCarthy's road and Prufrock's road, but also Frost's road not taken, Hawthorne's road through the forest, and Edgar Allen Poe's ramble through city streets in "The Man of the Crowd." "The father in *The Road* is like Frost," one student observed—"he makes up a reason why he has to keep going on the road, but he really believes in it . . . whereas Prufrock can't convince himself of anything." This facility was striking. Students seemed to be learning how to talk about literary works without fixating on the discussion-ending prize answer that would reveal all. Situating the poem within a broader field of literary works and drawing out both similarities and departures had established a "thick" aesthetic context for understanding the attitudes, themes, and form of Prufrock's love song.[4] Students knew "Prufrock," very, very well, evidenced by their fluency in linking new works back to the plot, sounds, and themes of Eliot's poem, but they also knew how to get *between* works.

Neither did we neglect literary history, but it had become less the subject of the course and more an active principle of reading. Grouping texts by their ability to illuminate one another rather than proceeding periodically exposed the ways in which period conventions spilled over their boundaries, remaining relevant long after the period that spawned the works had faded into the historical mist. Organizing the traditional, extensive materials of the survey course around an intensive examination of a single work of literature made me acutely aware of how much the meaning of any work of literature is derived from an awareness not just of what a work is, but also of what it is not. And, while not the point, but sometimes an indicator of whether a class worked or not, I had a ball.

I would characterize the reader-centered approach to literature I describe above with an older word—"appreciation."[5] By appreciation, I do not mean a superficial glance at the text buttressed by a nod to its fame. I mean what advocates of aesthetic education have called "percipience": a cultivated attentiveness to the object and an awareness of how one is responding to it, akin to what Louise Rosenblatt described as an "aesthetic attitude" toward the text.[6] The ability to cultivate a rich aesthetic response to a work of art, and to attach meaning or significance to that experience, has both a broad and a deep vector. Elliott Eisner, a leading advocate of art education in schools, frames the process of aesthetic engagement as analogous to wine-tasting connoisseurship, an exercise in distinguishing experiences from one another (which, as it turns out, leads to the development of highly desirable skills, applicable in any field that values the ability to make fine distinctions and attach significance to those distinctions).[7] Appreciation demands that we learn how to focus attention, but also that we see beyond the immediate quality of whether or not a particular text is "relatable" to us, to how it relates to a genre, to its audience(s), to a historical moment. For this, students need to learn to see the work both alone and alongside the other works from which it draws its energy in the mind of an engaged and knowledgeable reader.

I want to argue that instead of imagining appreciation as something a student does or does not have, it ought to be thought of as an entry-level skill like any other that depends on mastering certain movements of mind, and acquiring a sufficient store of material upon which to exercise this movement.[8] The deep learning of the class is embodied in the students' movement toward mastery of an aesthetic grammar: a language for talking about works of literature, for comparing them, for recognizing the ways in which they speak to one another, and that enables them to extend their moment of engagement with a work of literature.

For example, in a later edition of the "Prufrock" course, students wanted to discuss Beyoncé's song "Formation," in the news because of her controversial Super Bowl performance. Several students collaborated on a presentation breaking down the video and song, comparing Beyoncé's bold embrace of a visual identity—"Paparazzi, catch my fly, and my cocky fresh / I'm so reckless when I rock my Givenchy dress (stylin')"—with Prufrock's tentativeness—"My morning coat, my collar mounting firmly to the chin, / My necktie rich and modest, but asserted by a simple pin— / (They will say: 'But how his arms and legs are thin!')."[9] This led back to a contrast between the carpe diem genre's confident expression of desire and Prufrock's inability to play the part of bold ("fly") lover. Opening the field to students' own aesthetic contexts helps to frame the works we teach in relation to what they are already used to "appreciating." Indeed, much of their lives will be spent being entertained, and much of what they will be entertained by will be texts that can be better appreciated, and better used, by those who can connect what they consume to a broader tradition that is often a direct forbearer to these contemporary texts.

My approach—broad reading of literary works both inside and outside the traditional canon, covering a wide range of periods and styles, and framing those works as relevant to understanding a single work—is grounded in the belief that the breadth survey, despite having lost much of its status and function to increased disciplinarity, canon critiques, and simple logistical difficulty, still has a crucial role to play in making literature intelligible and meaningful to students.

Breadth and Depth: The Elephant in the Rabbit Hole

This argument comes at a moment when breadth in the survey seems to be breathing its last. Breadth's decline is linked to a broader set of pedagogical developments, including the movement toward forms of learning whose impact on students' short-term employment prospects can easily be measured. The last thirty years have thus seen the replacement of the "breadth" survey with a variety of courses that, while overlapping the survey's traditional functions, do other kinds of work as well.[10] Part of this work involves the shifting of the subject of the survey from texts to metacommentary on institutional uses of texts. Following Gerald Graff's 1987 call to teach the controversy, this work includes, for example, asking students to reflect on how canons are constructed in order to demystify the process by which texts get institutionalized.[11] Other recent suggestions for organizing the survey course include historicizing fewer texts, adjusting the pedagogy through strategies such as team teaching and guest lectures that provide historical background, or building around a transhistorical theme using "representative" works. Unfortunately, historicizing allows for intensive study of only a small number of texts and issues while theme-based approaches, by placing at the center of the course a central idea or abstract concern, risk dissipating the impact of individual texts. Both strategies reinforce an idea of literary works as having value not in the experience of them, but in the residue they leave behind.

But it is worth remembering that appreciation and breadth were once closely linked in the survey course. Appreciation was seen as a means of connecting students to a national life, and that national life was represented by a broad library of commonly held works. Susannah McMurphy, writing in 1921, argues that the survey is for "[t]he forming of a taste for literature, the acquisition of the power to read it intelligently, and the development of a perception in it of something vital and intimately related to the individual and national life."[12] As is clear in McMurphy's statement, the breadth survey was designed not necessarily to make students critical readers in our modern sense, but sensitive readers. Breadth familiarized a populace with the "great works" from which this sensitivity was derived, and to which students had not necessarily had access.

Today, we recognize the narrowness of such a conception. The idea of a coherent "national life" is problematic today for many reasons (as it was then). But such a fantasy promised not just a set of shared values that, from a privileged perch, could elide uncomfortable difference; it also promised commonly held texts that would anchor an ongoing conversation about those values, enriching both the public and private spheres. I fear that in abandoning the breadth survey, we have unlinked texts from the context that gives them life as objects of aesthetic value— that context being other texts—and from the kinds of reading that the pursuit of sensibility encourages. Ignoring appreciation as a valid aim and breadth as a means of achieving it has compromised our ability to shape courses that convey to students what it is that makes people want to interpret and analyze literature in the first place, and what makes them capable of doing so.

One of the most common criticisms of the breadth survey is that it leads to superficial reading as the price of coverage. What can a professor do except race through the centuries, cramming in the works he or she deems necessary? Albert Schinz writes in 1926 in response to the idea of a one-year French literature survey, "You cannot put an elephant in a rabbit hole."[13] Literature is vast, but the survey is small—you stuff the elephant in by deboning it. The survey certainly has the potential to be an exercise in skimming the surface. But this is not inevitable. It depends on what we are reading for: if we are reading texts as separate islands, representative of key themes, periods, or genres, then it is true, there is not much to do but touch down briefly and move on again. Or, if we are thinking historically in an uncritical sense, the lines of transmission and evolution we draw will be inevitably reductive, if not outright false. However, if we are thinking of texts as a network, and the survey as a mapping out of pathways of intelligibility and cross-textual illumination, the broad view makes more sense. My attempt to rethink the survey course is aimed less at questioning the premise that students need "breadth" alongside "depth" than at updating how we think about the interaction of those terms.

Students need both; the problem is how to solve this zero-sum game in a way that does justice to both forms of reading. I call my extensive/intensive approach "lateral" reading: a sideways slipping among texts, distinct from traditional notions of breadth and depth, where breadth implies broad coverage of a defined area, and depth the treatment of the individual text as a carrier of hidden meanings that must be recovered from below the text's surface. In this sense, lateral reading is a form of what Sharon Marcus and Stephen Best call "surface reading," which hews closely to manifest meanings—manifest at least to a careful eye—rather than latent ones.[14] I would extend Marcus and Best's focus on textual surfaces to the broader contours of the tradition: in the context of the survey, the surface to be studied is not just individual texts, but the patterns those texts form when made to fit together. Derek Attridge refers to the "singularity" of literature—its uniqueness as a form of communication, its articulation as an event involving readers and communities, and, in the reading of it, its ability to transform both its own meaning and the traditions of which it is a part (or not a part).[15] "Responding to a work of art means attempting to do justice to it as a singular other," Attridge writes. The "otherness" that allows the literary work to emerge as singular means positioning the work against "a set of contexts bearing down on the here and now."[16] By developing these contexts, the breadth survey done right does not turn away from deep textual engagement, it enables it. Depth supplies the rich and complex readerly relationship to a particular work that makes it indispensable, but breadth supplies the backdrop against which an individual work emerges.

The Lateral Survey Course and the Semester-Long Poem

What does this kind of reading practice look like in the classroom? I structure my survey course around lines from the central work. So, for example, a later class in the "Prufrock" semester deals with the line "Do I dare to eat a peach" (line 122). Assigned readings cluster around the theme of fruit—forbidden fruit, sexualized fruit, the fruit as symbol of nature. I begin with a few quotations, an example of the comic strip "Ms. Peach," a music video of Prince's song "She's a Peach," and Georgia O'Keefe's painting "Peach and Glass." From there, we identify categories of "peachiness." Then, we move to a "flight" of works: the Garden of Eden story from Genesis, Thomas Campion's seventeenth-century lyric "Cherry Ripe," Amy Lowell's "Apples of Hesperides," D. H. Lawrence's "Peach," William Carlos Williams's "This is just to say . . . ," Robert Graves's "The Bluefly," and so on. We read together as a class, analyzing each new work, comparing the treatment of the theme, the voice, the poetic attitude, to the other works under discussion. The discussion emphasizes the differences in each iteration; I ask comparative questions, such as "How is Campion's use of fruit as metaphor different/similar to Eliot's? To Williams's?" "Is O'Keefe's peach more like Eliot's or Lawrence's?" At the end of class, we turn all of this material back to "Prufrock," looking for the particular combination of carnality, embarrassment, sacralized sexuality, and lost nature that make Eliot's peach his own, even as his peach is nested within a complex literary history and set of associations.

Each class moves back and forth in a comparative, recursive manner. As the Beyoncé example suggests, students are encouraged to add their own analogous texts that they connect to the literary work. Frequently, I use the Internet to pull up a poem, a meme, a song or music video, or a YouTube video suggested by a student that highlights by analogy or contrast what is at stake in the central work. Sometimes I know the material they are referring to, but often I do not. Sometimes it works and sometimes it doesn't quite, but these excursions are the best part of the class. Students appreciate the opportunity to connect the material to their present, and I appreciate the window into the ever-changing culture of the students.

Here, it is important to note that the lateral movement I describe is distinct from intertextuality treated as an attribute of texts. The reader moves from text to text, discovering analogues and departures, through-lines and disjunctions, that thicken aesthetic response. This method treats the value of works of literature as differential; the manifest content is what the works say and do, in theme and style and the aim is to understand works in terms of their relative distance from other works. In practice, this means the classroom is oriented neither toward historical breadth nor interpretative depth in any conventional sense. Instead, the reading work of the class is oriented toward development of an aesthetic background against which a literary work can be read for formal, thematic, and attitudinal variations, and an aesthetic foreground, where a particular text becomes available for the "deep" reading that constitutes breadth's opposite pole.

Literary history looks very different through this lens. A comparative emphasis resists presenting literary history in abstract terms and instead privileges how periods operate *for readers.* For example, Romanticism might be best thought of not so much as an object of study, but as a set of expectations against which a text can be profitably read. By working always with a range of works, we can be attentive to how texts might fit, or not fit, within our understanding of a particular period. Comparing texts leads naturally to discussions of period conventions and attitudes. (My classes are twenty-five to thirty-five, which allows for discussion; a large lecture course would require some adaptation, such as assigning interpretive/comparison tasks to small groups beforehand.) Form is not treated as a set of independent, periodicized gestures to be memorized, but as a conversation that can be read meaningfully in either direction. One might compare, for example, a Romantic and a Modernist work in order to uncover their distinct sensibilities, tropes, genres, and attitudes. How does Eliot's portrayal of the walk swerve from Wordsworth's? How does Wordsworth's walk toward an epiphany of unity with nature help us understand Prufrock's journey through tedious streets that lead nowhere? How is Wordsworth's treatment characteristically Romantic, and Eliot's Modern? Various forms of history remain indispensable: we discuss canon formation, major shifts in material culture, the ways in which a work of literature functioned in a particular time and place. But history is subordinated to the artifacts it abstracts.

Just as historical direction does not matter, neither does the choice of central text in planning such a course. A pop song, a Shakespeare sonnet, a Romantic poem would all be equally compelling. A pop song might trace its precursors backward, a Shakespeare sonnet might trace its influence forward, and a Romantic poem might stretch out on both sides, encompassing precursors and progeny as well as texts that are neither. I try to include a wealth of canonical texts (i.e., the kind likely to appear in an anthology) in order to ground students in a more traditional history, but I also incorporate noncanonical works, including those suggested by students.

While some of the assessment methods for this class are quite conventional, there are crucial differences in how these methods are framed and the purpose to which they are put. For example, identifications are a retrograde staple of literature survey tests traditionally employed to ensure that students have done the reading and paid attention in class. But identifications can also serve another purpose. I want students to say, "that sounds like Langston Hughes," or "that looks like Woolf's stream of consciousness . . ." Apropos my earlier example, if students are reading Cormac McCarthy's *The Road* and someone mentions Frost, they need to be able to call up Frost's sense of purpose as something we conjure in order to keep at bay the nauseating emptiness of nature. But this requires students to recognize what a Frost poem is when they hear his name. When I tell students at the beginning of the semester that major tests will include identification of passages and short-answer questions associated with each work, they often complain they will never be able to memorize so many works. Most, however, quickly realize they do not have to; they need only learn to differentiate between writers by what the writers tend to say and how they tend to say it. Through spending time in class examining differences in style and theme, identifications become not a matter of memorization, but a test of students' ability to incorporate authors into their library of material for comparison. Sometimes, I will quiz students with works they have never seen and ask them to think about who the writer might be. At other times, I ask them to write a passage or poem using the style and themes of one of the writers we have studied. If other class members can guess the identity of the author is who is being imitated, the student "passes."

This work of comparison is a constant throughout the semester. Quick preclass quizzes set the stage for discussions ("How is the protagonist of Edgar Allen Poe's 'The Man of the Crowd' like Prufrock? How is he different?"). Quizzes test familiarity with the concepts, tropes, and themes we have discussed in class and provide review material that helps students recognize the characteristic voices, themes, and attitudes of the writers we study. I still assign papers in which students practice critical reading, research, and writing skills through analysis of particular works, but have found that privileging comparison as an ongoing area of assessment yields fruit in students' increased ability to recognize what is familiar and unfamiliar in new works introduced throughout the semester. With this in mind, I try not to focus too heavily on questions of "correct" interpretation. The hidden meanings we ask students to excavate may or may not come with aesthetic understanding. This is why I try to focus evaluation on students' ability to use comparisons and connections to think about works of literature. I think of all the texts I misinterpreted when young, and still misinterpret; I am less concerned with whether students get it right than whether or not they "get in the game." Interpretation will take care of itself.

I have noted several intriguing results of structuring the class in this way. First, the fluidity in connecting texts, mentioned earlier, is a striking difference in how students assimilate the material. They eagerly embrace the "this reminds me of" formulation, and become better at answering the follow-up "why" as they practice the language of comparison. Test grades tend to be higher, in part because we spend so much class time differentiating works. On a side note, I also note an increase in students who do not usually speak in class approaching afterward to tell me about something they have read or seen that fits in with something we have been talking about, and who seem genuinely excited to have found a connection between something they like and the subject of the course. These outcomes are consistent with the class's primary aim of providing tools to enrich students' encounters with texts.

To reiterate my main argument, it is important that the survey makes texts not only historically intelligible, but also *aesthetically intelligible*. The survey course outlined here is designed to help students understand the relational nature of literary works, for which a grounding in literary history and possession of a broad library of works is an initial step. Without material, students have no expectations; without expectations, they can never be surprised, appalled, or delighted by a wrench in the design. Returning to a central text throughout the semester and continuing to reread it in light of a wide array of other texts extends students' moment of contact with one work of literature. The lateral vector provides them with the breadth required for a comparative appreciation of the work's uniqueness and its continuities with other works; it helps them gain a feel for how bits and pieces of language, form, theme, and story recirculate through the tradition. At the same time, extended engagement with a single text helps students to consider the myriad aesthetic, ideological, historical, and social nodes of meaning that constitute a text, and thus models the depth and focus required for advanced critical work.

If we value something in the classroom we must be determined to teach it. The extended engagement survey provides a focal point for the introduction of a wide array of technical, thematic, critical, and contextual matter; however, such a structure lends itself particularly well to what I argue is the undervalued, but still relevant, and urgently needed, skill of appreciation. The course described here provides students with raw materials and a reader-centered framework for organizing them. I fervently hope this encounter creates for students some of the problems that our discipline so vigorously tries to solve.

NOTES

1. These texts are all available electronically, through sites like Bartleby.com and The Poetry Foundation; the approach I describe depends on this easy access to a wide range of materials; I also use an anthology for more contemporary materials.

2. T. S. Eliot, "The Love Song of J. Alfred Prufrock" ("Prufrock") in *The Norton Anthology of Modern and Contemporary Poetry*, vol. 1, ed. Jahan Ramazani et al. (New York: W. W. Norton, 2003), 463: lines 1–3.

3. "Prufrock," line 4.

4. My use of the word "thick" nods toward Clifford Geertz's concept of "thick description"; that is, the effort to understand and interpret cultural information within multilayered contexts of reception and participation. Clifford Geertz, "Thick Description: Toward an Interpretive Theory of Culture," in *The Interpretation of Cultures: Selected Essays* (New York: Basic Books, 2000), 3–30.

5. Appreciation as educational goal has a long history in English education. See, for example, Frank Hayward, *The Lesson in Appreciation* (New York: Macmillan, 1915). For my understanding of appreciation, I am drawing on the work of Elliott Eisner. See, for example, *The Nature of Aesthetic Education* (Sacramento: Sacramento County Superintendent of Schools Offices, 1968); "Getting Down to Basics in Art Education" in *Journal of Aesthetic Education* 33, no. 4 (1999): 145–59; and "What Education Can Learn from the Arts" *in Art Education* 62, no. 2 (2009): 6–9. See also Harold Osborne, *The Art of Appreciation* (London: Oxford University Press, 1970); Osborne and others associate appreciation with aesthetic education, and posit a specific set of skills, approaches, and processes.

6. Louise Rosenblatt, *The Reader, The Text, The Poem: The Transactional Theory of the Literary Work* (Carbondale: Southern Illinois University Press, 1978).

7. Eisner, *The Nature of Aesthetic Education*; Eisner, "What Education Can Learn from the Arts."

8. I explore the relationship between appreciation and the academy more fully in in my article, "Wine, Poems, and Song: Lateral Reading and the Pedagogy of Appreciation" in *Pedagogy: Critical Approaches to Teaching Literature, Language, Composition, and Culture* 17, no. 2 (April 2017): 203–34.

9. "Prufrock," line 44.

10. Phyllis Franklin, Bettina Huber, and David Laurence, "Continuity and Change in the Study of Literature," *Change* 24, no. 1 (January–February 1992): 42–48. Franklin et al. discuss how changes have been both significant and "overstated" (48).

11. Gerald Graff, *Professing Literature* (Chicago: University of Chicago Press, 1989); John W. Crowley, "Unmastering All We Survey," *ADE Bulletin* 100 (Winter 1991): 31–34.

12. Susannah J. McMurphy, "Backgrounds for a Survey Course," *The English Journal* 10, no. 2 (February 1921): 68–79.

13. Albert Schinz, "The Problem of the One-Year Literature Survey Course Again," *The Modern Language Journal* 10, no. 6 (March 1926): 345.

14. Stephen Best and Sharon Marcus, "Surface Reading: An Introduction," *Representations* 108, no. 1 (Fall 2009): 1–21. The turn in recent years toward alternative modes of reading that reframe how we value and encounter texts in both the classroom and in scholarship updates Susan Sontag's argument in "Against Interpretation" that "[w]hat is important now is to recover our senses. We must learn to see more, to hear more, to feel more" (Susan Sontag, *A*

Susan Sontag Reader [New York: Vintage, 1966, 1983], 104). Best and Marcus reject "symptomatic reading," and instead argue for reading that attends to "what is evident, perceptible, apprehensible" in texts. Similarly, Michael Warner historicizes the assumption that "critical reading" is the only proper way to read a text, drawing attention to how the modes of discourse associated with critical reading are "perversely antagonistic to the way our students actually read (Michael Warner, "Uncritical Reading," in *Polemic: Critical or Uncritical*, ed. Jane Gallop [New York: Routledge, 2004], 22, 14).

15.   Derek Attridge, *The Singularity of Literature* (New York: Routledge, 2004), 136, 128. As Attridge acknowledges, the idea that a text transforms its context echoes Eliot's imagining of a historical tradition that is ever-present for the well-trained reader: Eliot writes in "Tradition and the Individual Talent" (in *The Sacred Wood: Essays on Poetry and Criticism* [New York: Alfred A. Knopf, 1919], 42–53), the writer's "significance, his appreciation is the appreciation of his relation to the dead poets and artists" (44). Eliot's emphasis on the backward glance suggests the ultimate conservatism of his approach. Yet what is appealing in Eliot is his embrace of conflicting principles that remain relevant to current debates: on the one hand, that textual meaning and value do not derive from the work standing alone; on the other, that appreciation of a literary text requires aesthetic attention to the particular object.

16.   Attridge, *The Singularity of Literature*, 111.

BIBLIOGRAPHY

Attridge, Derek. *The Singularity of Literature*. New York: Routledge, 2004.

Best, Stephen, and Sharon Marcus. "Surface Reading: An Introduction." *Representations* 108, no. 1 (Fall 2009): 1–21.

Crowley, John W. "Unmastering All We Survey." *ADE Bulletin* 100 (Winter 1991): 31–34.

Eisner, Elliott. "Getting Down to Basics in Art Education." *Journal of Aesthetic Education* 33, no. 4 (1999): 145–59.

———. *The Nature of Aesthetic Education*. Sacramento: Sacramento County Superintendent of Schools Offices, 1968.

———. "What Education Can Learn from the Arts." *Art Education* 62, no. 2 (2009): 6–9.

Eliot, T. S. "The Love Song of J. Alfred Prufrock." In *The Norton Anthology of Modern and Contemporary Poetry*, vol. 1, edited by Jahan Ramazani et al. New York: W. W. Norton, 2003.

———. "Tradition and the Individual Talent." In *The Sacred Wood: Essays on Poetry and Criticism*, 42–53. New York: Alfred A. Knopf, 1919.

Franklin, Phyllis, Bettina Huber, and David Laurence. "Continuity and Change in the Study of Literature." *Change* 24, no. 1 (January–February 1992): 42–48.

Geertz, Clifford. "Thick Description: Toward an Interpretive Theory of Culture." In *The Interpretation of Cultures: Selected Essays*, 3–30. New York: Basic Books, 2000.

Graff, Gerald. *Professing Literature*. Chicago: University of Chicago Press, 1989.

Hayward, Frank. *The Lesson in Appreciation*. New York: Macmillan, 1915.

McMurphy, Susannah J. "Backgrounds for a Survey Course," *The English Journal* 10, no. 2 (February 1921): 68–79.

Osborne, Harold. *The Art of Appreciation*. London: Oxford University Press, 1970.

Rosenblatt, Louise. *The Reader, The Text, The Poem: The Transactional Theory of the Literary Work*. Carbondale: Southern Illinois University Press, 1978.

Rosenfeld, Aaron. "Wine, Poems, and Song: Lateral Reading and the Pedagogy of Appreciation." *Pedagogy: Critical Approaches to Teaching Literature, Language, Composition, and Culture* 17, no. 2 (April 2017): 203–34.

Schinz, Albert. "The Problem of the One-Year Literature Survey Course Again." *The Modern Language Journal* 10, no. 6 (March 1926): 345.

Sontag, Susan. *A Susan Sontag Reader*. 1966. Reprint, New York: Vintage, 1983.

Warner, Michael. "Uncritical Reading." In *Polemic: Critical or Uncritical*, edited by Jane Gallop, 13–38. New York: Routledge, 2004.

Sample Reading Blocks (some cover multiple class periods)

The Love Song of J. Alfred Prufrock . . .

c. 1348	Petrarch	"Sonnet XII (The Beauty of Laura . . .)"
1557	Thomas Wyatt	"Whoso List to Hunt"
1609	Shakespeare	"Sonnet 130 ("My Mistresses' Eyes . . .")"
c. 1633	John Donne	"The Flea," "Holy Sonnets. XIV"
1648	Robert Herrick	"Upon the Nipples of Julia's Breasts," "Upon Julia's Breasts"
c. 1650	Andrew Marvell	"To His Coy Mistress"
1845–46	E. B. Browning	"Sonnet 43 (How do I love thee?)"
1853	Gerard de Nerval	"El Desdichado"
1926	Dorothy Parker	"One Perfect Rose"
1940	W. H. Auden	"Lullaby"
1964	Philip Larkin	"Talking in Bed"
1969	Led Zeppelin	"Whole Lotta Love" (song)
1984	Leonard Cohen	"Hallelujah" (song)

Let us go then, you and I,
When the evening is spread out against the sky
Like a patient etherized upon a table . . .

1889	Thomas Eakins	"The Agnew Clinic" (painting)
1900	Thomas Hardy	"The Darkling Thrush"
1925	Virginia Woolf	Sky-writing scene from *Mrs. Dalloway*
1926	Gwendolyn Bennett	"Street Lamps in Early Spring"

1975	Paul Fussell	from *The Great War and Modern Memory* (criticism)

Let us go, through certain half-deserted streets,
Streets that follow like a tedious argument
Of insidious intent
To lead you to an overwhelming question. . . .

1798	William Wordsworth	"Tintern Abbey" ("Notes . . .")
1835	Nathaniel Hawthorne	"Young Goodman Brown" (short story)
1840	Edgar Allan Poe	"The Man of the Crowd" (short story)
1857	Charles Baudelaire	"To a Passerby"
1915	Robert Frost	"The Road Not Taken"
1953	Samuel Beckett	"Waiting for Godot" (drama)
2000	Cormac McCarthy	*The Road* (novel)

"I am Lazarus, come from the dead,
Come back to tell you all, I shall tell you all"

1797	Coleridge	"Kubla Khan"
c. 1860	Emily Dickinson	"Because I could not stop for Death," "I Died for Beauty," "The Bustle in the House," "I Heard a Fly Buzz"
1914	James Joyce	"The Dead" (short story)
1918	Wilfred Owen	"Strange Meeting"
1925	Zora Neale Hurston	"Spunk" (short story)
1962	Sylvia Plath	"Lady Lazarus"

. . . I have heard the mermaids singing, each to each.

I do not think that they will sing to me.

1830	Alfred Lord Tennyson	"The Sea Fairies"
1860	Walt Whitman	"Out of the Cradle Endlessly Rocking"
1920	Marianne Moore	"The Fish"
1934	Wallace Stevens	"The Idea of Order at Key West"
1946	Elizabeth Bishop	"The Fish"
1952	Ernest Hemingway	*The Old Man and the Sea* (novella)

PART TWO

Projects

Reacting to the Past in the Survey Course

Teaching the Stages of Power: Marlowe and Shakespeare, 1592 Game

JOAN VARNUM FERRETTI, NEW YORK UNIVERSITY

October, 1592
London

Master Tilney, Esteemed Members of the Privy Council, and Fellow Actors,

I am Will Kemp, an actor and clown in the Lord Strange's Men, the acting company of young playwright Will Shakespeare. I come before you today to argue for your support and licensing of his new play *Richard III*. I realize that you can choose only one play to produce at the Rose Theatre, and I believe that *Richard III* is the superior choice over Marlowe's *Doctor Faustus* for theatrical and poetical reasons.

Why, you may ask, am I, a talented comedic actor, promoting a play that is not a comedy? Permit me to explain. Some say that *Richard III* is a tragedy because it fits many of the standards of tragedy. Others say that it is a history because it refers to our fair Queen Elizabeth's ancestry (God save the Queen!). But, I submit to you that its selective use of comedic elements offers audiences a superb contrast to the other elements, making the tragic elements more poignant and the historical ones more significant. . . .

This speech and dozens of others like it have been delivered by the students in the Liberal Studies Program at New York University as part of a dynamic and innovative pedagogy called Reacting to the Past. Reacting to the Past (hereafter, referred to as Reacting) employs games, set in past historical periods, in which students take on the roles of authentic people who lived during those times. Through their arguments and game play, which are informed by classic texts, students endeavor to influence the ideologies and outcomes of historically based situations.[1] In the *Stages of Power: Marlowe and Shakespeare, 1592* game, for instance, one student might play the role of the amiable comedic actor Will Kemp as he works for the licensing of *Richard III*; another student might play the role of Ned Alleyn, principal tragedian in Christopher Marlowe's acting troupe the Lord Admiral's Men, who argues for the licensing of *Doctor Faustus*; yet another student might play the role of Edmund Tilney, Master of the Queen's Revels, who presides over hearings about both plays. In *The Threshold of Democracy: Athens in 403 BCE* game, a participant might play the role of a radical democrat or a Socratic. Or, in the *Greenwich Village 1913: Suffrage, Labor, and the New Woman* game, students could find themselves in roles arguing for women's suffrage and labor rights. Reacting games have the capability to open up traditional "coverage" types of survey courses by providing students with a unique, historically oriented, and immersive experience. In this way, the Reacting games are a little like scholarly time-travel.

Role-immersive game play forms the pedagogical blueprint of each Reacting game.[2] Mark Carnes, inventor of the Reacting pedagogy, explains: "Role-immersion games, when configured as an intellectualized pedagogical system, provide access to . . . often un-tapped wellsprings of motivation and imagination."[3] As a result, students learn more than content in the process of playing Reacting games; they cultivate skills such as formal public speaking, informal debate, writing, negotiation, critical thinking, problem solving, and teamwork (individual students must be ready to work for the benefit of the group in order to win the game).[4] As Meyers and Jones note, because simulations, exercises, and games "require the personal involvement of participants, students are forced to think on their feet, question their own values and responses to situations, and consider new ways of thinking."[5] Game play also allows students to "develop basic empathic skills (such as imagining the woes of a peasant in the French Revolution)" within a safe environment.[6] To win each Reacting game, students must be able to develop a level of mastery and understanding of texts, and to articulate their ideas in convincing, cogent oral and written arguments. The games require reasoning skills and a willingness to take on an opinion that may not necessarily be one's own. Reacting pedagogy epitomizes active and interactive teaching and learning.

Reacting has the potential to transform the classroom experience because it revises our traditional perceptions of what instructors should be and what students should do. Students must be willing to shift their conceptualizations of themselves from diligent notetakers to informed action-takers. In fact, for the duration of the game sessions, students suspend their own identities as twenty-first-century individuals in favor of adopting their respective roles, set in another place and time. This often acts as a liberating feature of game play for those students who customarily feel uncomfortable contributing in the usual modes of class participation. Consequently, instructors must be prepared to relinquish their usual perceptions of themselves as authoritative "sages on the stage" in favor of becoming more advisory, tutor-like "guides on the side."[7] In terms of game play, instructors become Game Masters who offer guidance before game sessions convene and after they close. The overall effect is that students are more inclined to identify as their main goals their own discovery of, learning of, and application of knowledge rather than to emphasize the reproduction of knowledge already delivered to them. In other words, Reacting games offer instructors and students the opportunity to develop a dynamic method of teaching and learning within the context of a survey course.

Teaching and Learning Goals

In 2009, I began searching for a relevant way to revitalize student learning in my Cultural Foundations courses. The Cultural Foundations courses function as a set of survey courses based on the Great Books of world literature, as well as world art, music, and the performing arts. Because these courses must coordinate as a sequence of required courses for all freshmen and sophomores in the Liberal Studies Program, certain areas of content must be covered each semester. And so, I wished to discover something fresh that would enrich the curriculum requirements and function within the existing course framework.

In the same way that history professor Sam Wineburg believes that students have "come to see history as a closed story when we suppress the evidence of how that story was assembled,"[8] I had observed that my students perceived literary analysis and interpretation as completely pre-established; they had become all too accustomed to having the Great Books digested for them. As Wineburg puts it, when "knowledge is detached from experience, it is certain and comes shorn of hedge and qualification, its source is textbooks and teachers, and it can be measured with tests in which every question has a right answer."[9] Lendol Calder calls for the development of a new sort of "signature pedagogy" for usage in history survey courses that would function in much the same way that interactive, question-driven methods are used to teach law and medicine.[10] According to Calder, this type of pedagogy would differ from the "coverage" model in which students depend upon receiving information from textbooks and professors.

For my students of literature, I sought a learning process in which they would feel motivated to make meanings for themselves, to understand that great works may be interpreted differently depending on one's perspective, that these works may have been produced during times of controversy and turmoil, that they may have been subject to sponsorship and censorship issues, and that they may have been produced with various purposes in mind. I wanted my students not simply to accumulate knowledge about literature, but to be able to apply that knowledge and to put it into practice.

Ideally, I wished to meet the challenge of motivating non-English majors to take a fresh approach to their active engagement with Shakespeare. As James Loehlin notes, "Teachers of Shakespeare have a singular opportunity to involve their students directly in the material being studied. Math students can reconstruct the proofs of their predecessors, art history students can copy a Vermeer— but students of Shakespearean drama can actually create the thing they study."[11] Several of my goals for my students coordinate with Loehlin's goals in teaching Shakespearean plays by situating them in historically contextualized performance: "to explore how the plays might have worked when they were new," and to realize how "an active engagement with a single text provides a uniquely vivid introduction to the way meanings are produced and contested in the crucible of theatrical representation."[12] Through a more direct experience with Shakespearean drama, Elizabethan playwrights, and acting troupes, as Loehlin states, students have the opportunity "to gain a grasp of Shakespearean language and rhetoric through close textual work; to explore a series of social, political, and ethical issues through interpretive work on scenes; to compare and evaluate different approaches to the play; and, finally, to bring together [their] work in a small-scale studio performance."[13] Although I valued Loehlin's vision of students' direct experience with Shakespeare's works, I had hoped to find a method of teaching Shakespeare more in keeping with the curriculum requirements of the Liberal Studies Program. And so, with the goal in mind of discovering one or two such active "signature pedagogies" that would privilege learning process and interdisciplinary study over preparation for public performance, I continued to attend conferences and professional development events.

Discovering Stages of Power: Marlowe and Shakespeare, 1592

I first discovered Reacting in 2010 during a professional development workshop sponsored by NYU's Center for Teaching Excellence where I met Mark

Carnes, professor of history at Barnard College, who invented the Reacting pedagogy in the 1990s and who has designed several of the games. Since the formal dissemination of the games began in 2001, hundreds of colleges and universities in the United States and internationally have adopted the Reacting pedagogy.[14] In 2004, Reacting received the Theodore Hesburgh Award for pedagogical innovation, and, most recently, the Reacting Consortium has announced a new grant initiative in collaboration with The Endeavor Foundation to support faculty who wish to incorporate the Reacting method of teaching and learning into their curricula.[15] As I talked with Mark Carnes during the workshop, I expressed my enthusiasm for the potential of this method and felt that it would complement the goals of our program. He suggested that I explore all of the game abstracts described on the Reacting website and that I try to attend a conference.

The website describes a number of games suitable for American literature courses. The *Frederick Douglass, Slavery, Abolitionism, and the Constitution, 1845* game (which can be accomplished in a one-day version or a three- to five-day version) opens with a review of *The Narrative of Frederick Douglass, an American Slave, Written by Himself* as its core text, and includes characters such as Sojourner Truth, members of the Auld Family, John C. Calhoun, Henry Clay, William Lloyd Garrison, and the Grimke Sisters. The *Trial of Anne Hutchinson: Liberty, Law, and Intolerance in Puritan New England* game would elucidate students' understanding of the Puritan world of Nathaniel Hawthorne's *The Scarlet Letter*; and *Red Clay 1835: The Cherokee Removal* would create historical context for the historical romances of James Fenimore Cooper and Catharine Maria Sedgwick.

I then attended the Reacting conference held at Barnard College in June 2011 hoping to discover more about a game that would fit into my existing courses: *Stages of Power: Marlowe and Shakespeare, 1592*. At the conference, I met faculty members representing colleges and universities across the nation who have employed the games in their classes with great success. Several instructors have used only selected elements of Reacting games; some instructors use the game materials as an anthology of primary sources for class discussions and essays; others use the game materials for the purpose of forming one or two session in-class debates, rather than to employ the entirety of a game together with its role-playing components. I played short versions of several games at that conference, but from the minute I met with Eric S. Mallin, the game designer of *Stages of Power*, and Paul V. Sullivan, who coauthored the game materials, both from the University of Texas at Austin, I knew that *Stages of Power: Marlowe and Shakespeare, 1592* would find another home in my classes.

In the *Stages of Power: Marlowe and Shakespeare 1592* game, the rival London acting companies of the established and seasoned playwright Christopher Marlowe and young upstart William Shakespeare must vie for sponsorship and licensing of their plays. Marlowe's acting company (the Lord Admiral's Men) and Shakespeare's company (the Lord Strange's Men) must compete to persuade the Privy Council (representatives of the peerage and government who are commissioned to investigate the plays) to grant an exclusive license to produce one play at the Rose Theatre in London. Each student plays a single role as a member of one of the acting companies or as a member of the Privy Council, and receives a role sheet at the start of the game that describes the historical person he or she will portray, as well as that role's goals in the game. By adopting the perspectives specified in each role, students must choose to advocate for, or argue against, a play based on its civic, moral, political, religious, or literary content. Students use a collection of interdisciplinary primary sources and the two plays to form their arguments in speeches and, in the cases of the acting companies, in the presentations of selected scenes as staged readings.

All students and the Game Master receive a Game Manual that specifies the historical situations and terms of the game, and contains the primary sources students will use as Renaissance authorities in order to shape their arguments. A number of games are published; if a game is designated as "in development" (not published), the materials may be downloaded free of charge into a specific course website, provided that instructors obtain advance express written permission via an online permissions form.[16] Game Masters receive an Instructor's Manual with role sheets and explanations of the game and its learning objectives. Companion texts may be selected according to each instructor's preferences. In the case of the *Stages of Power: Marlowe and Shakespeare, 1592* game, a number of texts fit the time frame of the game and may be used in combination. I have used the combination of Marlowe's *Doctor Faustus* together with Shakespeare's *Richard III* with excellent success. For Shakespeare, plays such as *Two Gentlemen of Verona* (1590), *Titus Andronicus* (1592), and *Taming of the Shrew* (1591–92), among others, would be appropriate to consider. For Marlowe, among others, *Tamburlaine* (1587–89), *The Jew of Malta* (1590–91), or *The Massacre at Paris* (1593) would work.[17]

What distinguishes *Stages of Power: Marlowe and Shakespeare, 1592* from many of the other Reacting games is that it does not rely upon the recreation of one historical moment and its time-honored arguments. Instead, "it imagines a contest between the acting troupes of these two great playwrights" that "culminates in a performance, by each troupe," of scenes before the Privy Council.[18] This imagined competition uses history as a context, rather than as its subject. As a result, the *Stages of Power* game opens new and dynamic avenues for students to engage in the processes of textual explication and interpretation for themselves.[19] Not only do students use the historical texts in support of their views, but they must use their understanding of the plays as evidence as well. As one of my students wrote anonymously in a postgame evaluation:

> This game gave me the license to scrutinize the plays and to seriously question the content, which broadened my understanding of them. That, along with learning about historical context, made me ask "why?" instead of settling with what would have been presented to me.[20]

In addition, those students who play members of the acting troupes must interpret and perform staged readings of scenes in collaboration with each other.

There are several options for playing the *Stages of Power: Marlowe and Shakespeare, 1592* game, as explained in the Instructor's Manual.[21] Initially, I was concerned about setting aside the number of class sessions that might be necessary to run the game, but, after a realistic review of my syllabus, I found that I had already been devoting five class periods to Shakespeare and his contemporaries in historical and cultural context. So, I began to run the game in five sessions. Ultimately, I added a sixth day to give students more time to process the meanings of the plays and to prepare scene presentations. Since then, I have been running the game in six sessions, as outlined in the game manual. With this three-week schedule, the *Stages of Power* game, like most Reacting games, can be interwoven into the fabric of an existing survey course.

I modify the game materials slightly to accommodate class sizes and to emphasize public speaking skills, as follows:

"Part I: Ideas and Words in London 1592"[22]

In session 1, each student is responsible for reading and reporting on one of the documents included in the Game Manual under "Texts that the Privy Councilors Might Plausibly Have Known in 1592." This excellent collection of primary source documents provides historical and cultural context for the game and ranges from excerpts of other plays by Shakespeare, Marlowe, and Kyd; to the writings of Erasmus and Machiavelli; and an excerpt from Philip Henslowe's Diary, which records expenses and receipts from plays produced in 1592. In brief, informal oral presentations, I ask each student to summarize the content of the document, to offer his or her response to it, and to connect one of the ideas in the document with a moral, political, religious, or literary idea in one of the plays we have studied.

"Part II: Disputation in the Commission on the Revels"[23]

During sessions 2–5, students receive their respective role assignments, most of which can be researched in the *Oxford Dictionary of National Biography*. Then, students meet in their groups to plan their speeches. Students must determine among themselves whether they will speak in favor of Marlowe, against Marlowe, for Shakespeare, or against Shakespeare. I require that all members of the acting companies present one speech during the disputations sessions and perform in at least one scene on the last day. To be sure that all students in the class have ample time to speak, I add a requirement to those specified in the Game Manual: all members of the Privy Council must give one longer speech (during disputations) and one shorter one (on the last day). In their speeches, all students (both acting companies and the Privy Council members) must weigh the merits and demerits of one of the plays in terms of its poetic, political, moral, or religious themes. Formal arguments, rebuttals, and disputations are presented in these sessions, followed by group meetings to plan and rehearse scenes for presentation. During the planning sessions, I charge the Privy Council with the creation of a pageant to be presented on scene day as a tribute to the Queen, which may involve readings, music, dance, or art. Students must hand in outlines of their speeches on their respective speech days.

"Part III: Performance of Scenes and the Final Vote"[24]

The crowning achievement of the game is the performance of selected scenes for the Privy Council. By this time, students are accustomed to the formality of the game and work beautifully within this framework. The Privy Council opens the proceedings with their pageant, followed by the presentations of scenes by the acting troupes. These presentations should be staged readings, but should be invested with theatricality. I ask each acting troupe to designate one person to give a prologue before each scene is presented and to explain the rationale behind the troupe's selection of each particular scene. Each member of the Privy Council gives a short speech following the scenes. The vote is taken to license one play and, ceremoniously, the results are announced. If time permits, a sort of postmortem session may follow the end of the game in which students drop their roles' personas and feel free to discuss their learning experiences.

After the close of the game, each student is responsible for writing one essay that argues, from his or her role's perspective, for the superiority or inferiority of one of the plays. Each paper should apply the standards set forth in one of the Renaissance texts we have read, as well as draw from one of the plays. In essence, the written essays may take on the voice, form, and style of the speeches delivered during the game sessions. A more writing-intensive option for the game is described in the Instructor's Manual, which offers additional opportunities for research papers, and which would be suitable for advanced courses. The Instructor's Manual outlines a number of types of writing assignments and exercises for both versions of the game.

Learning Outcomes

Reacting games connect academic learning with its future applications because they "[oblige] students to address messy, unstructured problems: these range from solving interpersonal dynamics within a team to devising arguments based on difficult texts and rapidly changing situations."[25] Specifically, the *Stages of Power* game succeeds in synthesizing the sort of content learning, critical thinking, teamwork, and verbal skills that students will need to apply to their academic lives and beyond. When I first encountered Reacting games, I was skeptical about the success stories I had heard. But, when I had witnessed the various ways in which students participate in the *Stages of Power* game, I saw peers supporting and helping each other in ways that I had not seen in other forms of class discussion or group work. As one of my students reflected, "This game forced me out of my comfort zone and to speak publicly in order to be a contributing member of my team."[26] Students begin to encourage each other in the game, and their collective success as a group sparks more energy and success. For this reason, through playing this game in ten different classes over the past five years, I have developed a "hands-off" policy in trying to direct students' staging of scenes; the aim in this course is not for students to generate performance-quality scene work, but for them to work together to develop their own understandings of the relationships between characters, the connections between Renaissance ideas and the play texts, and the meanings of the lines.

To be sure, Reacting games may not always be successful and they may not appeal to all students. As Mark Carnes states:

Reacting faculty routinely report unprecedented levels of student attendance, engagement, and participation. But not always. Sometimes the magic fails. Sometimes students, bound by an implicit pact against eager-beaver participation, stare sullenly at the gamemaster. Sometimes students who are accustomed to sitting and taking notes are baffled by the expectation that they go to the front of the room and address their peers. Sometimes students cannot get over their aversion to public speaking.[27]

Of course, difficulties with class participation may arise in any type of class. When I sense that a student is not ready to participate, just as I do with any class, I try to have a brief private conversation with the student. If needed, then I meet with the student to guide disputation ideas or to clarify line readings. When a group comes to a standstill, I task the group with specifics. These bits of guidance usually improve the comfort level of the students and the quality of game play for the entire class.[28] The advantages of the *Stages of Power* game's experience for students far outweigh its disadvantages.

One of my students exclaimed as he left our first session of speeches and debates, "I can't wait until Tuesday. I have so much I want to say to those Marlowe people!" Another of my students, when asked by her mother how her classes were going, explained, "Well, Mom, this week I'm the Archbishop of Canterbury in Cultural Foundations. By next Thursday, I have to decide, based on *Doctor Faustus*, whether Christopher Marlowe is an atheist." As time ran out for the last class period of the game, and with the votes yet uncounted, one of my classes insisted on staying to find out the results. "We can't go through the weekend not knowing," they said. Students often remark that these class sessions are among the most lively they have experienced.

Each time I have taught the *Stages of Power: Marlowe and Shakespeare, 1592* game, I have witnessed students' accomplishment of content-based learning objectives, such as "familiarity with the themes and language of (at least) one play by Shakespeare and one play by Marlowe," "general knowledge of late-Elizabethan history," and an understanding of the writings and ideologies that shaped this period.[29] But the game accomplishes much more. For me, one of the greatest privileges of teaching *Stages of Power* has been in seeing how well students interact with each other, how much their public-speaking skills improve, and how well they analyze multiple viewpoints of the same issue. The classroom becomes an organic place for fun, spontaneous student discoveries. In playing the *Stages of Power: Marlowe and Shakespeare, 1592* game, instructors need not feel obligated to explain in detail the meaning of texts to their students; via their immersion in Elizabethan England, students gain the knowledge and skills they need to experience and interpret the meaning of texts for themselves.

Acknowledgments

A previous version of this article appeared in the *Shakespeare's Globe* Colloquium website of the Liberal Studies Program of New York University. I wish to thank colleague Heather Masri for her meaningful comments on a preliminary draft of that article.

Permissions to include information from the game materials for *Stages of Power: Marlowe and Shakespeare, 1592* have been graciously granted by Eric S. Mallin and Paul V. Sullivan. Permissions to include references to the "Reacting to the Past" website at https://reacting.barnard.edu/ have been generously granted by the Reacting to the Past Consortium.

I also wish to thank New York University's professional development funding, which facilitated my attendance at two Reacting to the Past conferences held in 2011 and 2015. Based on my approximate recollections, I have included the words of some of my students in an anonymous way.

NOTES

1. Reacting to the Past website, "The Concept," https://reacting.barnard.edu/.

2. In addition to the works referenced in this essay, the values of pedagogical gameplay, including digital games, are discussed in Claus Nygaard, Nigel Courtney, and Elyssebeth Leigh, eds., *Simulations, Games, and Role Play in University Education*, Learning in Higher Education Series (Oxfordshire: Libri, 2012). See also James M. Lang's series of three articles published in *The Chronicle of Higher Education* beginning on July 21, 2014, with "Being Nehru for 2 Days."

3. Mark C. Carnes, *Minds on Fire: How Role-Immersion Games Transform College* (Cambridge, MA: Harvard University Press, 2014), 13.

4. Reacting website, "Curriculum, Basic Concept."

5. Chet Meyers and Thomas B. Jones, *Promoting Active Learning, Strategies for the College Classroom* (San Francisco: Jossey-Bass Publishers, 1993), 93.

6. Ibid., 96.

7. These terms come from the title of Alison King's article "From Sage on the Stage to Guide on the Side," which delineates a number of similar active and interactive methods of teaching and learning. Allison King, "From Sage on the Stage to Guide on the Side," *College Teaching* 41, no. 1 (1993): 30–36. More specifically, this shift in the customary functions of students and instructors is described by Mark C. Carnes, "The Liminal Classroom," *Chronicle of Higher Education* 51, no. 7 (2004): B6–B8.

8. Sam Wineburg, *Historical Thinking and Other Unnatural Acts* (Philadelphia: Temple University Press, 2001), 79.

9. Ibid.

10. Lendol Calder, "Uncoverage: Toward a Signature Pedagogy for the History Survey," *The Journal of American History* 92, no. 4 (March 2006): 1361.

11. James N. Loehlin, "On Your Imaginary Forces Work: Shakespeare in Practice," in *Teaching Shakespeare through Performance*, ed. Milla Cozart Riggio (New York: Modern Language Association of America, 1999), 286.

12. Ibid., 287.

13. Ibid.

14. Reacting website, "About Us."

15. Reacting website, "News" and "About Us."

16. The online permissions form is accessible through the Reacting website.

17. These and other eligible plays and poems are listed in the Appendix to the Instructor's Manual.

18. Eric S. Mallin, "On Game Playing and the Uses of Uncertainty," *English Language Notes* 47, no. 1 (Spring/Summer 2009): 127.

19. Ibid., 127–29.

20. As a part of the post-mortem session of the game, I customarily circulate a survey-questionnaire for students regarding what they feel they have learned or accomplished by playing the game. The student quotations included in this essay come from an anonymous student survey I circulated after the conclusion of the *Stages of Power* game, which was played in the Liberal Studies Program of NYU during the Spring 2016 semester.

21. When I began to teach this game, it was designated as a game in development, which is the version to which I refer here. Now, through additional revision and game-testing, the game is reaching its final form in preparation for publication by the Reacting Consortium Press, an imprint of the University of North Carolina Press.

22. I use the same titles of game segments, as stated in the Game Manual, in order to retain the game's original structure. However, I have reorganized several of the activities within each segment in order to accommodate class sizes that are usually larger than the game allots for.

23. I have rearranged a portion of the sequence of activities delineated in Part II so as to allow more time for all twenty-five students to deliver speeches and to participate in disputations.

24. All of these segments are delineated in the Game Manual under "The Play of the Game: Overview."

25. Carnes, *Minds on Fire*, 292.

26. See note 20 above.

27. Carnes, *Minds on Fire*, 142.

28. Ibid., 142–44.

29. These learning objectives, among many others, are described in the Instructor's Manual on pp. 2–5 under "What Students Can Learn."

30. At the time of this writing, the *Stages of Power: Marlowe and Shakespeare, 1592* game is scheduled to be published by the Reacting Consortium Press, an imprint of the University of North Carolina Press. The idea of the assignment described in the course documents at the end of this essay comes from Eric S. Mallin, who designed the *Stages of Power* game. Although this research-based project does not directly arise from the game and is not included in the game materials, it would work well as a supplemental and/or postgame assignment to enhance and update students' understanding of the Marlowe-Shakespeare relationship. The title of this assignment includes a quotation from Shakespeare's Sonnet 116.

BIBLIOGRAPHY

Calder, Lendol. "Uncoverage: Toward a Signature Pedagogy for the History Survey." *The Journal of American History* 92, no. 4 (March 2006): 1358–71.

Carnes, Mark C. "The Liminal Classroom." *Chronicle of Higher Education* 51, no. 7 (2004): B6–B8.

———. *Minds on Fire: How Role-Immersion Games Transform College.* Cambridge, MA: Harvard University Press, 2014.

King, Alison. "From Sage on the Stage to Guide on the Side." *College Teaching* 41, no. 1 (1993): 30–36.

Lang, James M. "Being Nehru for 2 Days." *Chronicle of Higher Education*, July 21, 2014. http://www.chronicle.com/article/Being-Nehru-for-2-Days/147813.

———. "How Students Learn from Games." *Chronicle of Higher Education*, August 25, 2014.http://www.chronicle.com/article/How-Students-Learn-From-Games/148445.

———. "Stop Blaming Students for Your Listless Classroom." *Chronicle of Higher Education*.September29,2014.http://www.chronicle.com/article/Stop-Blaming-Students-for-Your/149067.

Loehlin, James N. "On Your Imaginary Forces Work: Shakespeare in Practice." *Teaching Shakespeare through Performance*, edited by Milla Cozart Riggio, 286–94. New York: Modern Language Association of America, 1999.

Mallin, Eric S. "On Game Playing and the Uses of Uncertainty." *English Language Notes* 47, no. 1 (Spring/Summer 2009): 125–34.

Mallin, Eric S., and Paul V. Sullivan. "Game Manual and Instructor's Manual." In *Stages of Power: Marlowe and Shakespeare, 1592.* Reacting to the Past game. https://www.uncpress.org/book/9781469631448/stages-of-power/.

Marlowe, Christopher. *Doctor Faustus.* Edited by Sylvan Barnet. New York: New American Library, Signet Classics, 2010.

Meyers, Chet, and Thomas B. Jones. *Promoting Active Learning: Strategies for the College Classroom.* San Francisco: Jossey-Bass Publishers, 1993.

Nygaard, Claus, Nigel Courtney, and Elyssebeth Leigh, eds. *Simulations, Games, and Role Play in University Education.* Learning in Higher Education Series. Oxfordshire: Libri, 2012.

"Reacting to the Past." *Barnard College.* https://reacting.barnard.edu/.

Shakespeare, William. *The Tragedy of Richard III.* Edited by Barbara A. Mowat and Paul Werstine. New York and London: Folger Shakespeare Library, Simon and Schuster, 1996.

Wineburg, Sam. *Historical Thinking and Other Unnatural Acts.* Philadelphia: Temple University Press, 2001.

COURSE DOCUMENT: VARNUM FERRETTI

"Reacting to the Past in the Survey Course"

Appendix—A Shakespeare and Marlowe Research Assignment[30]

The idea of this assignment comes from Eric S. Mallin, who designed the *Stages of Power: Marlowe and Shakespeare, 1592 game.* Although this research-based project does not directly arise from the game and is not included in the game materials, it would work well as a supplemental or postgame assignment to enhance students' understanding of the possible complexities within the Marlowe-Shakespeare relationship. This project would heighten students' awareness of current topics in Shakespeare studies, and, depending on how much research would be involved, it could be quite suitable for advanced students with experience in literary research, especially research in the MLA database. Students should have good familiarity with the MLA-style documentation of sources for research papers.

Breaking News on Marlowe and Shakespeare

Rivals or a "Marriage of True Minds"?

As we have just seen in our *Stages of Power: Marlowe and Shakespeare, 1592* game, historians of literature and theater usually characterize the Marlowe-Shakespeare relationship in terms of artistic rivalry. But current literary scholars have researched a new possibility: that Marlowe and Shakespeare cowrote several plays, including the *Henry VI* plays (parts I, II, and III). Are they right?

To answer this question, first, you will need to investigate at least two or three news reports from reputable newspapers, wire services, or networks, such as the *Guardian* or the *New York Times,* dating from October 2016. What do these articles report? What claims are current scholars making? What reasons do they have for making these claims? (Summarize these views in a few paragraphs.)

Secondly, do some literary research on your own. Investigate at least two MLA articles that analyze one of the *Henry VI* plays and read that play. Which passages might lead you to believe that Shakespeare and Marlowe collaborated? What other types of evidence have scholars cited as proof?

How strong is the evidence you have discovered? (Record your findings and offer your analysis of several passages in two or three pages.)

Finally, write a few paragraphs that express your speculations. In light of the evidence you have gathered, how would you weigh the strength of linguistic and/or theatrical evidence to support this view? If you feel that this evidence is insufficient, what other types of evidence might you like to see? What other reasonable explanations might there be (other than collaboration) for these linguistic commonalities? How have your discoveries complicated your view of the Marlowe-Shakespeare relationship?

Please use MLA-style documentation to identify your sources.

The Blank Survey Syllabus

CHRIS WALSH, BOSTON UNIVERSITY

Have you practis'd so long to learn to read?
Have you felt so proud to get at the meaning of poems?[1]

I know Walt Whitman intends these questions rhetorically. Early in "Song of Myself," he is pushing for something beyond reading. He wants us to connect, even to commune with the poem and through the poem the poet ("who touches this," as he writes in "So Long," "touches a man"[2]) and through the poet all people (since he "contain[s] multitudes"), and also with nature itself, with the entire "kosmos."[3] Practice in reading may be necessary, but it is not sufficient for this profound endeavor, and pride in getting at the meaning of poems, or in believing we have, can get in the way of communion with them.

Still, I can't help but respond in the unrhetorical affirmative to Whitman's questions: Yes, I have in fact practiced so long to learn to read, so so long, and like most teachers of literature, I've been getting at the meaning of poems for years; I've actually gotten pretty good at it, thank you. Proud and practiced, I see it as my hard-earned honor to share with others what I've learned, and there is no place better to do that than in the literature survey class, where a central goal is to teach a range of writers and a range of work. This is both a privilege and a challenging duty, since there are so many works to choose from, and the semester is so short. Which poems, short stories, plays, sermons, to teach? Can I squeeze in a novel? Two? No? How about a novel and a novella?

Yet I have found that my students get the most out of the survey when I refrain from choosing all the texts, when I require them to choose some. Doing so makes them read, write, and converse better, and it deepens their engagement with literature, and with their own educations. It deepens my engagement with them too, and makes me read, converse, and teach better.

I call this approach the "blank syllabus"—a bit of Whitmanian bluster or twenty-first-century branding that emphasizes the real power it gives students in shaping the course. I don't leave the syllabus entirely blank, though, just some of the reading assignments for some of the class sessions. Here is what students see at the top of the calendar section of American Literature I: Colonial Period to the Civil War:

> You will notice some blank spots on the schedule below, beginning in late October. These will be filled in with your names and with the titles of the selections you choose to write about for the first essay (details to come). On the day your name appears, you will help me lead discussion of the text you chose, noting why you chose the selection, pointing us to a passage you found particularly striking, and concluding with questions or comments to spark discussion.

And here is what the schedule starts to look like on Tuesdays and Thursdays in late October (the "B" refers to the *Norton Anthology of American Literature 1820–1865*, volume B):[1]

October 19

Thoreau, *Walden*, Chapter 1, "Economy" (B 1807–50)

October 24

_____ & _____

October 26

_____ & _____

October 31

_____ & _____

November 2

Whitman, "Song of Myself" (B 2232–74)

November 7

_____ & _____

Sometimes, depending on the size of the class, every student gets to add something to the syllabus, usually from the course anthology. For larger classes, students can work in small groups to make their selections. It's also possible to make the process competitive by having students (either singly or in groups) make presentations advocating for their selections, followed by a class vote. In addition to considering some of the questions on the prompt above, I encourage presenters to recite a favorite passage or act out a scene, striving both to entertain their fellow students and to persuade them to vote for their selection.

However the class chooses the readings, the next step is to distribute a revised schedule with each new selection listed, accompanied by the name of the student (or students) who selected it:

October 19

Thoreau, *Walden*, Chapter 1, "Economy" (B 1807–50)

October 24

Irving, "Rip Van Winkle" (B 980–91; *Tess*)

Bryant, "Thanatopsis" (B 1072–74; *Calla*)

October 26

Thorpe, "The Big Bear of Arkansas" (B 1780–88; *Cece*)

Thoreau, *Walden*, chapters 12, "Brute Neighbors," and 15, "Winter Animals" (B 1924–31, 1948–54; *Mr. Walsh*)

October 31

Poe, "The Raven" (B 1518–21; *Carlos*)

Poe, "The Cask of Amontillado" (B 1592–97; *Malcolm*)

November 2

Whitman, "Song of Myself" (B 2232–74; *Mr. Walsh*)

November 7

Dickinson, "I Started Early–Took My Dog—" (B 2520); "My Life Had Stood—a Loaded Gun—" (B 2525) (*Mary*)

Endless variations of this approach are possible. David Gooblar chose all the prose pieces for his survey of American literature, but left blanks that students were required to fill with poems.[5] In a graduate survey of the Contemporary American novel, I asked students to write a short essay making a case for adding a novel to the syllabus. On the day these essays were due early in the semester, students made short pitches to the class. Then the class voted and the winner (it was Jonathan Safran Foer's *Everything Is Illuminated*) became the assigned reading for late in the semester. The approach can also work well in classes that aren't surveys. I have been using it for years in themed composition classes (on the poetry of war, for example, or on African literature). In an introduction to literature class that pivots on the concept of literary influence, Gillian Steinberg leaves readings "TBA" for the last month of the semester and asks students to find texts that show the influence of the books they read earlier in the semester. She assigned T. S. Eliot's *The Waste Land*, for example, and students assigned the class works influenced by that poem, including Pink Floyd's *The Wall* and excerpts from Evelyn Waugh's *A Handful of Dust*.[6]

Allowing students to select readings can present some challenges. Achieving coverage of the period under survey is the most obvious one. It is true, as Steinberg shows, drawing on the work of Elaine Showalter and Robert Scholes, that there are good reasons to question the idea of coverage.[7] It is an impossible goal, for starters, given how much there is to cover in even the narrowest time period, and even if it is possible, the pursuit of coverage can encourage a superficial engagement with literature and a false sense of completion when the term ends. ("Are you so proud," Whitman might ask, to have "'covered' 'American Literature I: Colonial Period to the Civil War'?") Yet a survey course that does not give students a rough sense of the lay of the land, that does not acquaint them with the most prominent historical and literary features of the period under focus, that does not identify commonalities and diversities of various kinds, is probably not doing its job. Panorama is not enough—"The panorama of the sea . . . but the sea itself?" Whitman asks.[8] But panorama can orient students and prepare them to navigate the sea.

Luckily, the blank syllabus can be structured to maximize coverage, however you define it. In addition to reminding students not to choose items already on the syllabus, an on-line sign-up sheet can delimit students' options in various ways, ensuring, for example, that only a certain number of slots are available for each third of the course anthology. Something similar can be done to keep students from choosing only short pieces. In the example above, Mary might have chosen only one Emily Dickinson poem for the class to read (on November 7), but the readings-must-be-at-least-one-page rule pushed her to choose two. Also, requiring students to select some readings does not mean allowing them to select all of them. Whitman's "Song of Myself" was on the syllabus from the start, and had no one selected anything by Dickinson, I would have done so. The teacher can also control the order and combination of readings, and supplement things as he or she sees fit, as I did in pairing Cece's choice of T. B. Thorpe's "The Big Bear of Arkansas" with *Walden*'s chapters on "Brute Neighbors" and "Winter Animals." Students had already been required to read the first chapter of *Walden*; Cece's selection gave us a chance to return to that book and examine two rather different mid-nineteenth-century attitudes toward animals.

Some students are taken aback by the blanks on the syllabus. Why are they, the novices, being asked to make decisions that the expert should be making? Isn't choosing readings the professor's job? Here again Whitman can offer some wisdom. In "When I Heard the Learn'd Astronomer" he tells of attending a lecture with "proofs . . . figures . . . ranged in columns before me" and "charts and diagrams, to add, divide, and measure"— until he "became tired and sick" and "wander'd off by myself, / In the mystical moist night-air, and . . . / Looked up in perfect silence at the stars."[9] As with the stars, so with literature: expert mediation can help us appreciate something we might not otherwise consider, or even notice, but sometimes it gets in the way of seeing (and thinking, and feeling) for ourselves.

Telling students about the transactional theory of reading can also brace them for the task of selecting readings and writing or presenting about their selections. As Louise M. Rosenblatt argues, "'The poem' comes into being in the live circuit set up between the reader and 'the text.'" Filling in the blank syllabus becomes an exercise in creating and sharing "literary event[s]," an opportunity for individual students to connect with individual pieces of literature, and then to connect with their fellow students via that literature.[10]

Less grand but perhaps more convincing for students is to tell them how the blank syllabus approach can benefit them practically. The first place students feel that benefit is in their reading—and this benefit comes even though the survey typically requires them to grapple with what may be the most assigned and most unread genre in all literature: the survey anthology. The *Norton Anthology of American Literature 1820–1865*, volume B, runs over 1,500 pages of Bible paper, with nearly fifty authors, and it is safe to assume that most students read only what they have to, leaving vast stretches of territory untouched, much less surveyed. But David Gooblar reports that requiring students to choose poems for his syllabus "got them to actually spend some time with the anthology apart from the assigned readings, and encouraged them to discover what sort(s) of poetry they might actually prefer to read. . . . [T]here's no question that the blank syllabus led them to engage better with those readings and each other than my previous classes. The students were much more enthusiastic about reading poetry—always a challenge, I find. . . ."[11] Looking for a selection, students read independently and actively, browsing in a way they rarely do if the teacher chooses all the readings.

Of course students may select a text for superficial reasons. Perhaps Mary chose Dickinson's "I Started Early—Took My Dog—" because she likes dogs. She likes the ocean, too, so she may have stayed with the poem because in the second line the speaker notes that she "visited the Sea." But the poem quickly becomes something more mysterious and disturbing than a walk on the beach, with talk of "The Mermaids in the Basement," of "Frigates" reaching out their sail-hands, and of the tide flowing "past my Apron—and my Belt / And my Bodice—too—[.]" What, Mary's classmates might wonder, has she gotten them into? Is this a poem about the fear of not loving ("no Man moved Me") or of being loved ("made as He would eat me up")? Or the fear of death? Or is it about the exhilarating and overwhelming—the oceanic—power of the imagination? Students may sometimes choose texts that seem easy or safe, but it often turns out that the waters they thought were shallow and still are deep and moving, even treacherous—until, in this case anyway, the poem concludes: "bowing—with a Mighty look / At me—The Sea withdrew—."[12]

The blank syllabus approach can improve student writing because it addresses a common problem in college essay assignments—that they seem, in the worst sense of the word, so academic. In the real world, including the academic real world, we write in order to communicate—to inform and persuade a specific audience. But students often write for no discernible audience except—perhaps—their teacher, who is usually already better informed about the subject than the students are, and the only consequence for being less or more persuasive is a grade. As Peter Elbow noted in discussing first-year composition classes, "unless we can set things up so that . . . students are often telling teachers about things that they know better than we do, we are sabotaging the essential dynamic of writers. We are transforming the process of 'writing' into the process of 'being tested.'"[13]

A blank syllabus writing assignment can set things up in a way that preserves the "essential dynamic" Elbow describes. Here's one for American Literature I:

In a 1250–1500-word essay, discuss a selection of your own choosing (one *not* already listed on the syllabus) from the *Norton Anthology of American Literature*. Choose a text that is at least one page long (so if you're interested in a short poem, you may have to select another short poem or two to meet the minimum) and craft an argument about the suitability of the piece for class reading. As you write, think about the questions we generated in class—the questions you would have about a classmate's selection, and answer them about your own. What is the piece about? Who wrote it, for whom, and why? What genre is it? What is the historical context? How does the piece advance our understanding of themes discussed in class or in the themes in the *Norton* introduction—religion and transcendentalism, for example, or immigration and xenophobia? How does it connect, or not, to life in 2016? You don't have to answer all of these questions, but your essay should tell us about the substance of your selection (so you'll need to include a brief summary) and about why reading it will be worth our time. As you draft, it may be helpful to have a working thesis that begins, "I recommend we read this text because . . ." Simply deleting the "I recommend . . ." may work for the final version of this claim, but the claim should also respond to the question or problem established in your introduction.

Even if it's just the teacher who ultimately reads the paper, and even if the class does not vote on the selections, knowing that the class will be reading the students' selection seems to give this assignment the concrete sense of audience that college writing so often lacks. Knowing they'll be called upon to help lead discussion of the text they have chosen can also have a bracing effect on students' writing. As a template or thesis-stub, "I recommend we read this text because" leads students to make specific arguable claims, and when in the body of the paper they try to execute these claims, awareness of their fellow classmates as audience makes the students more likely to adduce specific evidence and to explain how this evidence supports their points.

There are ways of making this sense of audience even more concrete. One is to have a class discussion about what sorts of questions students want answered in a paper about other students' selections. These questions can be incorporated in the assignment (as above) and in discussions with peers. In the first class after students choose their selections, but before they start writing, they have a ten-minute conversation with a partner about their selection, asking each other why they chose it, what the most striking passage is, and some of the questions noted in the paper prompt. The room buzzes with the excitement of students reporting to each other about their discoveries. Then I have them write in class for a few minutes to capture their thoughts and feelings— as well as the energy with which they were expressing them. After that I remind them of the challenge ahead: to write an essay that is academic in the best way—balanced, well-substantiated, carefully reasoned, and precisely focused, and to do so without losing the spirit so abundantly evident in their conversations.

In addition to helping students become better readers and writers, the blank syllabus can enhance the energy and dynamics of the class. Gooblar reported that "the open-mindedness and curiosity with which [his students] approached their peers' choices was great to witness. I think they found that they have a lot to learn from each other. . . ."[14] Selecting a text for the whole class to read makes students connect with their peers not just socially but intellectually. That student who always sits in the back wearing a baseball cap becomes the guy who picked that creepy Poe story about some Italian man getting sealed up in a wine cellar. The guy's name is there on the syllabus next to Poe's—Malcolm. And on October 31 (Halloween), when "The Cask of Amontillado" and "The Raven" are assigned reading, Malcolm and Carlos are the experts for the day, the students who will be able to tell their classmates what drew them to those texts, and, depending on what research they did, something about Poe's life and work.

Learning from each other does not mean that students always approve of their peers' choice of text. "The Cask of Amontillado" *is* pretty creepy, as invariably comes up in class discussions. Some students don't see the value of the creepiness, and I have found that they are more likely to raise objections when the reading they object to was selected by a classmate rather than by their teacher. But the teacher can bring focus and rigor to this discussion by drawing out students with questions (What do you mean by "creepy"?) and by bringing the larger scholarly conversation to bear on the given text. "Yes, some critics, especially during his time, also found Poe to be 'too fond of the wild—unnatural and horrible.' In 1836 one asked, 'Why will he not permit his fine genius to soar into purer, brighter, and happier regions?' "[15]

Even as we keep playing our role as teacher, though, the blank syllabus helps students learn by putting them in the teacher role, too. It is not news to teachers that a great way to learn something is to teach it, and research has shown that we learn deeply both not only when we actually teach, but also when we prepare to do so. A recent study showed that simply the expectation of teaching "enhances learning and organization of knowledge. . . ."[16] And it is possible to make the teaching role seem (and actually become) more real. Last semester, I had students write short multiple-choice quizzes and discussion questions for their classmates, and supply a link to a source related to their selection—anything (a video clip, song, website) that would help prime the class for a conversation about the piece they chose. Carlos, the student who chose "The Raven," for example, directed students to a clip from *The Simpsons* that dramatized this poem (with James Earl Jones narrating). Students received the links before class, and I would often project whatever it was as students filed into the room. Even when the link was not exactly scholarly, as was the case with *The Simpsons* clip, it helped get students focused on the subject of the day before class even began.

Putting students in the position of teacher also encourages them to adopt a mastery rather than a performance orientation to their education. Filling in the blanks on the syllabus and doing all the work associated with it, students do not forget about performance goals such as getting a good grade or doing better than their peers, but by giving students some sense of control and choice, the approach encourages mastery goals such as learning for learning's sake, or so that one can teach others. Cultivating the mastery orientation seems to enhance students' learning even after they complete a mastery-oriented educational experience. A study of "high ability" high school students who participated in a summer program that emphasized mastery goals found that "mastery goal orientation was sustained even when students returned to a more traditional classroom environment in which performance goal orientations might be more readily endorsed."[17]

Such sustained effects are an important consideration if survey teachers hope that their students will continue to survey literature after their class and even after their college experience is over. Independently and thoughtfully choosing what to read and (sometimes) advocating for your choices are, after all, fundamental skills for many professions, not to mention for a rich intellectual life. The blank syllabus helps sustain and improve students' engagement with literature, with their writing, and with each other, because it meets fundamental psychological needs for what motivation theorists Edward L. Deci and Richard Ryan call autonomy, competence, and relatedness. It cultivates autonomy by allowing students to choose; it cultivates competence by asking students to do a task that is challenging, but of which they are capable; and it cultivates relatedness by making them part of a team effort to create a survey together. None of these elements is an absolute good in itself, and they sometimes conflict. Too much autonomy can make students feel lost and incompetent, for example; too much relatedness can undermine the feeling of autonomy. In the right mixture, though, these elements contribute to students' intrinsic motivation to do the task—and that generally means that they will perform the task better. Intrinsic motivation also makes it more likely that students will do the same task again on their own.[18]

I have found that asking students to choose some texts enhances my own motivation, too. Sometimes a student selection renews my love for a text that had become stale to me. I had given up assigning "Rip Van Winkle," for example, until Tess assigned it to the class. The blank syllabus has also introduced me to texts that I had altogether avoided (who knew Bryant's "Thanatopsis" was so good?). It also brings a sense of collaboration to a profession that can sometimes be strangely lonely and exhausting. The teacher lives in a world parallel to his colleagues but separate from them, and separate also from his students, as the captain of a ship is separate from his crew. But when students select readings, a spirit of shared enterprise animates the classroom, and the teacher does not always have to supply the impetus to begin each class; it comes from students and from the readings they select, and from their enthusiasm about their selections. In my experience, distributing the revised schedule with each new selection listed and accompanied by the name of the student (or students) who selected it also provides a boost at a time of the semester when it's really needed. This is a big moment—when the blanks in the syllabus get filled up and the surveying ahead is not of sites predetermined by the teacher but of places that they have decided they want to go.

How many blanks should you give them to fill? How much autonomy should you give students before their competence is overwhelmed? Perhaps a good rule to follow is the greater the gap between your knowledge and the students', the fewer blanks you should leave. Looking back on my contemporary American novel course, I regret having left only one novel for the students to choose. Selecting eleven novels myself (we read a book a week) might have been justified had this been a class in early British Literature (from Beowulf to Milton, say). But surely a roomful of contemporary American graduate students interested in literature could have played a larger role in choosing contemporary American literature worth reading. I should have trusted them more.

Trust, in fact, may be the most important thing that the blank syllabus both requires from and fosters in teachers.[19] First comes the trust in our students' willingness and ability to take on the responsibility we give them. In this regard it is helpful to remember, and to remind them, that they've been choosing texts all their lives, and to remember also that we are not letting them loose into uncharted wilderness but into a world whose bounds we control through the options we give them in the anthology or otherwise. (Using a course anthology also means you trust its editors to have excluded total clunkers—though you can always exclude ones as you see fit.)

The blank syllabus also pushes us to trust in our own skills as able surveyors. We have practiced long to learn to read; we are right to take pride in our ability to get at the meaning of poems. Even if we don't know every nook and cranny of the territory our students might choose to explore, we still know the shape of the land, the main boundaries and contours, and we can offer guidance as the students take their own measures.

Finally and also foremost, the blank syllabus encourages us to trust literature's power to connect to students even before we offer our guidance to them. In that spirit, I will trust the inviting end of "Song of Myself" to have the last word here.

I bequeath myself to the dirt to grow from the grass I love,
If you want me again look for me under your boot-soles.
You will hardly know who I am or what I mean,
But I shall be good health to you nevertheless,
And filter and fibre your blood.

Failing to fetch me at first keep encouraged,
Missing me one place search another,
I stop somewhere waiting for you.[20]

NOTES

1. Walt Whitman, "Song of Myself," in *Norton Anthology of American Literature, 1820–1865*, 6th ed., ed. Nina Baym (New York: W. W. Norton, 2003), 2233.

2. Whitman, "So Long," *The Walt Whitman Archive*, http://www.whitmanarchive.org/published/LG/1891/poems/305.

3. Whitman, "Song of Myself" in Baym, *Norton Anthology of American Literature, 1820–1865*, 2274, 2248.

4. David Gooblar, "Filling in the Blanks," *Pedagogy Unbound*, November 13, 2013, https://chroniclevitae.com/news/144-pedagogy-unbound-filling-in-the-blanks.

5. Gillian Steinberg, "Literature and Influence: A New Model for Introductory Literature Courses," *Pedagogy: Critical Approaches to Teaching Literature, Language, Composition and Culture* 13, no. 3 (2013): 469–86, DOI: 10.1215/15314200-2266423.

6. Ibid., 481–82.

7. Walt Whitman, "[Song of Myself]," in Baym, *Norton Anthology of American Literature, 1820–1865*, 2181.

8. Whitman, "When I Heard the Learn'd Astronomer," in Baym, *Norton Anthology of American Literature, 1820–1865*, 2219.

9. Louise M. Rosenblatt, *The Reader, the Text, the Poem: The Transactional Theory of the Literary Work* (Carbondale: Southern Illinois University Press, 1994), 14, 161.

10. Gooblar, "Filling in the Blanks."

11. Emily Dickinson, "I Started Early—Took My Dog—," in Baym, *Norton Anthology of American Literature, 1820–1865*, 2520.

12.   Peter Elbow, "Being a Writer vs. Being an Academic: A Conflict in Goals," *College Composition and Communication* 46, no. 1 (1995): 81.

13.   Gooblar, "Filling in the Blanks."

14.   Anonymous review quoted in I. M. Walker, ed., *Edgar Allan Poe: The Critical Heritage* (New York: Routledge, 1986), 87.

15.   John F. Nestojko, Dung C. Bui, Nate Kornel, and Elizabeth Ligon Bjork, "Expecting to Teach Enhances Learning and Organization of Knowledge in Free Recall of Text Passages," *Memory & Cognition* 42, no. 7 (October 2014): 1038–48.

16.   Paul A. O'Keeffe, Adar Ben-Eliyahu, and Lisa Linnenbrink-Garcia, "Shaping Achievement Goal Orientations in a Mastery-Structured Environment and Concomitant Changes in Related Contingencies of Self-worth," *Motivation and Emotion* 37, no. 1 (March 2013): 51.

17.   Richard M. Ryan and Edward L. Deci, "Intrinsic and Extrinsic Motivations: Classic Definitions and New Directions," *Contemporary Educational Psychology* 25, no. 1 (2000): 54–67.

18.   Steinberg notes that asking students to choose some readings "forces us to trust [them] in a way that assigning readings and essays does not accomplish." Gillian Steinberg, "Literature and Influence: A New Model for Introductory Literature Courses," *Pedagogy: Critical Approaches to Teaching Literature, Language, Composition and Culture* 13, no. 3 (2013): 476, DOI: 10.1215/15314200-2266423.

19.   Whitman, "Song of Myself," in Baym, *Norton Anthology of American Literature, 1820–1865*, 2274.

BIBLIOGRAPHY

Baym, Nina, ed. *Norton Anthology of American Literature, 1820–1865*. 6th ed. 2 vols. New York: W. W. Norton, 2003.

Dickinson, Emily. "I Started Early—Took My Dog." In Baym, *Norton Anthology of American Literature, 1820–1865*, 2520.

Elbow, Peter. "Being a Writer vs. Being an Academic: A Conflict in Goals." *College Composition and Communication* 46, no. 1 (1995): 72–83.

Gooblar, David. "Filling in the Blanks." *Pedagogy Unbound*. November 13, 2013. https://chroniclevitae.com/news/144-pedagogy-unbound-filling-in-the-blanks.

Nestojko, John F., Dung C. Bui, Nate Kornel, and Elizabeth Ligon Bjork. "Expecting to Teach Enhances Learning and Organization of Knowledge in Free Recall of Text Passages." *Memory & Cognition* 42, no. 7 (October 2014): 1038–48.

O'Keefe, Paul A., Adar Ben-Eliyahu, and Lisa Linnenbrink-Garcia. "Shaping Achievement Goal Orientations in a Mastery-Structured Environment and Concomitant Changes in Related Contingencies of Self-Worth." *Motivation and Emotion* 37, no. 1 (March 2013): 50–64.

Rosenblatt, Louise M. *The Reader, the Text, the Poem: The Transactional Theory of the Literary Work*. Carbondale: Southern Illinois University Press, 1994.

Ryan, Richard M., and Edward L. Deci. "Intrinsic and Extrinsic Motivations: Classic Definitions and New Directions." *Contemporary Educational Psychology* 25, no. 1 (2000): 54–67.

"The Simpsons—Edgar Allan Poe: The Raven." YouTube. https://www.youtube.com/watch?v=bLiXjaPqSyY.

Steinberg, Gillian. "Literature and Influence: A New Model for Introductory Literature Courses." *Pedagogy: Critical Approaches to Teaching Literature, Language, Composition and Culture* 13, no. 3 (2013): 469–86. doi: 10.1215/15314200-2266423.

Walker, I. M., ed. *Edgar Allan Poe: The Critical Heritage*. New York: Routledge, 1986.

Whitman, Walt. "So Long." *The Walt Whitman Archive*. http://www.whitmanarchive.org/published/LG/1891/poems/305.

———. "Song of Myself." In Baym, *Norton Anthology of American Literature, 1820–1865*, 2232–74.

———. "[Song of Myself]." In Baym, *Norton Anthology of American Literature, 1820–1865*, 2147–89.

———. "When I Heard the Learn'd Astronomer." In Baym, *Norton Anthology of American Literature, 1820–1865*, 2219.

The Blank Syllabus Essay Assignment

In a 1,250–1,500-word essay, discuss a selection of your own choosing (one *not* already listed on the syllabus) from the *Norton Anthology of American Literature*, volume B. Choose a text that is at least one page long and craft an argument about the suitability of the piece for class reading. As you write, think about the questions we generated in class—the questions you would have about a classmate's selection. What is the piece about? Why do you like it? Who wrote it, for whom, and why? What genre is it? How does the piece advance our understanding of themes discussed in class or in the *Norton* introduction—religion and transcendentalism, for example, or immigration and xenophobia? How does it connect, or not, to life in 2017? You don't have to answer all of these questions, but your essay should tell us about the substance of your selection (so you'll need to include a brief summary) and about why reading it will be worth our time. As you draft, it may be helpful to have a working thesis that begins, "I recommend we read this text because . . . " Simply deleting the "I recommend . . ." may work for the final version of this claim, but, as we'll discuss in class, the claim should also respond to the question or problem established in your introduction.
Due September 29.

Initial Reading Schedule for The Blank Syllabus

[*At the beginning of the semester, students see the following text and schedule:*]

Reading assignments must be completed by the beginning of class on the day noted in the schedule below (where "A" refers to the *Norton Anthology of American Literature, Literature to 1820*, volume A; and "B" refers to the *Norton Anthology of American Literature, 1820–1865*, volume B). You will notice some blank spots beginning in October. These will be filled in with your names and with the titles of the selections you choose to write about for the first essay (details above). On the day your name appears, you will tell the class why you chose the selection, point us to a passage you found particularly striking, and conclude with questions or comments to spark discussion.

September 6
   Iroquois and Pima creation stories (A 19–33)

September 8
   Christopher Columbus (A 34–38)
   Bartolomé de las Casas (A 38–42)

September 13
   William Bradford, from *Of Plymouth Plantation* (A 156–83)

September 15
   John Winthrop, "A Model of Christian Charity" (A 205–17)

September 20
   Anne Bradstreet (A 239–40, 262–65, 269–70)

September 22
   Edward Taylor (A 356–62)

September 27
   Mary Rowlandson, "A Narrative of the Captivity and Restoration . . ."
   (A 308–40)

September 29
   Jonathan Edwards, "Sinners in the Hands of an Angry God" (A
   498–509)

October 4
   Benjamin Franklin (A 516–38)

October 6
   Abigail and John Adams (A 682–98)
   Thomas Paine (A 704–18)

October 11
   Thomas Jefferson (A 726–32)

October 13
Phillis Wheatley (A 808–24)
Ralph Waldo Emerson, "Self-Reliance" (B 1160–76)

October 19
_____ & _____

October 24
_____ & _____

October 26
_____ & _____

October 31
_____ & _____

November 2
Henry David Thoreau, *Walden* **(B 1807–50)**

November 7
Frederick Douglass, *Narrative of the Life . . . of an American Slave* **(B 2032–63)**

November 9
Frederick Douglass, *Narrative of the Life . . . of an American Slave* **(B 2063–97)**

November 14
_____ & _____

November 16
Whitman, "Song of Myself" (B 2232–50)

November 21
Whitman, "Song of Myself" (B 2251–74)

THANKSGIVING BREAK

November 28

_____ & _____

November 30

_____ & _____

December 6

_____ & _____

REVISED SCHEDULE for The Blank Syllabus

[*After students have completed "The Blank Syllabus Essay Assignment" (above), I distribute the revised schedule with their selections (and mine) followed by their names:*]

As you know, on the day your name appears, you will tell the class why you chose the selection, point us to a passage you found particularly striking, and conclude with questions or comments to spark discussion.

October 19

Irving, "Rip Van Winkle" (B 980–91; *Tess*)
Bryant, "Thanatopsis" (B 1072–74; *Calla*)

October 24

Nathaniel Hawthorne, "Young Goodman Brown" (B 1263–73; *Christine*) and "Rappaccini's Daughter" (B 1313–32; *Mr. Walsh*)

October 26

Harriet Jacobs, "Incidents in the Life of a Slave Girl" (B 1759–78; *Simone*)
Fanny Fern, "Male Criticism on Ladies' Books" (B: 1748; *Kandice*)

October 31

Poe, "The Raven" (B 1518–21; *Carlos*)
Poe, "The Cask of Amontillado" (B 1592–97; *Malcolm*)

November 2
> Thorpe, "The Big Bear of Arkansas" (B 1780–88; *Cece*)
> Henry David Thoreau, *Walden* (B 1807–50; *Mr. Walsh*)

November 7
> Frederick Douglass, *Narrative of the Life . . . of an American Slave* (B 2032–63; *Mr. Walsh*)

November 9
> Frederick Douglass, *Narrative of the Life . . . of an American Slave* (B 2063–97; *Mr. Walsh*)

November 14
> Abraham Lincoln, "Gettysburg Address" and "Second Inaugural" (B 1616–17; *Tim* and *Sylvie*)
> Thoreau, "Resistance to Civil Government" (B 1792–1806; *Melinda* and *John M.*)

November 16
> Whitman, "Song of Myself" (B 2232–50; *Mr. Walsh*)

November 21
> Whitman, "Song of Myself" (B 2251–74; *Mr. Walsh*)

THANKSGIVING BREAK
November 28
> Herman Melville, "Bartleby, the Scrivener" (B: 2330–54; *John T.* and *Sylvie*)

November 30
> Dickinson, "I Started Early—Took My Dog—" (B 2520) and "My Life Had Stood—a Loaded Gun—" (B 2525; *Mary*); "Much Madness Is Divinest Sense" (B: 2515; *Mr. Walsh*)

December 6
> Louisa May Alcott, "Transcendental Wild Oats" (B 2574–86; *Maria*)
> Emma Lazarus, (B 2597–601; *Lindsay*)

Errant Pedagogy in the Early Modern Classroom, or Prodigious Misreadings in and of the Renaissance

MELISSA J. JONES, EASTERN MICHIGAN UNIVERSITY

Although first New Criticism and now Presentism equally instruct us in the importance of adopting *some* flexibility in interpreting texts from the past, there's an unspoken agreement that this flexibility stretches only so far. In the survey classroom in particular, the instructor's role tends to be to help students to learn "right" versus "wrong" ways to read the text and its time. We would not, for instance, allow students to believe that Hamlet's big problem was that he was born a woman—in mind or body—yet was forced to act the part of a man in a man's world; we do, however, encourage students to tangle with the web of social and subjective questions that enmesh the seventeenth-century male body acting the part of Ophelia on the all-male stage. But what, really, would be the harm—or the salve—in allowing students to "fail" in their pursuit of a right reading? To let them misread, profusely and with gusto, such historically vested work? Taking my cue from nascent student inquiries and using personal recollections, shared anecdotes, and general hearsay as my evidence, this article takes seriously four different kinds of error across a range of survey classes: the errant ear in Shakespeare's *Romeo and Juliet* (Shakespeare Survey); a truant reading of Sidney's "Sonnet 69" (Renaissance Literature 1500–1660); an erratic pestle from Francis Beaumont's *Knight of the Burning Pestle* (Graduate Survey in Renaissance Poetry and Prose); and an awkward Freudian slip in the teaching of Milton's *Paradise Lost* (also Renaissance Literature 1500–1660). Errors like these, I argue, illuminate new pathways into the texts and their multiple contexts, and I insist on the queerness of this pedagogical practice because of its radical impact on the text's circulation in university circles, on traditional classroom dynamics, and on ideals of productivity and authenticity.

Mondegreen, Butt-Love

I raised the issue of learning from "failing" in the classroom at an academic conference recently, and several audience members took up the question by sharing stories from their own secondary and undergraduate days. One graduate student elaborated on how much her high school class had gained from a comical perversion of Romeo's line in Act Two, "Call me but love, and I'll be new baptiz'd; / Henceforth I never will be Romeo" (2.2.50–51).[1] The teens, she reported, were mostly bored by Shakespeare's star-crossed lovers, their lyrical repartee, and all of their thumb-biting friends and foes until one boisterous student misheard Romeo's imprecation as asking Juliet to call him "butt-love." He hollered out, "butt-love?!?" and for the rest of the term, all of the students in class referred to Romeo as "butt-love." On a very basic level, this misprision changed the students' relationship to the play, its characters, and its language by goading them to read and listen more closely in search of other hilarious homophones. Such attention readied the class to hear with greater nuance Mercutio's punning and sexually ambiguous bawdy, "stop[ping] my tale against the hair" (2.4.95–96), for instance, and it set them up to listen for the depth of Juliet's desire in her anticipation of "love-performing night" (3.2.5). For this reason alone, I encourage such playful and irreverent mishandling of Shakespearean language in the classroom as a matter of course.

However, I think that this particular homophonic error, the sort Sylvia Wright might term a "mondegreen," or mishearing that takes on its own persuasive meaning, is useful for more than just inspiring closer readings of what *is there already* in the text.[2] Romeo's "butt-love" might be just as important for the excess of meaning that it generates, and for the spotlight it shines on the play's inherent cultural biases and the problem of reproducing these biases unreflectively in our teaching of *Romeo and Juliet*, perhaps the most familiar and most frequently taught play in Shakespeare's repertoire. In an article on "Lyric Cryptography," John Shoptaw explores modes of listening that uncover such surplus words and ideas by attending to phonemic rather than graphemic "drifts," or to the sound rather than just the sight of a text's "markers" (the letters on the page). He makes his point using the line from *Hamlet*, "A serpent stung me," as the marker for the logically consistent cryptograph, "serpent's tongue [me]."[3] Shoptaw's argument makes sense for its attention to the "inherent expressiveness of sound" and for its effort to cleave "productive" reading from the infinite linguistic possibility of "paragrammatic" analysis.[4]

But I fear that Shoptaw's definition of "productive" listening still leaves much unheard, seeking as it does a logic of the poem limited by the cultural horizon of the text's author ("Yes, 'language writes,'" he affirms, "but it writes better with Dickinson").[5] Classroom emphasis on Romeo's "butt-love" operates contrarily, then, pointing up the importance of using the crypt phrase to uncover oblique relations that matter as much, if not more, in the world of the text's citation and circulation than in that of its original composition. With this in mind, two ways of reading the phrase "butt-love" emerge. The first, and most explicit, resonates provocatively with Jonathan Goldberg's sophisticated reading of "*Romeo and Juliet*'s Open Rs," which notes how the alliteration of Rs in Romeo and Rosaline's names, and in the name as well as image of the rose, are consonant with the play's repeated references to the "open-arse," a consonance—or assonance—that exposes a deep undercurrent of male and female anal eroticism.[6] Of course, we could simply revisit Goldberg's "open Rs" argument without the intervention of the colloquial "butt-love" to focus attention on the play's sodomitical potential. Even if the archaic sounding "arse" were to invite some disconnect between teens' recognition of their own sexual practices in the play's erotic structure, that gap could probably be bridged without too much effort, and the argument can even be made that it is perhaps important to maintain this linguistic distance, to signal that sexual acts and identities do not translate identically across time and place. Yet "butt-love" in modern parlance also refers to admiration of the buttocks as an emblem of feminine beauty, rather than merely as the means to an end (or end to a means?). This second version of "butt-love," holding no place in the play's critical history nor the early modern index of popular fetishes, might, in fact, be more immediately heard by today's youth, with songs like Sir Mix-a-Lot's "Baby Got Back" (1992), Destiny's Child's "Bootylicious" (2001), and J. Lo's "Booty" (2014) ringing in our ears.[7] The crypt phrase thus subtly challenges us to engage the racial politics of Shakespeare's *Romeo and Juliet* along with its queer affects, since the fetishization of butts in U.S. culture has for decades stood to differentiate African American from European American female body ideals.

Sir Mix-a-Lot succinctly captures this racial tension (and the shared patriarchal prerogative that subtends both perspectives on women's bodies) in the lyrics: "I'm tired of magazines / Saying flat butts are the thing / Take the average black man and ask him that / She gotta pack much back."[8] Tracie Morris's sound poem "Slave Sho' to Video a.k.a. Black but Beautiful" goes a step further, reclaiming this bodily part for black women with sound and word play that pushes back at all forms of hegemonic signification. "Signifying" with the same sort of errant ear and tongue-in-cheek that brings my discussion of *Romeo and Juliet* to this racially marked place, Morris riffs on and remixes the lines, "she too black aint she beautiful she bootiful she boot full booty she beaut boot bootiful /. . . / but black and beautiful and but full booty" (1:19–26).[9] Although Shakespeare's play does not explicitly represent racial difference (and barely nods to class distinction), "butt-love" draws our ear to these questions anyway, offering a vital opportunity for students in traditional "survey" settings to think about race—and, specifically, the often unseen construction of whiteness—in ways that aren't overtly scripted by plot or critical tradition.[10] The intersection of racial and sexual thinking evoked by "butt-love's" double-valence suggests an additional, queer axis along which to consider Benvolio's remonstrance to Romeo to compare "the fair Rosaline" to others in order to prove "the swan a crow" (1.2.82, 86), for example, a tainted metaphor that Romeo extends when he sees Juliet as "a rich jewel in an Ethiop's ear," whose beauty "shows [like] a snowy dove trooping with crows" (1.5.46, 48). The failure to talk about race alongside other issues like class, gender, and sexuality when opportunities like these present themselves, however obliquely, in courses dedicated to the unifying and homogenizing idea of "the survey" is not because race doesn't matter to an author or an era; yet it does suggest that race does not matter so much to us, accenting the very privilege that "butt-love" would sound out.

Sidney's Truant Pen and Our Missing Aim: Or, How to Be Super-Superficial

When time-traveling Bill S. Preston, Esq. and Ted "Theodore" Logan, from the movie *Bill and Ted's Excellent Adventure* (1989), meet real-time Bill and Ted outside of the San Dimas Circle K (where they had been asking strangers for help with a history assignment), they confirm their shared identities by "thinking of a number." The Bills and Teds reply in unison: "Sixty-Nine, dude!" Most of my students have neither seen nor heard of *Bill and Ted*, and yet I'm frequently reminded of—and instructed by—this scene when teaching Sidney's *Astrophil and Stella*, another tale about a slacker-cum-hero, with some history thrown in. As critics have noted, the poem's most poignant explorations of eros and politics are motored by the poet's recognition of his failures. Astrophil professes his romantic shame early and often, "Biting my trewand pen, beating myselfe for spite" (1.13), and he confesses his social abjection throughout: "Unable quite to pay even Nature's rent," (18.5), he now wears the "great promise" (21.9) of his youth as "a train of shame" (21.8). My students in my Renaissance Literature 1500–1660 survey embrace Ann Rosalind Jones and Peter Stallybrass's reading of how such Petrarchan tropes can work to reinforce the poet's authority over the woman-as-object; and they equally accept Catherine Bates's caution *against* seeing the debasement of the poem's narrator as certain evidence of the poet's writerly mastery, following her counterargument that the poem's masochistic affect also suggestively aligns with its rhetorical lapses, those moments of "unstable irony" and humor with no "inner content, signified or point of rest," in order to deconstruct any unified (masculine) self.[11]

I'd be lying, though, if I didn't confess that "Sonnet 69" often elicits extra attention in the form of snickers, head-cocks, or raised eyebrows, particularly if I'm injudicious enough to phrase my question: "So how does this apply to '69'?" Or, worse, "What do you all think of '69?' You know, the *sonnet*. Sonnet 69?" When I first started teaching, I pressed past these moments of levity and/or discomfort to return us to more serious academic points; yet I've come to believe that genuine entanglement with *Astrophil and Stella*'s "surfaces," as Bates urges, might need to risk contact with such *super*-superficial reactions if it is truly to elude, in her words, "the traditional Platonic categories of western metaphysics" that depend on a hermeneutics of depth.[12] Judith Halberstam reframes this critical injunction in more general terms as a call to "[p]*rivilege the naïve or nonsensical (stupid)*" in order to dismantle "the logics of success and failure with which we currently live."[13] In league with Bates and Halberstam and in the spirit of Sidney's companions in "Sonnet 23," those "curious wits" who with "idle pains, and missing aim, do guess [at his reasoning]" (23.4), I dare my students in classroom discussion to chase down their giggling reactions to "Sonnet 69," to value the insight that inexperienced or "stupid" readings might lend to this so-called anatomy of love.

Students begin by arguing that "Sonnet 69" is the most tumescent and ejaculative in the sequence, with its moaning assonance and pounding apostrophes: "O joy too high for my low style to show / O bliss fit for a nobler state than me" (69.1–2), "My spring appears, O see what here doth grow" (8), "I, I, O I may say that she is mine" (11).[14] Debate then ensues over whether or not this "sex" poem leaves any room for the mutuality of its titular "69" or if its erotic economy is simply masturbatory, since Stella's agency is described only in terms of "words" and permissions, whereas Astrophil's responses are characterized by physical action. He thus inveighs his "friend," likely Stella, to "Come, come, and let me pour myself on thee" (6), clarifying her role in this exchange, "Stella hath with words where faith doth shine,"

> Of her high heart given me the monarchy
> I, I, O I may say that she is mine
> And though she give but thus condition'ly
> This realme of bliss, while virtuous course I take,
> No kings be crownd but they some covenants make. (9–14)

Thinking about these bawdy descriptions within the framework of the "69" sex act begins the arduous task of challenging the assumption that the poem's fantasies are necessarily proscribed by critical questions of who is "on top"—even if a close reading ultimately fails to sustain the ideal of this mutual sexual action.

There are about a dozen additional reasons why the "69" fails to provide a master key to *Astrophil and Stella* in the easy way that it unlocked Bill and Ted's true identities. Only after students have thought through their own readings of the poem, however, do I mention that the sequence was not numbered in original manuscript or print copies, and that the number "69" doesn't seem to have stood for anything in particular in the Renaissance (despite Mercutio's complaint that Romeo is "for the numbers / that Petrarch flowed in"). More interesting is that I haven't been able to locate evidence of mutual oral sex as a "thing" at all in early modern sexual culture. Even Pietro Aretino's famed *Sonetti Lusuriosi* (1524) describe and depict only penetrative heterosexuality (despite a claim in Cassanova's memoirs that he spent New Year's Eve in 1753 with a nun doing Aretino's "straight tree" position, with the standing man holding the woman upside down for mutual oral sex). In spite of history, then, the novice focus opens up a range of refreshing questions that help students to think not just about the contours of Sidney's poem but also about the limits of the early modern sexual imagination—and/or the limits that modern readers instinctively place upon that imaginary. Even the masochistic self, which challenges the ideals of unity and empowerment so central to Western thinking, still finds in its embrace of disempowerment an implicit place for power. By contrast, student efforts to think about what a "69" poem would be about, and how it would work in the context of the rest of the sonnet sequence, makes room for fantasies of mutuality that could supersede the penetrative and reproductive paradigms of heterosexuality that still dominate thinking about early modern texts and times. Taking seriously, at least provisionally, these seemingly superficial or digressive readings, students learn to try on "ways of reading" that foster inquiry stances on both text and period. The teleology of courses dedicated to "surveying" the literary landscape from 1500 to 1660 might be similarly upended by chasing down and pursuing ahistorical and affective classroom reactions and readings like these.

Traumatic Malapropism

My final two mistakes are related, and I'm therefore categorizing them both as examples of classroom malapropism, though the first entails a persistent slip of the tongue and the second describes a misguided theatrical prop. Like

Freud's classic slips, both gesture to areas of the student and teacher's unconscious, and both point up how much is ultimately unknowable or unrecover-
able in classroom exchanges. My first gaffe I borrow from a good friend of
mine, who insists that her undergraduate Milton professor referred to the
Old Testament as the Old Testicle throughout his teaching of one whole two-
hour class on *Paradise Lost*.[15] She tells the story the way one talks about being
flashed on the subway: it's not threatening per se, but it's certainly perplexing, embarrassing, seedy, and memorable. This example of error in the early
modern classroom raises a host of pedagogical and practical questions. Did
this near-retirement male professor realize his error and persist in it, perhaps
as a joke, in self-aware misuse of language (or *mumpsimius*) that traces back
to Erasmus and leans forward toward sexual harassment?[16] Or was it an acci-
dental nod to the word's etymology, linking Milton's interpretation of Genesis to the root of "testament" in "testis"? We might even be dealing with a
"false memory" on the part of my witness, with remembered details mixing
into or amplifying other moments and histories. The only certain thing is
that her experience and my own subsequent teaching of *Paradise Lost* is for-
ever impacted by the remembered error.

In fact, graduate students in my Renaissance Poetry and Prose class might
tell a similarly traumatic story about our reading of *Knight of the Burning Pestle*, in which the boisterous "grocer errant" dons a blue apron and, wearing the
device of a burning pestle on his shield, amuses his Citizen masters with a chi-
valric romance of their design. Rafe's adventures weave in and out of the main
plot, comically offsetting the disturbing implications of Luce's orchestration of
her own "rape," and of her lover Jasper's mock-threat to kill her. I'm unsure
what turned classroom discussion one day to the idea that Rafe's heraldic pestle
resembled a dildo. Perhaps it was our effort to redirect conversation about the
"norm" of sexual assault into a counterpoint on female sexual autonomy, with
the emblazoned and bumbling dildo representing both ends of this spectrum?
Somehow, though, my students got the further impression that Rafe's dil-
do-pestle was not merely an image on a shield, but that this grocer errant was
costumed with an actual dildo on his helmet, like a unicorn. A weird, dirty
unicorn. This shared misunderstanding came out toward the end of our reading of the play, when students were as surprised to learn that this unicorn-dildo
livery was an invention of their imaginations as I was to hear that they some-
how thought I'd instructed them in this costumery.

"[B]e frivolous, promiscuous, and irrelevant," Halberstam urges: "lose one's
way, and indeed . . . be prepared to lose more than one's way."[17] In spite of their
humorous aspects, both of the above anecdotes hint at the reality of student

vulnerability, and the risks to students' feelings of safety when we set about to lose our way in the landscape of teaching early modern literature. This risk is recognized in recent debate over the benefits and drawbacks of syllabus "trigger warnings" that alert students to subjects that might provoke traumatic reactions.[18] Embracing error means that things might not always go where they should, academically or emotionally, which makes it all the more important that we clarify what we're aiming for from the start. I conclude on this note of caution not to curb the reach of errant pedagogy nor to discipline the lost, or the losers, in education, but to emphasize that our responsibility to the content of the period is always at the same time an obligation to the people in our classrooms.

Loose Ends

Although this is the place in my article for explicit recommendations, any careful reader up to this point should realize that there can be none. Being open to error and to failure doesn't come with an orderly playbook. However, I do have some thoughts on how to begin. As I've described above, re-seeing moments of error or failure are invitations for deeper exploration into disciplinary problems made visible through such errancy. For my students this invitation comes directly through exploratory and reflective writing assignments that span genres. John Bean argues that exploratory writing allows us to "present students with higher order critical thinking problems" and "immerse [them] in complexity without being threatening."[19] As with any pedagogical approach, assessment of student learning in both informal writing and more formal essays and exams can help to reveal how well allowing for error develops students' skill at close reading and analytical writing. This question of transfer is frequently at the center of arguments about student learning in higher education, and a growing body of literature suggests that reading and writing "different genres engage[s] different parts of the brain" and mixing exploratory and reflective writing with more traditional "academic" writing deepens student learning.[20]

To this end, my own students engage in a series of creative writing assignments aimed at giving them space to practice critical thinking in imaginative and nontraditional ways, where no "right" interpretation exists, but where they are pressed to reflect and analyze actively how their thinking is situated by and within larger questions of the text. By courting these playful and frequently multimodal responses, the assignments invite students to talk back to texts, modeling the kind of dialogic thinking required of advanced literary study. The assignments also force students to confront their own comfortable habits and practices as readers and writers, using different modalities and genres to help get at new ways of thinking. An early creative assignment, "In the mind's eye," works to help students visualize the psychic interior of three characters in John Webster's *Duchess of Malfi*. Students bring visual texts and accompanying short written rationales to class discussion to help demonstrate ways that the visual imagination colors textual reading practices. In "Talk back to Astrophil," students adopt the voice of Stella (the beloved of Sidney's sonnet sequence *Astrophil and Stella*) to respond in either poetry, prose, or dramatic dialogue to Sidney. Here they are exploring how voice and style work creatively and critically. "Shake It Up" invites a collaborative rewrite of Renaissance love poems in modern diction, again focusing on key aspects of the course: how language, style, and genre work. For the next iteration of the course, I've also been toying with passing these transliterated poems onto different peer groups to try to put them back into Renaissance diction and form, in keeping with Roger Ascham's celebrated humanist exercise of "double-translation" in Latin instruction. The fun would be to see how students understand what early modern poetry and language looks like and how it acts on its own, as lively and engaged expression, rather than just historical artifact. With each of these creative and exploratory writing activities, students always have an additional written reflective analysis on both product and process.

Students' reflective writing on the process of pursuing creative ideas as simultaneous wrong/right interpretations offers another rich site to study the advantages or disadvantages of this instructional mode. Regular mid-semester course evaluations can further help to gauge individual students' comfort levels and their intellectual engagement with course materials and structures. Some "wrong" readings in classroom discussion can be anticipated and built into the syllabus, like the snickering that frequently attends Sidney's "Sonnet 69." Others must be embraced when they arise, such as the mishearing of Romeo's "butt love." But what if an anticipated wrong reading doesn't transpire? My plan is usually to talk to students about where I thought they'd go wrong and then, together, we explore why my own expectations of a failed reading failed. Getting it wrong can be a lot of work, but it's ~~usually often~~ always worth it.

NOTES

1.   Immense thanks to Brianne Pernod for sharing this provocative example.

2.   Sylvia Wright, "The Death of Lady Mondegreen," *Harper's Magazine* 209 (1954): 48–51, derives the term from her youthful mishearing of the Scottish Ballad "The Bonnie Earl O'

Moray," where she confused "Lady Mondegreen" for "and laid him on the green" and compounded the error by building a convincing and sympathetic narrative around the character of Lady Mondegreen.

3.   John Shoptaw, "Lyric Cryptography," *Poetics Today* 21, no. 1 (Spring 2000): 221–62.

4.   Ibid., 240.

5.   Ibid., 241.

6.   Jonathan Goldberg, "*Romeo and Juliet*'s Open Rs," in *Queering the Renaissance*, ed. Jonathan Goldberg (Durham, NC: Duke University Press, 1994), 218–35.

7.   Will Fisher argues that buttocks are a fetishized object for the pleasure they provide on their own, but I'm not convinced that Fisher's examples from the early seventeenth century are erotic in themselves rather than for their proximity to the genitals. Will Fisher, "'Wantoning with the Thighs': The Socialization of Thigh Sex in England 1590–1660," *Journal of the History of Sexuality* 21, no. 1 (January 2015): 1–24.

8.   Sir Mix-A-Lot [Anthony Ray], "Baby Got Back" [Track 3], *Mack Daddy*, recorded 1991, Def American, 1992. compact disc. The song reached number one on the United States Billboard Hot 100 for five weeks in the summer of 1992, and it won the 1993 Grammy Award for Best Rap Solo Performance.

9.   Tracie Morris, "From Slave Sho' to Video," 1:17–1:30, https://mediamogul.seas.upenn.edu/pennsound/authors/Morris/Morris-Tracie_From-Slave-Sho-to-Video-aka-Black-but-Beautiful_2002.mp3.

10.   None of the essays in *Approaches to Teaching Shakespeare's* Romeo and Juliet, for example, talks about race thematically or in terms of student readership. Maurice Hunt, ed., *Approaches to Teaching Shakespeare's Romeo and Juliet* (New York: MLA, 2000).

11.   Catherine Bates, "Astrophil and the Manic Wit of the Abject Male," *SEL* 41, no. 1 (Winter: 2001): 10.

12.   Ibid., 10.

13.   Judith Halberstam, *The Queer Art of Failure* (Durham, NC: Duke University Press, 2011), 12, 2.

14.   Peter C. Herman, ed., *Sir Philip Sidney's* An Apology for Poetry *and* Astrophil and Stella: *Texts and Contexts* (Glen Allen, VA: College Pub., 2001).

15.   My profuse gratitude to friend and colleague Christine Hume for sharing this story and for helping me to think through its myriad implications for teaching and learning about literature.

16.   In his *Letters*, Erasmus complains about the "mass-priest who refused to change the word *mumpsimius*, which he had used for twenty years, when someone told him *sumpsimius* was what he ought to say." Quoted in Peter Marshall, *Religious Identity in Henry VIII's England* (New York: Ashgate, 2006), 159.

17.   Halberstam, *The Queer Art of Failure*, 6.

18.   See the spate of blog posts and articles in last year's *Chronicle of Higher Education*, in particular Peter Schmidt, "AAUP Says 'Trigger Warnings' Threaten Academic Freedom," September 8, 2014, http://www.chronicle.com/blogs/ticker/aaup-says-trigger-warnings-threaten-academic-freedom/85573.

19.   John C. Bean, *Engaging Ideas: Integrating Writing, Critical Thinking, and Active Learning in the Classroom*, 2nd ed. (San Francisco: Jossey-Bass, 2011), 121.

20.   Ibid., 63–64.

BIBLIOGRAPHY

Bates, Catherine. "Astrophil and the Manic Wit of the Abject Male." *SEL* 41, no. 1 (Winter: 2001): 1–24.

Bean, John C. *Engaging Ideas: Integrating Writing, Critical Thinking, and Active Learning in the Classroom*. 2nd ed. San Francisco: Jossey-Bass, 2011.

Fisher, Will. "'Wantoning with the Thighs': The Socialization of Thigh Sex in England 1590–1660." *Journal of the History of Sexuality* 21, no. 1 (January 2015): 1–24.

Goldberg, Jonathan. "*Romeo and Juliet*'s Open Rs." In *Queering the Renaissance*, edited by Jonathan Goldberg, 218–35. Durham, NC: Duke University Press, 1994.

Halberstam, Judith. *The Queer Art of Failure*. Durham, NC: Duke University Press, 2011.

Herman, Peter C., ed., *Sir Philip Sidney's* An Apology for Poetry *and* Astrophil and Stella: *Texts and Contexts*, Glen Allen, VA: College Pub., 2001.

Hunt, Maurice, ed. *Approaches to Teaching Shakespeare's* Romeo and Juliet. New York: MLA, 2000.

Marshall, Peter. *Religious Identity in Henry VIII's England*. New York: Ashgate, 2006.

Schmidt, Peter. "AAUP Says 'Trigger Warnings' Threaten Academic Freedom." *Chronicle of Higher Education*, September 8, 2014. http://www.chronicle.com/blogs/ticker/aaup-says-trigger-warnings-threaten-academic-freedom/85573.

Shoptaw, John. "Lyric Cryptography." *Poetics Today* 21, no. 1 (Spring 2000): 221–62.

Wright, Sylvia. "The Death of Lady Mondegreen," *Harper's Magazine* 209 (1954): 48–51.

COURSE DOCUMENT: JONES

LITR 314//Undergraduate Renaissance Literature 1500–1660: Creative Writing Sequence

Description: A series of creative short-writing assignments and one longer creative essay to enable students to engage canonical literary texts on equal footing and with a deeper investment in the process of critical reading and writing.

Goal: To hone students' critical reading and thinking skills by asking them to interact with a text creatively and personally, to open up space for error and exploration by destabilizing the text's authority and building the student's own sense of agency in critical reading and writing. Quite literally, students will learn to "talk back" to texts, modeling the kind of dialogic thinking required of advanced literary study. Each assignment will also develop students' writing skills by asking them to attend to different genres, styles, and writing conventions as they spin their creative webs.

Justification: Most of you are English majors who feel quite comfortable within the parameters of the formal essay—perhaps too much so. After years of honing your craft, your hard-won competency risks turning into inflexibility in how you think about writing in general and genres in particular. It is precisely this level of comfort that this assignment aims to unsettle in order to encourage greater flexibility with reading and writing, to lead students to innovative ways of seeing and engaging a text, and to recognize the place of creativity—and even failure—in all critical work.

- *"In the mind's eye"*: Visualize the psychic interior of three characters from John Webster's *Duchess of Malfi.*" For this homework assignment, bring in visual texts that describe or support an interpretation of different characters from the play in order to demonstrate ways visual imagination colors textual reading practices. Write short paragraphs explaining each choice; we will discuss these choices and rationales in class. I will individually grade and comment on these creative and self-reflexive pieces.
- *"Talk back to Astrophil"*: This independent homework assignment asks students to respond to Sir Philip Sidney's sonnet sequence *Astrophil and Stella* in the voice of Stella (the poem's beloved). Choose what form this dialogue should take—poetry, prose, dramatic dialogue—

but specify (as Stella) which parts of Sidney's poem you are responding to. Students must think about how style works in their creative responses to Sidney, and they must articulate a fully developed critical position on the original poem in the voice of Stella. This will help you to think about how voice works creatively and critically. To reinforce this habit of thinking, the assignment also calls for a "coda" paragraph in the form of a critical self-reflection. You will share your creative work in groups, and the group will do a collaborative peer-review. (I will grade it, too.)

- *"Shake It Up"*: Rewrite Shakespeare's "Sonnet 116," John Donne's "The Flea," or Marvell's "To His Coy Mistress" in modern diction. This is a collaborative, in-class exercise that requires students to deconstruct the poem and to assume equal footing with Shakespeare, Donne, or Marvell in the process of reauthoring. You will need to pay special attention to the ways that language, style, and genre work in your particular poem so you can effectively make these tools your own. This exercise will be peer-reviewed both in the composition stages and through each group's oral presentation of their poems. In-class discussion will provide some assessment of the process, but you will also be required to reflect collaboratively on your group's style and content choices in a separate paragraph intended to reinforce self-reflexive writing habits.

- *"Paradise Losers"*: This final, longer creative assignment (4–6 pp.) asks students to invent a new character for John Milton's epic poem, *Paradise Lost*. You will need to think of how the new character works in the poem in terms of its characterizations, philosophy, and the larger narrative. What book does he/she appear in? Whose side is he/she on? This creative characterization can take whatever form you choose, but you must theorize your choices either simultaneously or in a final reflection paragraph.

Digital Tools, New Media, and the Literature Survey

JENNIFER PAGE, NORTHWESTERN OKLAHOMA STATE UNIVERSITY

Introduction: The Digital Curation Project

Planning a compelling, engaging, and thorough early British literature survey course can be more than a little daunting. The challenge of teaching even just the highlights of more than a thousand years of literature in sixteen weeks might strike some instructors as Herculean. As a result, many of us take the classic coverage approach to conquer this beast: We get through as many texts and authors as possible in the time we have, providing quantity sometimes at the expense of quality. The unfortunate result of this tactic is that students are introduced to the literature, but they rarely develop any deeper, more detailed understanding of these works' significance. Although the coverage model allows us to provide a foundation to students for later literature classes or later educational testing, we cannot be sure that such a whirlwind tour of early Britain makes a lasting impression in a significant way.

Seymour Papert's theory of constructionism provides an alternate pedagogical model that can supplement the coverage approach and ensure more student engagement with the course material, the instructor, and their peers. This school of thought

> shares constructivism's connotation of learning as "building knowledge structures" irrespective of the circumstances of the learning. It then adds the idea that this happens especially felicitously in a context where the learner is consciously engaged in constructing a public entity, whether it's a sand castle on the beach or a theory of the universe.[1]

In other words, constructionism encourages student ownership of a particular aspect of a subject. The theory holds that constructing or generating something, from a model to a digital gallery, is a key component of effective learning. Instead of compiling and regurgitating what others have written about a specific text in a traditional essay, students building a constructionist project become generators of knowledge themselves. Through their research, self-reflection, and creative output, students take on the role of expert and critic on a given topic and display much more investment than they might in more traditional survey assessments, like the standard essay model.

Many instructors of literature, from surveys to more specialized single-author courses, rely on the research essay as a way of assessing students' critical thinking about the assigned works; it is, after all, a process for developing depth of knowledge about a small portion of the course reading list.[2] While I have assigned research essays in every survey I've taught, over the last two years or so, I've noticed that my students are increasingly challenged by this assignment; it seems as though they don't really develop an attachment or deep interest to motivate the production of an engaging, thoughtful research essay, at least not in the way I would hope. As a result, I set out to develop an assessment that would:

1. be more engaging and creative for students whose entire lives are immersed in media;
2. require students to assess their knowledge about course content as they generated unique narratives about a specific work or issue; and
3. help me better understand students' learning processes and their ability to create connections between literature and culture.

Because I model engagement with and analysis of media related to literature throughout the semester, it only seemed natural that this new task should ask students to do the same. The assignment I developed to address these particular needs is something I called a digital curation project.[3]

On the first day of my early British literature survey in August 2015, I gave students an assignment sheet that outlined the parameters of the digital curation project without giving rigid specifications—after all, I didn't want to provide a template or lead students to produce stagnant, unimaginative projects. The assignment sheet indicated that "Each student will be tasked with compiling a multimedia gallery for one author, work, literary period, and/or genre featured on our course reading list." For this description, I chose language that I thought would be familiar to students. After all, they have all been exposed to visual galleries on various websites, and I orally compared this multimedia gallery to a photo album on social media, with which all students were intimately familiar. Students were allowed to choose their own topics in order to increase their interest and engagement in what would surely be a lengthy research process.[4] I didn't want to assign students topics because I felt that would increase resistance to the project and any resulting learning. In discussing the objective of this project, some students seemed hesitant or even suspicious. This assignment was not the boring research project they were told to expect in a literature course.

The assignment sheet also suggested programs that students could use, including: Microsoft Word, Microsoft PowerPoint, Prezi, InDesign, (or) any comparable program that will allow the side-by-side inclusion and manipulation of multimedia files and text. In our discussion of the assignment, I elaborated that students could use any software or tools available to them to make this digital gallery with the caveat that I must be able to open the file in order to respond to it. I tried to make it clear that I would be happy to install an application or software to see these projects if it meant that students would produce a unique, fun, creative gallery. The only required components listed for the project were:

1. a brief introduction to the author, work, period, or genre itself (350–500 words);
2. compilation of 10–12 multimedia pieces (images, videos, graphical representations, music files, etc.), each followed by appropriate citations and the student's unique, original caption (100–200 words each) that explains the item's significance to the topic being researched; and a
3. complete works cited page.

From the assignment sheet, students knew that they would have to propose their topic and chosen software by midterm, October 8, and that the project would be due before their final exam on December 11. I encouraged the students, however, to think about this topic throughout the semester as they read for class and participated in discussion. Twice before midterm, I deviated from our course schedule to initiate group brainstorming so students could share their opinions about the texts and historical issues we had discussed so far and give each other feedback about their potential topics' cultural significance. In one of these sessions, for example, a student decided to focus her project on the portrayal of magic in Medieval literature and culture vis-à-vis *Sir Gawain and the Green Knight* and the later pop culture portrayal of magic in the British television program *Merlin*. After students chose their topics, we spoke as a group twice more about their research progress and whether they had met any challenges. The students seemed to be facing the same difficulties with finding media to fit their topics, and so in one of these sessions, they shared different techniques and sources they thought might help each other. These conversations seemed to be very productive, and I think the students enjoyed the collaborative aspect of this project. Unlike a research essay, which can sometimes feel like an independent effort separate from the day-to-day function of a course, the development of this project encouraged students to produce and share knowledge in real-time conversations.

I understand that some instructors may find the flexible parameters for this assignment to be too relaxed or unstructured. Granted, this project placed a lot of responsibility on students as decision-makers, researchers, and producers of content; however, there are ways to add more structure to this project while still allowing digital natives to embrace their interests through familiar media. A popular digital compilation project that many literature instructors use is the playlist assignment, wherein students must develop a playlist of a specific amount of time or number of songs to score a literary work and explain how the songs relate to themes, symbols, plot points, or characters (e.g., developing a Spotify playlist for *Romeo and Juliet*); students demonstrate their knowledge about a work and relate its important points to other texts (songs) in order to create a musical narrative. Instructors who want to refocus this type of curation project for visual learners or through multimodalities might instead direct students to create a Pinterest board for a specific author, work, or literary movement; functioning as a digital scrapbook, the Pinterest board allows students to identify key aspects of a course element, providing necessary organization, without imposing such a rigid or linear structure the way a playlist or the digital curation project does.

Results and Students' Inquiry Stances

Overall, the final project submissions demonstrated thoughtful, detailed analysis and engagement with the chosen topics. As with any written assignment, some digital submissions showed a great deal of polish while others were not quite as refined. Despite the variety in quality, the different approaches students took to understand their chosen topics demonstrated unique and interesting ways of conceptualizing the intersection of literature and culture. Four students in particular—Mike, Raquel, Brittany, and Nora—submitted projects that demonstrate the versatility of this assignment and some of the many inquiry stances students can take to become successful knowers and designers of their own knowledge.

Figure 8. An excerpt from Mike's digital curation project that shows how William Blake visually interprets *A Midsummer Night's Dream.*

Mike: The Traditional/Canonical Cultural Legacy Approach

Mike, a junior English education major and football player, used Prezi to create his multimedia gallery of artistic representations of scenes from *A Midsummer Night's Dream (MND)*. Instead of including any available images of modern iterations or pop culture references to *MND*, Mike organized his gallery around more traditional artistic renderings—paintings by well-known artists and prints by William Blake, a figure he likely recognized from taking the second half of the British literature survey during a previous semester (see Figure 8). Mike made connections not only between literature and art in his gallery, but also between prominent literary figures, which suggests thoughtful application and a greater likelihood of internalizing information about Shakespeare and Blake. Throughout the semester, Mike was taciturn and seemed uninterested in many of the readings—a condition that isn't exactly uncommon in early British literature surveys—but the digital curation project seemed to have given him the freedom to express himself in a way that classroom discussion and standard written assignments did not.

While Mike focused his gallery on one type of media in a traditional survey of the literature, other students used a combination of historical, canonical, and cultural images as well as other digital files (audio and embedded video, for example) that demonstrated the broad cultural significance—including the inherent academic value—of their chosen topics. The following students used media from classical art, as well as more recent literature, film, and pop culture to give the impression of their topics' relevance and viability.

Nora: The Extended Cultural Legacy Approach

Nora's project, compiled using desktop publishing software, focused on John Donne's textual and artistic legacy. A columnist and graphic designer for the university's student newspaper, Nora capitalized on her external experiences to make her project read more like a spread in a literary magazine than a novice scrapbook (see Figure 9). Nora's introduction demonstrated her familiarity with Donne's poetry and the critical response to his works, but her connections to later writers and more contemporary culture demonstrated a sort of generic mastery. In creating an expansive timeline tracing the development of modern romantic poetry from Donne to twentieth-century songwriters, Nora had to define the qualities of Donne's verse and apply this standard, with varying degrees of success, to later writers.

Brittany: The Literary Historian Approach

Taking a somewhat more traditional approach to media research than Nora was Brittany's PowerPoint presentation on social structures during the High Medieval period. An English education major, honor student, and athlete, Brittany relied on rigid scheduling and organization to keep her life on track, and so it came as no surprise that her project was also quite methodical. Instead of searching for modern interpretations of life during the Middle Ages, Brittany found images that demonstrate the way a modern-day individual might document items or images for inclusion in a museum gallery or textbook. I found

In 1966, American singer and songwriter John Renbourn released his folk album titled, *John Renbourn.* One of the tracks on this album is called "Song," which contains the lyrics from a poem written by John Donne. John Renbourn is thought of as an extraordinarily talented folk guitarist and an introspective songwriter. His track, titled "Song," is in tribute to Donne's literary works, particularly his work emphasizing the complications of female sexuality. Donne's poem, "Song" focuses on the elegiac sentiment that the female sex is extraordinarily fickle. Could there possibly be a more fitting subject matter for a folk song?

"Song" can be found at:
https://www.youtube.com/watch?v=yhmw

Figure 9. An excerpt from Nora's digital curation project that demonstrates her thoughtful integration of image, text, and multimedia links in her analysis of Donne's legacy.

this approach particularly fascinating because it seemed almost meta-archival. She created a gallery that implicitly studies the way that we preserve and study past cultures (see Figure 10).

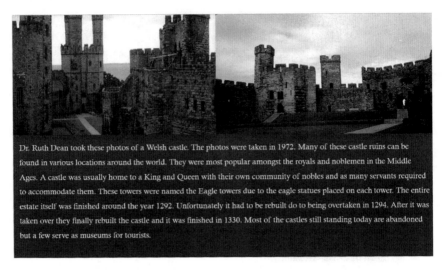

Dr. Ruth Dean took these photos of a Welsh castle. The photos were taken in 1972. Many of these castle ruins can be found in various locations around the world. They were most popular amongst the royals and noblemen in the Middle Ages. A castle was usually home to a King and Queen with their own community of nobles and as many servants required to accommodate them. These towers were named the Eagle towers due to the eagle statues placed on each tower. The entire estate itself was finished around the year 1292. Unfortunately it had to be rebuilt do to being overtaken in 1294. After it was taken over they finally rebuilt the castle and it was finished in 1330. Most of the castles still standing today are abandoned but a few serve as museums for tourists.

Figure 10. An excerpt from Brittany's digital curation project that illustrates her historically focused approach.

Raquel: The Pop Culture Critic Approach

Raquel's project, a video uploaded to YouTube, explored different modern representations of courtly love. Because her subject was not as focused as some of the other students', her resulting gallery was a bit more diverse and perhaps even more whimsical (see Figure 11). Without strict parameters, she was able to include many film excerpts and images that she was familiar with before she began the project. Just as Nora chose her particular software and approach because it built on her existing skill set, Raquel's project also played to her strengths. An avid fan of Japanese animation and member of many fan communities (fandoms), Raquel chose to create a video for this project because it's something she does in her free time for the other members of the online forums she frequents. She later commented that she "greatly enjoyed being able to choose" which software she would use for this very reason.

Challenges and Remaining Questions

Beyond internalizing and retaining course content, I wanted students to create something, to construct a unique multimedia representation of their individual research and understanding in order to feel some ownership and

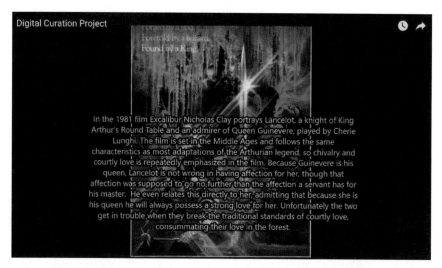

Figure 11. An excerpt from Raquel's digital curation project that demonstrates her critical analysis of a media source that might not typically be considered academic (the film *Excalibur*).

responsibility for their education. The idea that students learn better when they create something unique and representative of their understanding is a foundational principle of constructionism. Edith Ackermann elaborates that Papert's theory considers "how learners engage in a conversation with [their own or other people's] artifacts, and how these conversations boost self-directed learning, and ultimately facilitate the construction of new knowledge."[5] While the potential for student misapprehension is vast in a project that requires novices to originate information, the benefits of generating knowledge are abundantly clear.[6] Sharon Bertsch and Bryan J. Pesta describe the "generation effect," an important element of learning, as "the finding that, in most cases, information is more likely to be remembered when it was studied under conditions that required learners to produce (or generate) some or all of the material themselves, versus reading what others had prepared."[7] The process of constructing a digital presentation, I also thought, would be a useful training exercise for the English education majors in the course who in a few short semesters would have to prepare lessons and presentations for their own students on a regular basis.[8]

My overarching goal for the digital curation project was to create an opportunity for students to engage with seemingly dry, out-of-reach texts in interesting, unconventional ways. While the submitted projects fulfilled this goal in varying degrees, they also held several unexpected, although quite welcome, implications for my understanding of the student population I serve. First, in assessing my students' submissions, I was able to gauge their familiarity and skill level with the technology they chose to employ. Before I set out to review these projects, I assumed they would be elaborate, sophisticated, thoroughly researched portfolios made with software I had never encountered. Without even realizing it, I fell into the admittedly ageist trap of assuming that because my students were all traditional college students, aged nineteen to twenty-two, that they would be extremely digitally savvy. What I found upon opening the projects suggested a different story, at least superficially. Although I know firsthand that the students in this particular course section were very adept at using social media, specifically image-sharing sites like Instagram or Snapchat, and had been constantly exposed to infographics and other visual media, the projects they submitted—for the most part—relied on software that students usually encounter in their high school and early college years. Of the nine projects submitted, five were formatted with Microsoft PowerPoint, one used Microsoft Word, and one used Prezi—all of which were suggested on the assignment sheet. The remaining projects used somewhat less mainstream techniques: One student used video-editing software to screen capture a PowerPoint presentation set to music, which she then uploaded to YouTube, and another student's project was created using Microsoft Publisher.

It is apparent that in choosing these software types, students were following what they perceived to be requirements for the project, but I have also come to expect students' creative, and in some cases extremely liberal or even wildly bizarre, interpretations of assignment directions. Despite my irreverent expectations, there were no social media accounts made for Beowulf, no digital comic strips about *Astrophil and Stella*. The students relied on familiar, supposedly classroom-appropriate technology to carry out the digital curation project rather than making the project more complicated and time-intensive by trying to learn a new software in addition to compiling all the research about their topic. Brittany later commented, "I chose to use PowerPoint because I was comfortable with it and I could make it appeal to me visually the way I wanted. Media research such as this was totally new to me." I can't say that I find this reliance on familiar software surprising, especially given the fact that the assignment itself—media research and digital compilation—was a new challenge for everyone involved; however, I was surprised by the resulting implication that students might have perceived a divide between digital tools used for entertainment and those used for academic purposes.

I am disappointed that I relied on my assumptions about the tech skills and innovation of Millennials instead of talking more with the students about the actual design and execution of the project. The thought of relegating class time to demonstrating makerspace software rather than progressing in the reading list does, I'll admit, make me a bit squeamish; but really, all students in this digital age could benefit from an introduction to new software that might be used in future classes or careers. The literature survey does not just introduce students to the literary "greatest hits" of a period; the survey is also a space for students to be initiated into academic and discipline conventions, including technological methods. Had I worked more diligently with the students on the presentation aspect of the project, I think the resulting submissions (and their future productions) would have been far more engaging and instructive.

Rather unexpectedly, the digital curation project also made me reassess how students value and understand the vast array of works presented over the course of a semester. Through the narratives the students composed in these projects, I realized a new way to determine if students were absorbing the key information from my lectures and the assigned readings. If the connections they drew between the work or figure and its resulting place in Western culture were tenuous or weak, as some of them were, I was clued in to areas in my instruction that can be improved before I teach the course again.

While all four projects had their strengths and weaknesses (for example, Brittany's rushed proofreading job that led to the typo "it had to be rebuilt *do* to being overtaken . . ." in Figure 10), each contributed a thoughtful and unique interpretation of what it is to digitally curate a text, figure, or cultural issue.

Through these projects and final reflections on their work, the students indicated that this project, while somewhat unorthodox for their expectations of a literature class, was refreshing and unique. On the due date of the digital curation project, I asked students for their opinions of the project, including its scope, difficulty, and ability to inspire interest. Students responded to the following prompts:

1. What did you like about the process/assignment?
2. What didn't you like about the process/assignment?
3. How did this project require you to engage with texts/authors differently than a research essay would?
4. Did you like being able to choose the software you used?
5. Are you comfortable performing media research, or was this a new/unfamiliar experience?

Overall, the students' reflections demonstrated that they enjoyed completing a research "non-essay" and that the task forced them to be more creative and engaged than they typically would in a final research project for a comparable college course. "I found it to be an enjoyable experience," Mike wrote. "It's nice to break the monotony with something fresh every now and then. This also gives insight into different ways that a text can be interpreted." Interestingly enough, other students appreciated the "freshness" of the text because it some-how seemed to be less work than writing an essay. Raquel "enjoyed the opportunity to make something digital that didn't involve writing out an entire essay." This comment makes me feel pedagogically duplicitous; the amount of research, composition, design, and revision these students had to do for the digital curation project was likely more time-consuming and detailed than what they would have prepared for an essay, and yet the assignment appeared to be more engaging. Most surprising to me was Nora's response about the project's appeal: "I found the digital curation project to be highly enjoyable, as it allowed me to combine poetry, history, communications, and design into one project." While designing the project, creating a unique aesthetic and resulting visual appeal, was certainly a "fun" aspect that most students brought up in their reflections, Nora's enjoyment of the task seemed to lie in her ability to think in an interdisciplinary capacity. A challenge that I think many professors of literature surveys face is trying to find a balance in instruction so that students are not only aware of significant literary texts and figures of a given period but also the historical, social, and political events that influenced the development of these texts; Nora's acknowledgment that this "unique" project forced her to think about "John Donne's cultural legacy (in addition to) his historical or literary legacy" was quite validating. Although other students didn't make such an overt statement in their reflections, their projects seemed to demonstrate a similar awareness of the intersection between literature, history, and culture. Through this project, at least, these students developed a deeper understanding of what we mean when we tell them that literature is not created in a vacuum, independent of any outside influences.

Conclusion

Even though the students seemed generally pleased with the digital curation project, their reflections held some constructive criticism and suggestions that likely will not surprise anyone who has taught a literature survey before. Despite my best efforts to keep students on track throughout the semester with several check-in conversations and brainstorming sessions, it appears that all of the students—yes, all of them—waited until the last week or two of the semester to start working on the project. As a result, the students perceived that they had a tremendous amount of work to accomplish in a brief window. Brittany opined, "Having (the project) due right before or near the final was a little stressful," and both Brittany and Raquel expressed dismay at the amount of text required for the project. Brittany thought that each image's caption should only have been "50 or so words," while Raquel hinted that "shorter captions might have been better." The student complaint of working too hard within a short time frame, as I noted, should not be surprising. Unfortunately for me, I *was* surprised at these responses. During the repeated checkups, brainstorming sessions, and individual meetings with students during office hours, I was under the impression that students were working diligently all semester long. It was clear that they were thinking about their projects in significant ways, but evidently this extensive research and cognition did not translate into usable narration or design. I'll admit that I'm torn about the students' procrastination. On one hand, I gave out the assignment sheet for this project on the first day of class and spoke with the students regularly about their progress. If they chose not to manage their time wisely by working throughout the semester, then the "stress" of the situation, to use Brittany's designation, was a direct consequence of this choice. On the other hand—the hand that remembers what it's like to be at the beginning of my college career—I realize that I should have expected at least some degree of procrastination and reticence and as a result should have made the digital curation a multiple-part project with several drafts bearing point values. While I have no doubt that I would like to do this project again with future early British literature survey courses, I will most definitely plan to divide the project into several smaller assignments with due dates throughout the semester.

I incorporate media and technology in every class I teach, from freshman composition to literary criticism. Not only does technology engage my students, but it allows me to keep learning about and considering new viewpoints. It's exhilarating to work through an issue alongside my students, to truly feel like we are learning together in our conversations, and technology makes that possible. Using media and digital tools in any capacity will engage students, but the digital curation project and tasks like it move students in the literature survey away from complacency or reactionary participation and toward active, effective learning. To truly improve student learning, educators can't simply trust that engagement equates to critical thinking and internalizing. We have to provide opportunities, digital or not, in which students can "impose meaning on content" and feel connected to the information they encounter.[9]

NOTES

1. Seymour Papert, "Situating Constructionism," *Papert.org*, 1991, http://www.papert.org/articles/SituatingConstructionism.html.

2. Robert Davis and Mark Shadle, "'Building a Mystery': Alternative Research Writing and the Academic Act of Seeking," *College Composition and Communication* 51, no. 3 (February 2000): 419. Davis and Shadle likewise concede that the traditional research essay carries both benefits and complications. Davis and Shadle "would like to believe that research writing teaches valuable skills and encourages students to commit to the academic ideals of inquiry and evidentiary reasoning. However, it may be as often the case that the research paper assignment teaches students little more than the act of producing, as effortlessly as possible, a drab discourse, vacant of originality or commitment." Davis and Shadle have thus employed what they call a "multi-genre/media/disciplinary/cultural research project" to help students research and synthesize knowledge in a method that may be more applicable to students' skill sets and interests outside the classroom. This project is actually quite similar to the digital curation project I outline below.

3. Adeline Koh, "Introducing Digital Humanities Work to Undergraduates: An Overview," *Hybrid Pedagogy* (August 14, 2014), http://www.digitalpedagogylab.com/hybridped/introducing-digital-humanities-work-undergraduates-overview/. Koh notes that this type of assignment "might be an attractive project to some instructors. Many are used to getting students involved in creating physical exhibitions—the curation and presentation of materials being a useful pedagogical exercise in examining questions of cultural value. Furthermore, adding a digital component to a physical exhibition extends its reach and its audience. It also provides an easy way to get students involved with digital tools."

4. Chris Friend and Sean Michael Morris, "Listening for Student Voices," *Hybrid Pedagogy* (October 15, 2013), http://www.digitalpedagogylab.com/hybridped/listening-for-student-voices/. Friend and Morris explain some potential drawbacks and benefits of allowing students to follow their interests: "If we give students the freedom to choose their own path, they might choose poorly or make mistakes on our watch. But we must be willing to allow them the challenge of this authority, the dignity of this risk, and the opportunity to err and learn from their mistakes. They learn and gain expertise through experimentation."

5. Edith Ackermann, "Piaget's Constructivism, Papert's Constructionism: What's the Difference?" *Sylvia Stipich: Technology Educoach*, http://www.sylviastipich.com/wp-content/uploads/2015/04/Coursera-Piaget-_-Papert.pdf.

6. Sharon Bertsch and Bryan J. Pesta, "Generating Active Learning," in *Applying Science of Learning in Education: Infusing Psychological Science into the Curriculum*, ed. Victor A. Benassi, Catherine E. Overson, and Christopher M. Hakala (Washington, DC: Society for the Teaching of Psychology, 2014), 74. Bertsch and Pesta rightfully point out that "discerning more important from less important information appears to be a general problem, particularly among poorer academically performing students. This issue is not only with what students choose to study but also in the notes they take from lectures or text sources in the first place," which is why professorial oversight is necessary for generative projects to become successful.

7. Ibid., 71.

8. Susan Ambrose et al., *How Learning Works: 7 Research-Based Principles for Smart Teaching* (San Francisco: Jossey-Bass, 2010), 84. Ambrose et al. attest that "Students often focus on specific course content without recognizing how the skills and abilities they develop across courses . . . will benefit them in their professional lives. . . . We can help motivate students by explaining how various skills will serve them more broadly in their professional lives." I had

hoped that by demonstrating this task's usefulness to their future profession, I might engage education students in a way that essays usually do not. For the most part, I believe this was an effective part of our conversations and brainstorming sessions.

9.   Paul Bruno, "How People Learn: An Evidence-Based Approach," *Edutopia*, para. 5, October 9, 2015, https://www.edutopia.org/blog/how-people-learn-evidence-based-paul-bruno.

BIBLIOGRAPHY

Ackermann, Edith. "Piaget's Constructivism, Papert's Constructionism: What's the Difference?" *Sylvia Stipich: Technology Educoach*. http://www.sylviastipich.com/wp-content/uploads/2015/04/Coursera-Piaget-_-Papert.pdf.

Ambrose, Susan A., et al. *How Learning Works: 7 Research-Based Principles for Smart Teaching*. San Francisco: Jossey-Bass, 2010.

Bertsch, Sharon, and Bryan J. Pesta. "Generating Active Learning." In *Applying Science of Learning in Education: Infusing Psychological Science into the Curriculum*, edited by Victor A. Benassi, Catherine E. Overson, and Christopher M. Hakala, 71–77. Washington, DC: Society for the Teaching of Psychology, 2014.

Bruno, Paul. "How People Learn: An Evidence-Based Approach." *Edutopia* 9 (October 2015). https://www.edutopia.org/blog/how-people-learn-evidence-based-paul-bruno.

Carr, Nicholas. "Is Google Making Us Stupid?" *The Atlantic*, July/August 2008. http://www.theatlantic.com/magazine/archive/2008/07/is-google-making-us-stupid/306868/.

Carrington, Victoria, and Muriel Robinson. "Introduction." In *Digital Literacies: Social Learning and Classroom Practices*, edited by Carrington and Robinson, 1–9. London: Sage Publications, 2009.

Davis, Robert, and Mark Shadle. "'Building a Mystery': Alternative Research Writing and the Academic Act of Seeking." *College Composition and Communication* 51, no. 3 (February 2000): 417–46.

Downing, Kevin, et al. "Problem-Based Learning and the Development of Metacognition." *Higher Education* 57, no. 5 (May 2009): 609–21.

Friend, Chris, and Sean Michael Morris. "Listening for Student Voices." *Hybrid Pedagogy* (October 2013). http://www.digitalpedagogylab.com/hybridped/listening-for-student-voices/.

Hobbs, Renee. *Digital and Media Literacy: Connecting Culture and the Classroom*. Thousand Oaks, CA: Corwin, 2011.

Koh, Adeline. "Introducing Digital Humanities Work to Undergraduates: An Overview." *Hybrid Pedagogy* (August 14, 2014). http://www.digitalpedagogylab.com/hybridped/introducing-digital-humanities-work-undergraduates-overview/.

Lang, James. "The Best-Laid Teaching Schemes." *The Chronicle of Higher Education* (March 11, 2012). http://www.chronicle.com/article/The-Best-Laid-Teaching-Schemes/131105.

Leonard, David C. *Learning Theories: A to Z*. Westport, CT: Greenwood Press, 2002.

Mayer, Richard E. "Research-Based Principles for Designing Multimedia Instruction." In *Applying Science of Learning in Education: Infusing Psychological Science into the*

Curriculum, edited by Victor A. Benassi, Catherine E. Overson, and Christopher M. Hakala, 59–70. Washington, DC: Society for the Teaching of Psychology, 2014.

Papert, Seymour. "Situating Constructionism." *Papert.org*, 1991. http://www.papert.org/articles/SituatingConstructionism.html.

Prensky, Marc. "Digital Natives, Digital Immigrants." *On the Horizon* 9, no. 5 (October 2001). http://www.marcprensky.com/writing/Prensky%20-%20Digital%20Natives,%20Digital%20Immigrants%20-%20Part1.pdf.

―――. "H. Sapiens Digital: From Digital Immigrants and Digital Natives to Digital Wisdom." *Innovate* 5, no. 3 (2009). http://nsuworks.nova.edu/cgi/viewcontent.cgi?article=1020&context=innovate.

English 2543, Fall 2015

Syllabus Addendum: Digital Curation Project

This project comprises 40% of your participation grade.

Each student will be tasked with compiling a multimedia gallery for one author, work, literary period, and/or genre featured on our course reading list. Students should seek the professor's permission before starting work on a particular topic.

Important Dates

- October 8: Deadline to propose project topics, including software to be used
- December 11 (by 10 a.m.): Deadline to submit project via email

Suggested Programs to Use

- Microsoft Word
- Microsoft PowerPoint
- Prezi
- InDesign
- Any comparable program that will allow the side-by-side inclusion and manipulation of multimedia files and text

Required Components

- A brief introduction to the author, work, period, or genre itself (350–500 words)
- Compilation of 10–12 multimedia pieces (images, videos, graphical representations, music files, etc.), each followed by appropriate citations and the student's unique, original caption (100–200 words each) that explains the item's significance to the topic being researched
- Complete works cited page

PART THREE

Programs

Thematic Organization and the First-Year Literature Survey

KRISTIN LUCAS AND SARAH FIONA WINTERS

The introductory survey in English has always been a complex course.[1] In Canadian universities, it traditionally serves as an introduction to the different literary periods, helping to clarify for students their characteristic forms and features; it simultaneously acts as a gateway to the discipline, a tool-box course that helps students to develop the vocabulary, critical acumen, and writing skills that are foundational to English programs. The first-year survey, then, performs numerous roles within English departments, and no doubt in many universities a chronologically organized introductory survey continues to accomplish what programs ask of it. But for us it stopped working. And our response was to set aside a coverage model and introduce thematic survey courses, capped at forty students (one of the lowest caps for an introductory course in Arts and Science at our institution). These courses function as surveys in that they provide students with an introductory overview of English literature, one that is focused on literary forms and features. Employing the same evaluation scheme and assignment parameters, including outcomes and expectations, these new first-year surveys are taught by different faculty members and are organized around different themes. What follows maps the experience of revising our introductory survey at the departmental level, and at the level of the individual course; we consider the key processes that guided the reconfiguration of our program's gateway curriculum, and detail the design of two such courses—Love and Loss (Kristin Lucas) and Friendship in Literature (Sarah Fiona Winters).

Curricular Pressures

A number of pressures, both internal and external, contributed to the revision of our introductory survey. Nipissing University, in North Bay, Ontario, is primarily an undergraduate university of approximately four thousand students, many of whom are first-generation students from small towns in southern Ontario. Historically, most of our English Studies students aspire to be teachers, and after the BA they go on to the Faculty of Education. One consequence of being closely tied to the Faculty of Education is that when teaching jobs in Ontario waned, our enrollments declined. A recent province-wide change, which saw the bachelor of education degree expand from one to two years, also weighs on our program's numbers: our students now undertake a four-year plus two-year (4 + 2) course of study instead of the previous four-year plus one-year (4 + 1).

While changes to the Faculty of Education have had a significant impact on our program, there are other issues internal to the Faculty of Arts and Science at work. Although Academic Writing (Composition) has been a staple in the United States context for years, it is not particularly widespread in Canada: Nipissing only recently introduced a first-year course on Academic Writing that is required across the Faculty of Arts and Science. This course counts as three humanities credits, half the number required by all first-year students. The math, alas, is not hard to do. We'd previously resisted dismantling our six-credit introductory survey (twenty-four weeks, seventy-two contact hours); however, decreasing numbers of English majors and student demand for the flexibility of three-credit courses (twelve weeks, thirty-six contact hours), combined with the Academic Writing requirement and a proliferation of other three-credit humanities electives, made it impossible for our program to continue with a full-year six-credit course. A three-credit course was necessary.

It may be tempting to think of this change to our introductory curriculum, and thus to our program, as imposed by pressures external to our department and in a sense that is accurate. But in another sense, curricular and programmatic changes by their very nature respond to shifts within the discipline, faculty research, institutional climate, and student needs and interests. "The English Major," as Sidonie Smith has remarked, "is always changing, even when it is not being revised."[2] As a department we responded to all of the aforementioned pressures with the same discussion, review, and planning as we would with any programmatic change. The decision to set aside chronology as an organizing principle was not an easy one, and nor, initially, was it the evident outcome. But in rethinking our introductory survey, we were aware of the brevity of a twelve-week semester, and the tripartite need to (a) set a foundation for our majors, (b) draw additional students into regarding English as a minor, and (c) attract students looking for electives. Certainly the option of six to eight first-year courses to choose from intrigues students at open houses much more than one compulsory course titled Introduction to English Studies, and the list of course titles alone functions as advertising.[3]

Appealing to student interest may seem frivolous, and humanities disciplines don't often talk about affective response (except to discourage it) but surely most students who take English courses do so, at least initially, because they like, or love, to read. And for some there can be an alarming gap between reading for pleasure and academic study. A part of that gap is bridged when a first-year survey is chosen out of curiosity about the topic. Meeting students "where they are,"[4] and developing an introduction to our program that allows for choice and makes room for popular or contemporary texts certainly engages student interest, but it does more than that: it tacitly underscores the relevance of English studies to our students and invites them into the discipline.

From Chronology to Theme

In our department, programmatic needs sparked pedagogical innovation: thematic organization facilitates the development of skills and introduces students to the discipline as effectively as our historical survey did. The gateway courses need to serve majors as well as students who want to take electives, and both groups are important to our enrollment numbers. In light of that consideration we thought carefully and creatively about how we could address the requirements of our students and our program. Undertaking a process akin to what Grant Wiggins and Jay McTighe refer to as "backward design"[5] or "*results*-focused design,"[6] and Linda Nilson calls "outcomes-centered course design"[7] enabled our decisions. By thinking through and prioritizing "desired results"[8] over specific content, our goals became clear: what we, as a department, wanted most from an introductory survey was to facilitate students' development of core disciplinary skills—the critical reading, analysis, and argumentation that will help them to be successful in upper years. For us, disciplinary literacy emerged as the most essential goal of our gateway courses. This goal is reflected in our common evaluation scheme, and in the expectations and outcomes (skills measured by assignments) that are shared by all our first-year surveys:

a) By the end of the course, students will be able to
   1. identify the defining features of major literary forms;
   2. identify and use key literary and critical terms in the process of analysis;

3. apply basic critical and theoretical methodologies to close, critical readings of a wide variety of texts;
4. discuss texts and ideas comfortably and respectfully in class;
5. construct and sustain analytical arguments in clear, coherent prose and proper essay format.

b) Students who successfully complete this course will demonstrate:
1. an introductory knowledge of some key concepts and methodologies of English studies;
2. a promising ability to comprehend primary texts and offer analytical commentary;
3. a promising ability to analyze texts and propose persuasive answers to interpretive questions;
4. a promising ability to communicate in clear, correct prose.

These shared features make our departmental goals and priorities explicit, helping to ensure parity, and the perception of it, across courses. Our approach encourages our students to work beyond mere summary of plot and theme, to master and apply discipline-appropriate terminology and concepts, and to be attentive to form and genre. These are capacities that, in our experience, first-year students improve upon appreciably in twelve weeks, improvements that can, in turn, foster a sense of accomplishment and pride in the discipline.

With disciplinary skills identified as an outcome priority, theme became the connective tissue of our first-year surveys. It is worth remembering that theme is not foreign to the period-based survey.[9] When Victorian Literature, for instance, is taught through the lens of Faith and Doubt, it is not an esoteric choice, but rather one that conveys an idea about the period and its preoccupations. Our introductory surveys utilize theme to facilitate the discovery, in Laura Dittmar's words, of "formal and conceptual interrelations."[10] Indeed, we have found that thematic organization provides lively and accessible through-lines that enable our students to learn the discipline's foundational skills. As such, our experience of teaching these courses leads us to disagree with the suggestion that thematic organization is inherently confusing.[11] Theme is capable of providing shape and continuity to our first-year surveys—as it has in graduate teaching for years.[12] That said, one result of foregoing literary history as an organizing principle is that there is a different onus placed on course design and text selection, both of which require a pedagogically sound rationale rooted in clear programmatic aims. In our program, the emphasis on disciplinary literacy shapes our curriculum and all our introductory surveys must teach multiple forms (both Love and

Loss and Friendship in Literature covered five forms each), familiarize students with material from before 1800, and introduce the two streams of our program: literature and culture.

Course Design

The curricular changes that underpin our first-year surveys make sense for our program in part because for many of our first-year students the most challenging aspect of starting their undergraduate career is the discipline's strong emphasis on analysis and argument. In our departmental grading criteria, these are an essential component of essays that receive a grade of 70 percent (B–) or over, yet many students begin university without a firm grasp on what literary argument means or entails. To help students gain an understanding of literary argument, both Love and Loss and Friendship in Literature have a simple framework, a series of questions with which to approach our texts. They include the following: What kind of love—romantic/erotic, friendship/*philia*, filial/*storge*, or divine/*agape*—is considered in this text? Is this text primarily about love or primarily about loss? If there is more than one kind of love in the text, which one is constructed as more powerful than the others? When love of any kind is represented in a text, what kind of love is the contemporary Western audience trained to see? These are straightforward questions, and that is the point—the students are able to formulate an answer. The questions elicit interpretation, guiding the response away from summary, and asking each student to come to a conclusion about the orientation and emphasis of a given text. Indeed, a shared objective of these courses is to help students realize that neither love nor friendship is neutral or timeless.

The work we do in these courses, through lecture and discussion, ranges further than the scope of these questions and many students are able to provide increasingly nuanced responses as the semester develops. In both courses, the framework has a number of benefits. For proficient students, the questions become a springboard to more nuanced analysis, and for those whose skills are not yet as advanced, they provide a consistent access point to the material and reinforce the pedagogical aims of the course. For all students, having familiar concepts or questions to return to while reading, especially in advance of class, provides a means to approach each text and a means to think about the relationships between texts.

Although we have reoriented our introductory surveys, literary history is not absent from our program. Jennifer Summit has written about the value of historical literacy for English majors; in our program, upper-level courses serve as the training ground where students work to acquire that literacy. For example, our second-year core requirement for majors, British Literature Before 1800, teaches the development of British literature and encourages students to think of early texts not as museum pieces, but as, in Summit's words, "the building material of the present."[13] Anchoring disciplinary literacy in literary history, this course freed us to alter our first-year course so significantly and now draws upon the skills students establish in our introductory surveys.

Love and Loss (Kristin Lucas)

The text selection for Love and Loss is genuinely fun and the theme's breadth allows for material to be added and altered yearly. While my course texts span the sixteenth century to the twenty-first century, their sequence does not follow chronology. Instead, John Milstead's suggestion that "difficulty of comprehension increases pretty much in direct proportion to distance in time"[14] informs the organization of Love and Loss. Starting with Blake's "The Sick Rose" (1794), Chopin's "The Story of an Hour" (1894), Gilman's "The Yellow Wallpaper" (1892), and Hemingway's "Hills Like White Elephants" (1927) accomplishes several things. Shorter texts, particularly fiction and lyric poetry, allow us to work in depth on close reading, attending to the ways detail accrues and supports a work's theme. These texts lend themselves readily to discussion, and students note that they appreciate the amount of discussion in class. Pragmatically, beginning the course with short works makes it easy for students to keep up with the reading and catch up if they fall behind, while also providing considerable variety in the first weeks of the course. With these early texts, we begin to think critically about relationships of love, though to be sure, that lens is introduced gradually and for many students it becomes graspable in the second half of the course. These are results-based decisions.[15]

The course covers lyric poetry from a number of periods. The early modern sonnets, which I tend to change yearly, are drawn from Spenser, Shakespeare, and Donne and include the English and Italian forms. We also read Ondaatje's sonnet "Bear Hug" (1979), and several other lyrics, including Blake's "The Garden of Love" (1794) and Stevens's "Sunday Morning" (1915). The sonnet in particular is pivotal to Love and Loss because as a form it emerged to convey the tension between desire and absence. If students begin the course with an idea about sonnets, it is typically that they are love poems. And so students are routinely intrigued to learn that separation and longing are also ingrained in the form. There is, of course, nothing earth-shattering about this point. Its utility in my first-year survey is to suggest new ways of seeing and reading, and to provide a paradigm with which to approach the form. When, after studying the convergence of desire and distance in early modern sonnets, we turn to *Romeo and Juliet*, some of the ground of the *liebestod* motif has been established. We are able to consider Romeo and Juliet's pilgrimage sonnet in relation to Donne's *Holy Sonnets*, comparing Donne's use of physical and erotic imagery to convey intense spiritual longing with Shakespeare's use of the spiritual journey to convey human love. Later in the semester, when we read Ondaatje's "Bear Hug," the students are able to see that while it is neither English nor Italian in form, it does take some of its structural cues from both. The modern form departs from earlier renderings, and so too the love between father and son departs from the erotic love of early modern sonnets. What remains, which students always apprehend, is the deep contemplation of distance between two people.

Romeo and Juliet is important to help facilitate the introduction to university-level study because, like the sonnets, it helps students to see differently. Although most of the class reports having read *Romeo and Juliet*, they are quite surprised when I introduce it as a play about masculinity. They have studied the heterosexual love story, but not the homosocial dimension of the text. In class we address the ongoing perception of Romeo as sodden, teary, and formless, while Romeo bemoaning his own "effeminate" behavior[16] echoes the implicit and explicit criticisms of him that resound in the play. The point of this critical tack is to encourage students to begin to grapple with an often difficult concept—that heterosexual romantic love is not neutral or timeless, and neither are its related social institutions. Ibsen's *A Doll House*, which we read after *Romeo and Juliet*, helps to solidify for students that love is ideologically contoured. For numerous reasons, *A Doll House* helps to sharpen students' ability to think about gender roles and expectations, which paves the way to considering the (social) ways love and loss imbricate in these plays. When, near the end of the course, we read Alison Bechdel's *Fun Home* (2006), students are prepared to engage with the graphic memoir's examination of sexuality and gender identity. The memoir's two interwoven stories—Alison's coming out and Bruce's suicide—enable an examination of pre- and post-Stonewall experience, and affirm desire and the ways it is allowed to flourish, or not, as contingent.

I often conclude with Craig Gillespie's *Lars and the Real Girl* (2007), a film that allows us to reflect upon the short fiction studied early in the course, especially "The Story of an Hour" and "The Yellow Wallpaper." That reconsideration is possible because of the two axes of *Lars and the Real Girl*. The film depicts the various ways that Bianca, the silicone sex doll that Lars purchases online, helps Lars to accept change and loss—his deep resistance to them stems from the death of his mother—and also the important ways that she enables the community to change by learning to accept Lars on his own terms (a point made by Nicole Markotić).[17] In class, we attend to both of these aspects of the film. Then, looking back to "Hour" and "Wallpaper," we discuss the social space afforded to difference in those late nineteenth-century stories. Most of the students recognize immediately that the world depicted in *Lars* differs markedly from that conveyed by Chopin and Gilman, where non-normative views are held privately, but gain little social purchase.

Our department sees the introductory survey as a means to introduce students to a variety of literary forms that they will encounter in greater depth in upper years. In Love and Loss, students study five forms: poetry, short fiction, drama, the graphic memoir, and film. While material is drawn from the early modern period to the twenty-first century, the majority belongs to the nineteenth and twentieth centuries. That choice, somewhat narrow in literary historical terms, enables me to augment diversity. It means that I can include male and female, British, Canadian, and American writers, alongside queer and Indigenous writers, acquainting students with a range of upper-year courses and research interests in our department.

Friendship (Sarah Fiona Winters)

Because this course was inspired by C. S. Lewis's chapter on "Friendship" in *The Four Loves*, I designed it around not only his theories of friendship but also his biographical experiences of it. That is, I taught his friendship with J. R. R. Tolkien as well as two texts by Tolkien: the short story "Leaf by Niggle" and the film adaptation of *The Lord of the Rings* (a three-credit first-year course is not the place to teach Tolkien's long novel). This real-life friendship between writers who wrote about friendship was an aspect of the course I was eager to teach since I had responded with such fascination to this kind of biography (one could just as accurately call it literary gossip) in my own first year as an English student.

I began my course readings with the stanzas from *The Song of Roland* that tell of the death of Oliver. Since the approximate date of *The Song of Roland* is 1100 and the most recent work on my course was the film trilogy *The Lord of the Rings* (2001–03), I was thus able to cover a nine-hundred-year period in this non-chronological course. I thought it would be exciting for my students to be able to boast that they were starting their university English career with something so old, something they would have been unlikely to encounter in high school. I followed *The Song of Roland* with Lewis's chapter titled "Friendship," Tolkien's "Leaf by Niggle," and Shakespeare's *Much Ado About Nothing*. This sequence of texts worked beautifully for the thematic development of the course and for teaching different forms. The remainder of my texts covered two centuries and four forms: Jane Austen's *Pride and Prejudice* (1813) was my novel; Christina Rossetti's *Goblin Market* (1862) my second narrative poem; Ivor Gurney's "To His Love" (1917), Robert Graves's "Two Fusiliers" (1918), and Wilfred Owen's "Strange Meeting" (1919) my three lyric poems; Oscar Wilde's "The Happy Prince" (1888) and four Sherlock Holmes stories ranging from 1893 to 1924 my other short stories; and *The Lord of the Rings* (2001–03) my film.

I departed from chronological order twice in my course, once based on the principle of "backwards" or "results-focused design" celebrated by Wiggins and McTighe, the other based on the idea of inviting affective response into the classroom. The first departure took place right at the beginning: the progression from a text written c. 1100 (*Song of Roland*) to one published in 1960 (*The Four Loves*) to a third published in 1945 ("Leaf by Niggle") to one written in 1599 (*Much Ado About Nothing*) certainly demonstrates a cavalier approach to literary history and chronological development. As I have already said, I did so in part to introduce four different forms quickly, but my other reason for this choice was to set the first essay on a short story ("Leaf by Niggle"), a manageable task for my students. The second departure from chronological order in the course was scheduling my lectures on World War I poetry during the week of November 11, Canada's Remembrance Day, an appeal to the emotions that turned out to be powerful and effective.

In the past, one of our tasks in the first-year survey had been to introduce our students to our two separate streams of study: literary history and cultural studies. I wanted my thematic course to continue to perform this function. Therefore I taught the Sherlock Holmes stories not as examples of the short story or prose fiction but rather as a way of introducing the cultural studies stream of English studies for those students who wanted to become majors. By teaching various television and film adaptations of the Conan Doyle stories as well as the responses of fandom to the friendship of Holmes and Watson, I was able to expose the students to the kind of work we do in cultural studies; for example, in my third-year course on Fan Vids, I include a consideration of slash (the eroticization of same-sex friendships by fans). While Conan Doyle did not write his Holmes stories as an exploration of a human relationship, many twentieth- and twenty-first-century readers and viewers seem to want to treat those stories as episodes in the saga of a great friendship or a great love affair rather than as many separate stories detailing the solving of puzzles. I took this question of authorial intent and reader reception to the last text on the course, *The Lord of the Rings*, and examined the different readerly interpretations of Frodo and Sam's friendship as informed by *eros* or informed by *agape* and the likelihood that Tolkien saw it as infused by the latter.

Focusing on theme did not mean I had to sacrifice an introduction to form or to critical terminology in my thematic course: as well as five forms (poetry, drama, prose fiction, prose nonfiction, and film) the course covered many different critical terms I would have taught in a traditional first-year survey. I did, however, sacrifice some chronological coverage: apart from *The Song of Roland* and *Much Ado About Nothing*, all the texts on the course were from the nineteenth, twentieth, and twenty-first centuries. I felt free to do so in the knowledge that any English majors in my class would be introduced to literature from earlier centuries in the second year of the program.

Conclusion

We hope that the brief discussion of our curricular changes and their role in our program will prove useful for other departments considering abandoning the chronological first-year survey for thematic courses. We acknowledge that for our particular department, which is small and collegial, this approach to disciplinary literacy works in ways it might not in other departments with a different faculty complement and a different student demographic: we all regularly teach first year, and are committed to setting a strong foundation for our students so that they are successful from the very beginning of their degree. Anecdotal evidence from both students and faculty suggests that this strong foundation has been realized; our new focus on skills means that students are no longer as lost in their first year as they were previously in the chronological course.

One unanticipated benefit of employing theme to concentrate on skills is that when students take more than one course (which a number do, although it is not required), they experience directly that what they learn in one course is applicable to another. They realize that success is an effect of their understanding of disciplinary skills, and not a quirk of the material or instructor. Responses from students who took both Love and Loss and Friendship in Literature provided us anecdotal evidence of this gain.

Students at our university now have a range of courses to choose from, that is, until and unless administrative pressure comes to bear upon us to revert back to a large course in the first year. (As at almost all institutions, resources are always an issue.) But because of this choice, we have students in our classes who have selected to be in this or that English course, usually because they are interested in the topic. It is productive to think of each course as "a hub of intellectual interests and affective attachments."[18] For example, Love and Loss includes texts addressing queer love as well as heterosexual love, a choice that speaks to the current generation of students who are widely attuned to sexual orientation as a human right, while Friendship in Literature appeals to those many students who do not find romantic love in their first year at university but do find and rejoice in new and powerful friendships. Robert Scholes has long advocated expanding the purview of literary studies, and recently argued for the importance of "devis[ing] pathways into that wider world [of culture] that will make it interesting and accessible."[19] Thematically organized introductory courses are our attempt to do just that.

NOTES

1.   We would like to thank our colleague and Chair Gyllian Phillips (who teaches the Sports in Literature and Film course) for her generous feedback on a draft of this chapter.

2.   Sidonie Smith, "The English Major as Social Action," *Profession* (2010): 198.

3.   Sports in Literature and Film; The Family in Literature; Love and Loss in Literature; Friendship in Literature; Monsters, Madness, and Malice; Photography in Literature; Music in Literature; Science and Literature; Rebels and Rogues in Literature and Media.

4.   Gregory Roper, "Making Students do the Teaching: Problems of 'Brit Lit Survey I,'" *Studies in Medieval and Renaissance Teaching* 9, no. 1 (2002): 123.

5.   Grant Wiggins and Jay McTighe, *Understanding by Design*, exp. 2nd ed. (Alexandria, VA: Association for Supervision and Curriculum Development, 2005), PDF e-book, 13–34.

6.   Ibid., 15; italics original.

7.   Linda Nilson, *Teaching at Its Best: A Research-Based Resource for College Instructors*, 3rd ed. (San Francisco: Jossey-Bass, 2010), 17–31.

8.   Wiggins and McTighe, *Understanding by Design*, 17.

9.   John Milstead, "On the Matter of Literary Surveys," *College English* 36, no. 6 (1975): 675–80; Timothy J. Viator, "Which American Dreams? A Constructive Approach to Teaching American Drama," *Teaching American Literature: A Journal of Theory and Practice* 3, no. 2 (2009): 57–72.

10.   Laura Dittmar, "Literature as Art: Sequencing Learning in the Core Curriculum," in *Teaching Literature and Other Arts*, ed. Jean-Pierre Barricelli, Joseph Gibaldi, and Estella Lauter (New York: Modern Language Association of America, 1990), 78.

11.   Rebecca Olson and Tara Williams, "Reimagining the Literature Survey through Team Teaching," *Pedagogy* 14, no. 2 (2014): 21; Roper, "Making Students do the Teaching," 41.

12.   J. D. Isp, "Lose the Chronology, Lose the Anthology: Clearing the Way of Innovation in American Literature Survey Courses," *Teaching American Literature: A Journal of Theory and Practice* 4, no. 3 (2011): 58.

13.   Jennifer Summit, "Literary History and the Curriculum: How, What, and Why," *Profession* (2010): 147.

14.   Milstead, "On the Matter of Literary Surveys," 675.

15.   Wiggins and McTighe, "Understanding by Design."

16. William Shakespeare, *Romeo and Juliet*, in *The Oxford Shakespeare: The Complete Works*, 2nd ed., ed. Stanley Wells, Gary Taylor, John Jowett, and William Montgomery (Oxford: Clarendon Press, 2005), 3.1.114.

17. Nicole Markotić, "Punching Up the Story: Disability and Film," *Journal of Canadian Film Studies* 17, no. 1 (2008): 2–10.

18. Smith, "The English Major as Social Action," 198.

19. Robert Scholes, "English Curriculum after the Fall," *Pedagogy* 10, no. 1 (2010): 232.

BIBLIOGRAPHY

Dittmar, Linda. "Literature as Art: Sequencing Learning in the Core Curriculum." In *Teaching Literature and Other Arts*, edited by Jean-Pierre Barricelli, Joseph Gibaldi, and Estella Lauter, 78–85. New York: Modern Language Association of America, 1990.

Isp, J. D. "Lose the Chronology, Lose the Anthology: Clearing the Way of Innovation in American Literature Survey Courses." *Teaching American Literature: A Journal of Theory and Practice* 4, no. 3 (2011): 39–62.

Markotić, Nicole. "Punching Up the Story: Disability and Film." *Journal of Canadian Film Studies* 17, no. 1 (2008): 2–10.

Milstead, John. "On the Matter of Literary Surveys." *College English* 36, no. 6 (1975): 675–80.

Nilson, Linda. *Teaching at Its Best: A Research-Based Resource for College Instructors*. 3rd ed. San Francisco: Jossey-Bass, 2010.

Olson, Rebecca, and Tara Williams. "Reimagining the Literature Survey through Team Teaching." *Pedagogy* 14, no. 2 (2014): 199–223.

Roper, Gregory. "Making Students do the Teaching: Problems of 'Brit Lit Survey I.'" *Studies in Medieval and Renaissance Teaching* 9, no. 1 (2002): 39–57.

Scholes, Robert. "English Curriculum after the Fall." *Pedagogy* 10, no. 1 (2010): 229–40.

Shakespeare, William. *Romeo and Juliet*. In *The Oxford Shakespeare: The Complete Works*. 2nd ed. Edited by Stanley Wells, Gary Taylor, John Jowett, and William Montgomery, 369–400. Oxford: Clarendon Press, 2005.

Smith, Sidonie. "The English Major as Social Action." *Profession* (2010): 196–206.

Summit, Jennifer. "Literary History and the Curriculum: How, What, and Why." *Profession* (2010): 141–50.

Viator, Timothy J. "Which American Dreams? A Constructive Approach to Teaching American Drama." *Teaching American Literature: A Journal of Theory and Practice* 3, no. 2 (2009): 57–72.

Wiggins, Grant, and Jay McTighe. *Understanding by Design*. Exp. 2nd ed. Alexandria, VA: Association for Supervision and Curriculum Development, 2005. PDF e-book. 13–34.

COURSE DOCUMENT: LUCAS AND WINTERS

Friendship in Literature (ENGL 1007) and Love and Loss (ENGL 1017)

Evaluation Scheme (common to both courses)

Essay 1: 10%

Essay 2: 20%

Brief in-class assignments: 15%

Participation: 10%

Midterm: 15%

Final Exam: 30%

(ENGL 1017) Love and Loss

Description: This course provides an introduction to the discipline of English studies through a consideration of the intertwined themes of love and loss. Our readings address three main facets of love, romantic, filial, and divine, as well as the profound loss that so often accompanies relationships of love. The texts we study are drawn from a range of historical periods—the sixteenth century to the twenty-first century—and include the genres of poetry, short fiction, drama, graphic novel, and film. Our different genres facilitate familiarity with a wide range of formal literary features, and the shared theme provides a basis for comparative analysis. More broadly, the course focuses on learning the disciplinary skills required to move from an initial impression of a literary work to a clear, coherent written analysis. Particular attention is therefore given to genre, formal literary features, critical terms, correct grammar and usage, argumentation, and proper essay format.

Schedule of Readings and Class Meetings

Week 1

Introduction

reading poetry (William Blake, "The Sick Rose")

Week 2

reading short fiction (Kate Chopin, "The Story of an Hour")

short fiction (Charlotte Perkins Gilman, "The Yellow Wallpaper")

Week 3

short fiction (Ernest Hemingway, "Hills Like White Elephants") / *in-class assignment*

early modern sonnets (Shakespeare "Sonnet 73"; John Donne, "Batter My Heart")

Week 4

sonnets (Shakespeare and Donne)

Shakespeare, *Romeo and Juliet*

Week 5

Romeo and Juliet / Essay 1 due in class

Romeo and Juliet

Week 6

Romeo and Juliet

midterm test

Week 7

Ibsen, *A Doll House*

A Doll House

Week 8

A Doll House; Alison Bechdel, *Fun Home*

Fun Home / *Quiz 1*

Week 9

Fun Home

short fiction (Ann Beattie, "Snow") / *Essay 2 due in class*

Week 10

dir. Chris Eyre, *Smoke Signals*

Smoke Signals

Week 11

reading poetry (Michael Ondaatje, "Bearhug"; Blake, "The Garden of Love")

reading poetry (Wallace Stevens, "Sunday Morning")

Week 12

dir. Craig Gillespie, *Lars and the Real Girl* / *Quiz 2*

Review

(ENGL1007) The BFF and the Bromance: Friendship in Literature

Course Description: Students engage in the study of literature through a particular theme or topic of literary study. Students gain necessary skills for literary analysis, critical thinking, and writing at the university level.

C. S. Lewis claims that "When either Affection or Eros is one's theme, one finds a prepared audience," but that "very few modern people think Friendship a love of comparable value or even a love at all." This course studies historical and contemporary attitudes to friendship as a form of love in poetry, drama, fiction, nonfiction, and film.

Schedule of Readings and Class Meetings

Week 1

Introduction

Sayers, *Song of Roland* (selections)

Week 2

Lewis, "Friendship"

Tolkien, "Leaf by Niggle"/ *Quiz 1*

Week 3

Tolkien, "Leaf by Niggle"

Shakespeare, *Much Ado About Nothing* / *Quiz 2*

Week 4

Shakespeare, *Much Ado About Nothing*

Shakespeare, *Much Ado About Nothing*

Week 5

Shakespeare, *Much Ado About Nothing* / *Essay 1*

Austen, *Pride and Prejudice* / *Quiz 3*

Week 6

Austen, *Pride and Prejudice*

Austen, *Pride and Prejudice*

Week 7

Austen, *Pride and Prejudice* / *Passage Analysis 1*

MIDTERM TEST

Week 8

Rossetti, "Goblin Market"

Rossetti, "Goblin Market"

Week 9

Graves, "Two Fusiliers" and Gurney, "To His Love"

Owen, "Strange Meeting"

Week 10

Conan Doyle, "The Final Problem" and "The Empty House" / *Quiz 4*

Conan Doyle, "The Devil's Foot" and "The Three Garridebs" / *Quiz 5 / Essay 2*

Week 11

Wilde, "The Happy Prince" / *Quiz 6*

Jackson, *The Lord of the Rings / Quiz 7*

Week 12

Jackson, *The Lord of the Rings / Passage Analysis 2*

Review

Fear and Learning in the Historical Survey Course[1]

GWYNN DUJARDIN, QUEEN'S UNIVERSITY

On the first class meeting of the History of Literature in English, upon welcoming the students and telling them my name, I direct them to the handout containing four lettered passages. *I'd like you to read through these samples from across our syllabus and hypothesize in what order you think they were produced. Which do you think is the earliest? Which two come next? Which was written most recently? Order them by letter on your handout.* When a critical mass of students begins committing to choices, I pause the activity to ask them to write down why they ordered the texts in the chosen sequence. *On what basis did you decide one came before or after another? What were you seeing in each work that distinguished it from others?* When they finish I ask for volunteers to share their proposed order, and record a number of suggested sequences on the board with no indication of which is right.

Instead I ask them to share what they noted in the different works that suggested their chronological relationship. I have varied the four texts over the years, but collectively they feature descriptions of nature, so much as to seem indistinguishable on first read, despite ranging from an Anglo-Saxon elegy to contemporary experimental verse.[2] So the students look for other clues. *"The language in B seems older than the others." "C seems more personal, more about the author's feelings." "There's a reference in A to a civil war in Africa." "D is broken down. There's no rhyme. Isn't that more modern?"* I record their impressions on the board until patterns in observed differences begin to cohere, which I then abstract into a more formal list: language; form, genre, and style; persona and/or authorial voice; setting; historical context, etc. Directing their attention here, I point out that they have generated an inventory of features that distinguish literature as a specialized form of discourse. In doing so, I add, they have identified elements we'll examine as we study the ways literature changes through time, and shown that they possess the critical abilities needed for that work. Only a handful of students lists the correct sequence, but the rest don't leave the class discouraged. To the contrary, the students are surprised and relieved to learn what they are capable of knowing by the end of the course.

The historical study of literature has long been the defining feature of our undergraduate program. Up until recently, the storied "British survey" was our first-year course, anchoring a curriculum comprised of progressively smaller courses organized around the conventional literary periods. When the threat of diminishing resources demanded that we rethink how to deliver our curriculum, debate centered considerably—urgently and passionately, for many—on what place, if any, "history" should continue to have in our program. The discipline had changed unmistakably since our existing curriculum had been implemented a generation ago. How were we to reflect those developments, many of which involved the expansion of areas of study and the emergence of new methodologies such as cultural studies, while maintaining our brand among peer (which is to say, competing) institutions, all on a more stringent budget? At the crux of the debate was our introductory course: for decades, ENGL-110 had introduced Queen's students to the study of literature through the historical survey. Was that still the appropriate starting point for an expanded, more diverse curriculum, and for students entering university at a younger age (secondary school in Ontario previously extended to grade 13), with less preparation?

The outcome of these discussions at once reinforced our commitment to the historical survey course and intensified the challenges of teaching it. Where our new first-year course would consist of a genre-based introduction to literary study, focusing on critical terminology and techniques in analysis and writing, the new "History of Literature in English" would be a year-long required course for majors and minors in their second year. Still organized on chronological principles, the new course would cover more material "in English" to encompass colonial, postcolonial, and Indigenous literatures. The class itself would also be larger, as we boosted enrollment (to roughly one hundred students) to make teaching resources available for majors to take a complementary "slow reading" seminar the same year. Indeed it is precisely because our department made small classroom teaching a priority during curriculum reform that we increased the size of this particular course.[3] Paradoxically, at the same time we declared the foundations offered by the historical survey sufficiently important to make it a requirement,[4] we put our students in conditions making learning in it potentially more difficult.

The course stands out in the curriculum in ways that cause many students to enter it with trepidation.[5] In other courses we lay stress on developing students' analytical skills, and indicate that we care about their ideas. Entering the historical survey course, students often believe they're supposed to know what they're told, and that what we'll tell them is the history that explains what texts "really" mean. They worry about the amount of reading. They worry they won't understand the reading. They worry that the course will consist in the memorization of trivia, and that their grade will come down to a very large exam. They worry they'll be bored. Put the perceived scope, method, and object of the course together, and students may enter the class comparatively daunted, unmotivated, or disengaged.

This essay offers a series of principles and related practices I follow to facilitate learning in the historical survey course by teaching to students' fears and preconceived expectations of it. Two ideas in pedagogical research guide my approach. The first holds that meaningful learning occurs under conditions of "expectation failure." In his influential book *What the Best College Teachers Do*, teaching and learning specialist Ken Bain advocates an approach to teaching undergraduates that targets the "mental models" that limit their preliminary thinking. Bain writes that "when we encounter new material, we try to comprehend it in terms of something we think we already know," and that students "bring paradigms to the class that shape how they construct meaning."[6] Arguing that "deep" learning results from helping them build new models of reality, Bain posits that effective teaching involves leading students to confront their faulty expectations. With this principle in mind, I purposefully capitalize on students' preconceptions of literary history to present them with fresh ways to understand literature from the past.

Yet students are also often inhibited by expectations of how the historical survey course itself will operate. Perceptions of its scope and size, methods of instruction and assessment, and the availability of support critically affect student motivation. Detailing the role of affect in cognition, Sarah Rose Cavanagh's recent book *The Spark of Learning: Energizing the College Classroom with the Science of Emotion*[7] proposes that instructors consider ways to mobilize emotion in order to help their students learn. Concerned to relieve anxieties that might interfere with learning, I challenge students' preconceptions about the construction of the course to free them to concentrate on our historical inquiry—and thus earn the good marks that concern them. As Bain notes, we often cleave to preconceived ideas because they are familiar and more comfortable. In this case, by contrast, students are relieved and excited to discover that literary history and the historical survey course are not what they fear. Designing the course around elements of it that concern students can lead to a surprisingly effective and enduring learning experience.

I challenge the students in the course's opening moments both to confront their assumptions about literary history and to subvert their expectations about the methodology of the course. The reading and discussion establish our subject matter in historical artifacts of language and render explicit the underlying premise of the course, which is that such artifacts change through time. This should seem obvious, and yet students often expect the history to consist primarily in important events and social developments that the course readings will unilaterally, and subordinately, reflect. Asking them to consider the chronological sequence of four passages instead prompts them to consider literary texts *as* history, and not just verbal repositories of it. Asking them to pinpoint which features locate the texts in time also signals that their course readings will provide them information with which to develop their own historical insights. To be sure, immediately setting the students to such an activity disrupts their expectations of how the class will proceed. Instead of "going through the syllabus," which foregrounds my agenda while they sit back to listen, I prompt them to consider themselves intellectual agents in the course.[8] Leading with an exercise in critical discrimination in particular notifies them that the historical study of literature involves analysis and that they can look forward to using skills they learned in their introductory course. Rendering the logic of the curriculum thus explicit, the first class aims to mitigate students' fears of being overwhelmed by indicating what they will have under their control.[9] I often hear them leaving the room encouraged, whispering, "that was *not* what I expected."

Within a day, we're up against another source of worry, though, as we approach our first readings in the Medieval period. Some programs have moved the historical survey out of the first year in part to avoid "scaring off" potential majors with *Beowulf* or Chaucer. While moving the course to the second year enables students to enter it with practice in literary analysis, it does little to prepare them for the challenges of older forms of English. Most courses build up to the most complex material; the historical survey course presents students with some of its most difficult reading while they're still decorating their new dorm rooms. It is tempting to start later in the period, the sooner to get to more comfortably modern, if early modern, material. Many instructors have also devised alternative chronologies or dispensed with chronology entirely. I start at the very beginning, with Bede's *Ecclesiastical History of the English People* and "Caedmon's Hymn," recorded in Bede's chronicle. Besides endeavoring to pique their interest in one of the earliest known works in English, I use the poem to reframe students' perceptions of older forms of language as aides, not obstacles, to understanding.

I approach the "Hymn" as a problem of translation. First I ask the class to write down the following words: father, roof, house, might, guardian, work.

How would you describe these words? "They're nouns. Things." "Tangible things." "Things you live with." "Things that protect you." From there I acknowledge that the Anglo-Saxon lexicon, a term I introduce, consisted mostly of monosyllabic terms used to describe everyday things. Next question: *How would you use these words to convey the Christian concept of God? Of Heaven?* The class is puzzled at first, until someone inevitably hits upon the idea of putting terms together to create a new idea. "*Might-father.*" "*Guardian-father.*" "*Guardian-roof.*" "*Might-work-house.*" In short order, I point out, they have discovered for themselves how Old English developed as a language, i.e., through compound word formation. Now (I intone) imagine the challenge for the Roman Christians and others looking to convert the Anglo-Saxons, when no words existed for abstract Christian concepts in a language of concrete everyday things. Some of the religious words we use in English, e.g., lord (from OE *weard*), were adapted from terms in Anglo-Saxon social structure. But compound word-formation could be also deployed to represent novel spiritual concepts. As we open our anthologies to the story of Caedmon, the cowherd turned divine poet, the meaning and composition of the prayer come to light as the students recognize our base words on the page. Just as the students built new words for God and heaven, Caedmon builds a poem about the idea of God as a builder.[10] Presenting Old English as a linguistic challenge for the Christian missionaries presents students the opportunity to solve its difficulty for themselves.[11]

With some insight into the roots of their own lexicon, they are ready to take on the original Anglo-Saxon. Viewing the Modern and Old English versions side by side, I teach them the orthography (*thorn* [Þ], *eth* [ð], and *ash* [æ]) that renders the language strange. Explaining the concept of the *scop,* I then ask them to envision themselves reciting the poem to stir other Anglo-Saxons to conversion, and read the nine-line poem a half line at a time, for them to repeat back (you can find good readings on YouTube). Vocalizing the poem reinforces the orality of Anglo-Saxon verse through example while providing occasion to discuss the half lines and alliteration, which I accentuate in my delivery. Enabling students to perceive critical features of the poetry, our collective recitation builds intellectual confidence as well as classroom community, as they certainly never expected to belong to an Anglo-Saxon chorus. I can measure the students' increasing trust in themselves and the course with every successive and rousing rendition.

Thus getting over their fear that language will be an impediment to understanding, the class appreciates how learning historical features of English will help them grasp what constitutes literary uses of it.[12] From "Caedmon's Hymn" they are primed to look for *Beowulf*'s kennings and tensions between Christian and pagan social values; they appreciate the contrast of Marie de France's polysyllabic Anglo-Norman and the mellifluous cadences of her rhymed *lai*; and they pick out where Anglo-Saxon and Anglo-Norman–based words appear as part of Chaucer's satire of Medieval estates.[13] And while the approach may seem old-fashioned, making language a focal point from the beginning pays off most in the areas where our department substantially reformed the course. Encompassing both linguistic features and cultural perceptions of English, our study of language extends beyond eighteenth-century British prescriptivism or the "common language" of Wordsworth's poetics. Denaturalizing students' experience of their own language early on prepares them to weigh depictions of linguistic alienation in the postcolonial writing of Derek Walcott or Chinua Achebe or the Indigenous poetry of Armand Ruffo. Teaching to students' fears of older forms of English helps them comprehend literary developments in each historical period and over the *longue durée*.[14]

Assuaging students' concerns about language does not suffice to extinguish other worries about "keeping up" with the material, however. Interpreting the historical scope of the course in terms of volume of material, virtually every student enters the class concerned about the amount of reading. Students also assume the reading will be more challenging to "get through," not only because it includes literature from the past, but also because they intuit that each sequential item on a chronological coverage syllabus has been selected to represent something new and different. Some instructors break their syllabus down into accessible themes or topics to moderate the wearing effects of constant change. In my experience, when students worry about "keeping up with all the reading," the pragmatic terms in which they voice their concerns—typically, whether they "have the time"—mask more serious doubts about their *ability* to "keep up"—that is, to process and master new ideas.[15] This is where the foreignness of the past figures in their worries, as students question whether they can truly comprehend that which they perceive as alien. Insisting on the value of diachronic study, I conduct another exercise in expectation failure to counter students' beliefs that they are intellectually unequipped to grasp even the most remote material in the course.

Deep in our dive into Medieval England, I open a class by asking the students to reflect on writing in present-day society. *What does it mean to write, or "be a writer," today? If someone tells you that he or she is a writer, what do you assume about that person? What do you imagine that person doing?* Delighted with an unexpected discussion of the present, students are bemused at how, even as English students, they haven't given much thought to contemporary literary culture. For my part, it's surprising just how old-fashioned many of their ideas are (*"They're creative." "They write novels." "They're published."*) Despite living much of their lives online, many of our students still perceive "legitimate" writing to involve a solitary genius-type who publishes fiction in print. I needle them to update that impression, first by drawing attention to other genres and subgenres as well as public and collaborative forms of authorship, and then by noting how digital publication is now an authorized means of circulation. I also question where they derive the idea that some forms of writing are more creditable than others, and we discuss how the word *literature* itself codes for elevated forms of writing and occludes oral modes of expression. My point is that these elemental components of literary culture—language, medium of publication, genre and form, and concept of authorship (elements we had singled out on the first day of class)—are dynamic and transitory. My purpose, however, is to give students a framework with which to compass the differences and revolutions of the past.

I thus have them turn to reconsider the Medieval period through the lens of what we've just discussed: *Now, how would we characterize these four elements in our readings thus far?* The air suddenly goes out of the room, as students realize just how different those elements are. In addition to Bede's Latin, there were over three different historical forms of English; "texts" circulated orally and in manuscript; there were myriad distinct and unfamiliar forms of expression; and the modern concept of authorship simply did not exist. Of course the students came into the course expecting Medieval literature to be different; the difference now is that they grasp *how* it is different, and thus *know* it in a deeper, meaningful way. Expectation failure—here, their recognition of how their mental model is insufficient—functions to facilitate learning, in part because the students can now relate personally to the components that define the differences of the past.[16] As they apprehend these variations together, a composite picture of the period comes newly into view. I assist them in this awareness by consolidating the four elements into a rubric:

Table 2. **Transhistorical rubric for the History of Literature in English**

Analysis to Synthesis

MEDIEVAL LITERATURE

Text	Language	Medium of Circulation	Genre/Form	Concept of "Author"
"Hymn" Cædmon seventh century	Anglo-Saxon (Old English); vernacular	oral (later recorded in ms.)	poetry hymn: song of praise alliterative verse	reverent, inspired (lay) creator
Ecclesiastical History of the English People Bede eighth century	Latin language of church	manuscript	prose historiography religious chronicle	learned church figure records/promotes Christian conversion
Beowulf ninth to tenth century (?)	Anglo-Saxon influenced by Norse	oral (later recorded in ms.)	narrative poetry epic alliterative verse	*scop* (shaper) recites legend to community; story retold/remade

Text	Language	Medium of Circulation	Genre/Form	Concept of "Author"
Chevrefoil (Lais) Marie de France twelfth to thirteenth century	A Anglo-Norman language of court	(*lai*=song) manuscript	narrative poetry Breton lay; romance rhyme; couplets	individual voice narrates chivalric legend; female author
The Canterbury Tales Geoffrey Chaucer fourteenth century	Middle English London dialect	manuscript	narrative poetry estates satire; tales vary iambic pent./couplets	social observer/critic authorial persona writing as avocation
Crucifixion play York pinners' guild fourteenth to fifteenth century	Late Middle, Early Modern English Northern dialect	public performance	drama mystery play/ *Corpus Christi* cycle	community stages episodes in Christian history

I time our discussion and the presentation of the first table partly to re-assure students that we will review material as we go along. But the day's exercise principally serves to give them intellectual confidence moving forward. Newly possessed with fresh historical insight, they see how the set of longitudinal coordinates I've presented provides them diverse entry points into each new reading, and will enable them to accomplish more than just "get through" the syllabus. The class meeting motivates the students at a critical juncture, as, in lieu of fatiguing at the thought of how much still lies ahead, they perceive the gulf separating the Middle Ages from their own culture in a way that sparks their curiosity about how we'll get from the past to the present.[17]

Supporting them in this discovery, the rubric helps students understand individual texts relationally while also indicating diachronic patterns and developments. Read laterally, the tables offer a generic description of each text, e.g., how the York Crucifixion play is a Christian mystery play performed by one of the town's guilds in late Middle/Early Modern English. Reading one of the components vertically, students can observe significant developments within a period, e.g., how at the beginning of the Renaissance, poets such as Thomas Wyatt write as a courtly avocation and circulate their work in manuscript, where by the end John Milton prints his work and writes full-time. Reading multiple components relationally helps students formulate synthetic statements about a particular literary period or movement, e.g., how the satire and epigrammatic wit of the Restoration and eighteenth century often target new social groups (Grub Street hacks, the emergent merchant class) in an evolving public sphere. Read vertically in succession over the duration of the course, the rubrics help students discern trend lines as well as significant variations, e.g., how the individualism fostered by empiricism and early capitalism figures in the development of the novel, the spirit of Romanticism, and the fragmentation of self in Modernist and postcolonial texts; or how the conditions of female authorship vary in distinct historical periods. Students arrive at a deeper, more dynamic understanding of literary history by seeing their course readings figured in multiple dimensions over time.[18]

A diversified, transhistorical framework also enables students to enjoy the insights of long-term historical study without mistaking literary history as a linear, univocal narrative. While the discipline has debunked the idea of a singular (British, white, male) tradition, historically authors work in, with, and against multiple discrete traditions. Providing for their legible appearance in the course not only represents the history, or histories, of literature more accurately but also allows students the delight of recognition—and felicitous sense of mastery—in the experience of seeing the familiar in something new (*How does Milton's Eve figure in Wollstonecraft's argument in "Vindication of the Rights of Woman"? What is Wordsworth doing here with the Petrarchan sonnet?*). Cognitively, the students benefit from the play of repetition and variation such a model affords: the more and more different ways a student encounters, say, pastoral, the more she knows it deeply, not as a static glossary definition but as a rich and pliant mode whose conventions signify differently under different cultural conditions. Students surprise themselves with their facility to perform informed close readings on new material while the course models an updated, more historicist approach.[19]

I head the rubric with the phrase "Analysis to Synthesis" to define the nature of their work. Entering a one-hundred-seat lecture hall, students come into the course thinking they know more about what to expect from me than what they need to do to succeed in the course. Calling on them to use the critical abilities they demonstrated on the first day of class, I counter their expectations by continuing to approach the majority of our class periods as large-scale seminars, reserving lectures for occasions when students will particularly benefit from, and enjoy, having diverse ideas dynamically synthesized before them. In some classes, we focus on individual texts (as with "Caedmon's Hymn"), as close analysis may set up a problem useful to understanding the period (devoting occasional classes to slow reading also helps stem the perception that the historical survey course is "all a blur"). In others, we read across a set of texts (e.g., sixteenth-century sonnets, descriptions of the industrial North in Gaskell and Dickens) to make inferences about what defines them as a group, and then use those inferences to develop interpretations of individual works. Our synthetic work at the end of each unit follows the same pattern of induction and deduction. Plotting details of the texts in the rubric, the students survey the charts to draw conclusions (modeled above) about features characterizing each period or movement. Indeed the sparse language of the charts is intended to engender prose, as we use them to practice formulating historical claims in writing.[20] Endeavoring to redefine the term *survey* to connote depth instead of surface, our classroom activity progressively intensifies students' knowledge of each text and literary period.

One limitation of designating the historical survey course as "foundational" is that students suspect they won't enjoy the rewards of what they do in the course until they're sitting in another class. All things considered, I believe the best way to ensure that students carry historical knowledge into their future classes is to make its production and acquisition a transparently gratifying experience. I embrace that commitment especially in our department, where the historical study of literature, and this course, have such a venerable history of their own. Foregrounding textual analysis, my approach defies students' expectations that the course will consist wholly in my presenting historical facts that they need to commit to memory. Stressing the dialectic between text and culture, my methodology also resists treating texts as static illustrations of history, which can constrain interpretation instead of stimulating it.

And yet *exposition*—of terms, facts, historical events, social conditions—is necessary for our analytical and synthetic work. No amount of Donne's *Holy Sonnets*, as much as the students enjoy them, is going to teach them the English Reformation, and it's our responsibility to name devices like the metaphysical conceit so students can employ them in their analyses. I come prepared to class with critical information I present to spark or punctuate our discussions. But I also happened upon a strategy to have the students themselves come prepared with that material and feel personally connected in an unusually large class. A couple of years ago I felt I hadn't communicated an idea very effectively in a lecture, and was compelled to write the students an email, using our online learning platform, to clarify the concept and reinforce its importance. This quickly grew into a habit, not of correcting myself, but of writing my classes to review what we had covered in the last class, and introduce important material for the next one, with a set of questions the students should use to prepare. Effectively moving exposition from our class meetings to another medium the students are using, these interclass communications don't add to my prep time: they constitute it. I set the agenda I'm obliged to follow, and once in class, students are already reviewing the new information I've presented as we dedicate the class period to making use of it.[21] Far from encouraging students to skip class (thinking they can follow the course on-line), the emails reportedly motivate them more to come. Students justifiably perceive my initiative to write them as personally encouraging—perhaps the last thing they expect from a professor, in a class of one hundred students—when my goal is to support them intellectually in order to demand much more from them in class.[22]

Challenging them often with frequent assessments is another strategy intended to sustain their motivation while contributing further to their learning. It is tempting to offset the volume and difficulty of reading in the historical survey by giving the students less work in other areas. Research has nonetheless shown that numerous assignments aid in the mastery and retention of material, suggesting that checking against that instinct is all the more beneficial for students in this course.[23] More to the point here, there is nothing our students fear more than a large, all-the-marbles final exam. The challenge lies in designing assignments so that students experience their accumulative benefits and we don't overwhelm ourselves and our teaching assistants with grading.

A palette of assorted, multimodal assignments can economize on work hours, offer students repeated and diverse modes of engagement, and, if scaffolded effectively, teach them how to make use of the knowledge they progressively acquire. First, I make use of our university's online learning platform to create multiple-choice quizzes that the system grades and automatically records. Like most quizzes, these quick assessments test students on the reading, terms, and facts, and encourage students to consolidate instrumental knowledge as we go along. Next, following up on our stirring Caedmon performances, a recitation requirement asks that students memorize and recite two texts of their choice, one each term, in scheduled, private appointments held during my and the teaching assistants' office hours. Requiring them to work with a text closely at two distinct points in the history of the language and the literature, the process of memorization entails breaking the texts down into parts—i.e., analysis—and the TAs and I follow up the students' recitations with a discussion of how their delivery reflects their interpretation of the text. These conversations feed directly into discussion of the students' essays: in the fall term, they analyze a text using critical vocabulary native to a particular historical period (e.g., kenning, Petrarchan conceit); in the winter term, they build a critical analysis using a contemporary historical source. Five brief in-class writing exercises also prepare them for these essays by helping them practice writing critical analyses using historical terminology and information. Far from claiming they were annoyed or overwhelmed—what I initially expected—students have commented positively on the number and structure of assessments more than any other aspect of the course.

Besides reinforcing learning through repetition, and rendering their final grade a product of multiple, lower-stakes assignments instead of one or two large ones, the assessments provide other forms of positive affirmation. First, the quizzes are basic enough to build students' confidence through the good marks they earn on them. Further, while students believe I am sufficiently naive to think they aren't getting together when they take them outside of class, I've accepted that development as part of a covert design to encourage class community. Set at the lowest course percentage, the quizzes prompt students to gather voluntarily to teach one another, which develops into a course-long habit of mutual support. Next, while students are initially daunted by the recitation assignment, fear turns readily to pride as they exit our offices jubilant at having memorized both, say, a Shakespeare sonnet and Keats ode. Giving the teaching assistants a meaningful task in the early, lonely days of required office hours, the recitation appointments jump-start their relationship with the students long before the first paper is due, and give us an occasion to speak one on one with each student to see how he or she is faring in the course, and intervene when needed.[24] Finally, these personal consultations involve helping students identify the course readings they would most like to write on, to make their own mark in the course.

By the time we get to the final exam (my department requires them), students should expect no surprises, and I don't give them any. Indeed, that students single out the number and structure of assignments in their course evaluations, just prior to writing their cumulative exam, speaks to their relative comfort level heading into it. Far from being panicked at having to remember who Caedmon is in April, they are generally assured about the depth and extent of their learning, and eager to show it, both in the final exam and their ensuing coursework. As an instructor of third- and fourth-year courses, I can testify to the depth and amount of knowledge they come in with, and former students are generous to report how much they "use what we learned in ENGL-200." They are justified in feeling a tremendous and well-deserved sense of accomplishment.

The historical survey course is exceptional—and we should make no apologies for that. In this era of hyper-specialization, I am aware that students are not alone in their apprehensions about the course; many instructors are also hesitant to teach it. I am passionate about this course precisely because it is difficult: I enjoy learning more about periods other than my own and consider myself a better scholar for it; and I deeply enjoy the process of helping young people surmount that which they initially perceive as intellectually and academically insurmountable. Critics of the contemporary university might believe that teaching with emotion in mind is a sign that we are coddling our students when in fact I approach teaching empathetically to challenge students more. Compassion and rigor are not antithetical values but mutually essential to the greater project of the humanities. From beginning to end, the historical survey course can constitute a model of that enterprise.

NOTES

1.   I would like to thank Shelley King for her generous insights during the composition of this essay. I dedicate it to the students of ENGL-200, who have supported me in the teaching of the course with their insight, generosity, and hard work. Always remember to "show what you know."

2.   Thus far they have included, in various combinations, "The Seafarer," an Anglo-Saxon elegy; Christopher Marlowe, "The Passionate Shepherd to His Love"; Robert Herrick, "Corinna's Going A-Maying"; William Wordsworth, "Lines Written Above Tintern Abbey"; a passage from Susanna Moodie's *Roughing it in the Bush*; Derek Walcott, "A Far Cry from Africa"; and Al Purdy, "The Country North of Belleville."

3.   I credit my colleagues for this commitment, but will also note that research institutions, sector-wide, are also placing a greater priority on teaching "outcomes" and accountability.

4.   I highly recommend John Guillory's eloquent disquisition on the historical survey course as "knowledge base" in a presentation Guillory delivered to the MLA, and which is posted on the ADE website. John Guillory, "Discipline and Knowledge Base: The Uses of the Historical Survey Course," https://ade-adfl.mla.hcommons.org/files/2016/03/John-Guillorys-Discipline-and-Knowledge-Base.pdf.

5.   I base statements in this essay about students' fears and expectations on two written sources: first, students express their concerns coming into the course through an index-card exchange system I institute on the first day of class; and second, I have collated reflections on my approach from over three hundred course evaluations.

6.   Ken Bain, *What the Best Teachers Do* (Cambridge, MA: Harvard University Press, 2004), 26–27.

7.   Sarah Rose Cavanagh, *The Spark of Learning: Energizing the College Classroom with the Science of Emotion* (Morgantown: University of West Virginia Press, 2016).

8.   James M. Lang recommends devoting an early class to "assessing students' current state of knowledge" in *Small Teaching: Everyday Lessons from the Science of Learning* (San Francisco: Jossey-Bass, 2016), 101–3; 101. Having assigned the syllabus for the second day, I use that class meeting to explain how I've designed the course to help them learn what we discussed.

9.   See Cavanagh, *The Spark of Learning*, 148–49, on the importance of perceived control in student motivation.

10.   Indeed a "might[y]" "glory-father" who "shaped . . . heaven as a roof" to guard "mankind."; in James Black et al., eds., *The Broadview Anthology of British Literature, Volume One: The Medieval Period*, 3rd ed. (Peterborough, ON: Broadview Press, 2014), 23.

11.   See Cavanagh, *The Spark of Learning*, 124–26, on the value of puzzles and mysteries for stimulating "epistemic curiosity" (125).

12. I often introduce segments on language using the comical one-minute videos on "The History of English in 10 Minutes" posted online by Open University, https://www.youtube.com/watch?v=H3r9bOkYW9s.

13. The Medieval volume of the *The Broadview Anthology of British Literature* noted above contains excellent side-by-side translations.

14. I also believe that incorporating some history of the language in the course provides a context in which to slip in helpful lessons about grammar and syntax. See Guillory, "Discipline and Knowledge Base," 8, for a defense of the study of language in the historical survey course.

15. In practical terms, after all, we shouldn't assign daily reading amounts in excess of what students have in their other courses.

16. Cavanagh describes Reinhard Pekrun's control-value theory of learning, which measures "to what degree students feel in control of the activities and outcomes that are important to them" as well as "to what degree the activity of material represents meaning or worth to students," to encourage bringing to students' attention the ways course material has "relevance" to their "daily life or their eventual career." Cavanagh, *The Spark of Learning*, 148–49.

17. As Cavanagh writes, the "knowledge deprivation hypothesis" holds that "interest is often engaged when one realizes a gap in one's knowledge." Ibid., 115.

18. Indeed I use the rubrics to select the course readings, and to ensure that I include a representative assortment of texts in each period while also building diverse forms of intertextuality into the course.

19. In many respects, my course falls into the category of those that Jennifer Summit describes as having "historical literacy" as its objective. See Jennifer Summit, "Literary History and the Curriculum: How, What and Why," *ADE Bulletin* no. 149 (2010), https://ade.mla.org/content/download/7905/225668/ade.149.46.pdf.

20. This is critical as writing enables students to develop their ideas in the form in which they will be asked to demonstrate their knowledge. My index-card exchange system also provides students the opportunity to get ongoing feedback on their writing and ideas.

21. As an additional benefit, these emails model ways to write using critical terminology and historical information.

22. To my surprise the practice did not invite a raft of emails in return. As my emails are sent through the campus learning website versus my personal account, the interface defines the communication as academic, and the point is to direct students to bring their questions to class.

23. See Peter C. Brown, Henry L. Roediger III, and Mark A. MacDaniel, *Making It Stick: The Science of Successful Learning* (Cambridge, MA: Belknap Press, 2014).

24. I am grateful to the numerous teaching assistants who have taken on both the academic and pastoral roles of this exercise. For their part, the TAs enjoy the opportunity to get to know their students well over the duration of the course, and see the reward of their counsel in the quality of the students' work. Expanding their roles within the allowances of their stipulated work hours—treating them as colleagues, not just graders—makes an enormous difference in the students' perceptions of the availability of support as well as their sense of our class as a community. I include an in-take sheet that one of my former teaching assistants, Tara Hilman, developed for the recitation exercise in my course documents following this essay, and would like to thank her as well as Gabrielle ("Ellie") Berry for their permission to reproduce this work.

BIBLIOGRAPHY

Ambrose, Susan A., Michael W. Bridges, Michele DiPietro, Marsha C. Lovett, Marie K. Norman, and Richard E. Mayer. *How Learning Works: Seven Research-Based Principles for Smart Teaching.* San Francisco: Jossey-Bass, 2010.

Bain, Ken. *What the Best College Teachers Do.* Cambridge, MA: Harvard University Press, 2004.

Black, Joseph, et al., eds. *The Broadview Anthology of British Literature.* Vol. I, *The Medieval Period.* 3rd ed. Peterborough, ON: Broadview Press, 2014.

Brown, Peter C., Henry L. Roediger III, and Mark A. MacDaniel. *Making It Stick: The Science of Successful Learning.* Cambridge, MA: Belknap Press, 2014.

Cavanagh, Sarah Rose. *The Spark of Learning: Energizing the College Classroom with the Science of Emotion.* Morgantown: University of West Virginia Press, 2016.

Guillory, John. "Discipline and Knowledge Base: The Uses of the Historical Survey Course." https://ade-adfl.mla.hcommons.org/files/2016/03/John-Guillorys-Discipline-and-Knowledge-Base.pdf.

Lang, James M. *Small Teaching: Everyday Lessons from the Science of Learning.* San Francisco: Jossey-Bass, 2016.

Open University. "The History of English in Ten Minutes." YouTube. https://www.youtube.com/watch?v=H3r9bOkYW9s.

Summit, Jennifer. "Literary History and the Curriculum: How, What and Why." *ADE Bulletin* no. 149 (2010). https://ade.mla.org/content/download/7905/225668/ade.149.46.pdf.

COURSE DOCUMENT: DUJARDIN

ENGL 200 FW » Forums » News forum » For Wednesday, October 28: The Language of Love

For Wednesday, Oct. 28: The Language of Love
by Gwynn Dujardin—Monday, October 26, 2015, 9:42 p.m.

Dear class,

First, a reminder to those of you who haven't completed your recitations on Medieval material to book your appointments with your TAs this or next week in advance of when office hours will be wholly dedicated to papers. Our readings for this week—sonnets and *King Lear*—are excellent choices for recitation as well as for the term essay.

To those ends, I have posted a number of audio and video files on our Moodle featuring British villains, superheroes, and wizards of two varieties reciting our particular course readings. I choose these actors' readings not just because of their star power (Hiddleston! Cumberbatch! . . . Snape?!) but because of their education—a number of them were educated in the very kind of humanist grammar schools we have been talking about—as well as their theatrical training: they know what they are doing in enunciating the language and representing the poetry through voice. For the sonnets, you should be listening for and aiming to capture the iambic pentameter, accentuate the rhyme, and otherwise seek to render your interpretation through your delivery.

I also post two video clips of *King Lear* for two reasons: first, if you recall from our discussion of the York Crucifixion Play, it is important to assess and analyze drama in the medium in which it was performed; and second, it is useful and important to see the different interpretive choices different performances make, not only in line readings but in every other aspect of staging. I was delighted to see the full Ian McKellen Lear posted online, and you are welcome to read along with it. It contains subtitles, which irritated me at first, before I realized they're a wonderful way to follow along with the language and indeed see how the actors are interpreting their lines. Enjoy.

The theme of Wednesday's class is the "language of love." As we discussed on Friday, poets such as Thomas Wyatt adapt the sonnet from the Italian poet Petrarch to the English language (a common feature of Renaissance writing, i.e., imitating classical and continental authors). Petrarchan sonnets feature paradoxes and oxymorons (e.g., "I burn and freeze like ice"), blazons (which list a mistress's physical features in comparison to other objects of beauty), and *conceits*, or extended metaphors that often govern the idea of an entire poem. Some of you might be interested in writing your term essay on a sonnet conceit, such as that in "Whoso List to Hunt." We began to develop an interpretation in class, but for your own essay you would mount your own interpretation of the deer/hunt conceit using evidence and reasoning from the rest of the poem to support your reading.

At the end of class I posted sonnet 1 from Philip Sidney's sonnet sequence *Astrophil and Stella*. Where Thomas Wyatt adapted fairly random poems from Petrarch, Sidney is the first to write an entire sequence, a loosely related series of sonnets, in English. As I noted as we were packing up, Sidney appears to favor inspiration over the method of writing in which a poet follows previous models. But there's an irony in this in that the sonnet itself is defined by rigid constraints in form, and Sidney not only matches but also exceeds his predecessors with the addition of an extra foot (alexandrine).

In reviewing Shakespeare's sonnets for Wednesday, ask yourself how Shakespeare approaches all of these sonnet conventions. As you may or may not know, the first 127 sonnets are dedicated to a male figure, not a female; right there we have a significant variation. But even the sonnets written to the mistress appear to vary from the form: How? What comments do you see Shakespeare making about the language of love?

Identify a particular sonnet in our reading that appears to imitate and vary upon previous texts or models in the way we have been discussing how Renaissance authors learned how to write. Or, given the topic of the day, select the one you love most, and consider why.

Until then,
Prof. Dujardin

ENGL 200 FW » Forums » News forum » Accounting for the whole

For Friday, January 15: "Accounting" for the whole in *Robinson Crusoe* by Gwynn Dujardin—Thursday, January 14, 2016, 8:24 p.m.

Dear class,
Tomorrow will have two sides to it.

First, we will want to consider everything we have been tracing in view of Crusoe's return to England and the book's eventual conclusion. The main threads of our conversation have related to:

- *Robinson Crusoe* and Restoration and eighteenth-century mercantile culture: Crusoe's own "station" in the emergent merchant class, as indicated to us in the early section in the book
- The status of the book as an early novel, which we can break down into three areas connected to the so-called "rise of the novel":
  - the book's own status in the literary marketplace and how it is sold both as an account of "strange surprising adventures" (frontispiece) and something worthy of providing "instruction" to the reader
  - its recounting of details and their bearing on Crusoe's "character," as we've assessed whether the book subscribes to empiricist conceptions of "human understanding"; the different forms of "accounting": narrative; material; and spiritual
  - the book's perspective on individualism, which we've approached chiefly in terms of Crusoe's self-interest
- The ways *Robinson Crusoe* relates to the history of English and British exploration and colonialism, and Britain's standing as a major naval power and principal actor in the transatlantic, a.k.a. triangular, slave trade

The book pulls us in two directions. On the one hand, we might view Crusoe as a distinct individual, a first-person narrator with unique experiences. On the other, we can see him as representative of broader social categories and forces, i.e., as a prototypical merchant-tradesman, colonist, and even slave owner. One of the challenges in analyzing the book lies in being clear about what approach you're taking, and considering how aspects of each relate and sometimes challenge the other.

I'd like to talk about the book as a whole by returning to the beginning and specifically the editor's preface on page 45. In what ways do you think the book is "worth making Publick"? The Editor claims a particular didactic function for the book, i.e., that it will furnish "Instruction to the Reader."

In the end, what "instruction" do you think it offers—on its own terms, in its own right?

From there we'll turn to considering ways that we could (and could not) use historical sources to define and augment our own claims and analysis. There are four, two in two sets:

- Brief excerpts from two other publications by DeFoe, "An Essay Upon the Trade to Africa" and "A Review of the State of the British Nation"

- Slightly longer material from two accounts from the voyages of Alexander Selkirk, which DeFoe used as sources

In reading these sources, look for connections you can see between them and the book. What do you see that they have in common? In what ways, if any, do the sources shed light on any aspect of the book?

Remember that we are most concerned with making our analytical claims about the literary text, i.e., Robinson Crusoe. In doing "historical research," that research should support and advance those claims. This discussion will represent only the beginning of ways to go about this.

See you then,
Prof. Dujardin

ENGL 200 FW » Forums » News forum » For Wednesday, March 23

For Wednesday, March 23
by Gwynn Dujardin—Tuesday, March 22, 2016, 4:58 p.m.

Dear class,
Tomorrow we turn to the second half of our study of the twentieth and twenty-first centuries to consider postcolonial literature in the form of Derek Walcott's poem "A Far Cry from Africa" and J. M. Coetzee's *Foe*. Indeed as we near the end of this study of The History of Literature in English we are now reading texts in the English language by and/or about those for whom that language is not indigenous but that of British colonialism.

We will discuss two important concepts pertinent to postcolonial writing: *alterity* speaks to the condition of other-ness experienced by those in relation to a dominant colonial culture; and *hybridity* to the condition of being of mixed race and culture. How do you see those ideas represented in and by Walcott's "A Far Cry from Africa"? How do you see Modernist perspectives on form manifesting in this example of postcolonial poetry? Select a section of the poem that answers one of these questions.

We'll devote most of our time to Walcott to establish a framework for postcolonial literature but then introduce our last novel, J. M. Coetzee's *Foe*, in which we have a radical retelling of Daniel DeFoe's *Robinson Crusoe*. In *Robinson Crusoe* we read only Crusoe's "account" of his "adventure." General questions we will discuss in the coming classes: Whose story is being told, and by whom, in *Foe*? How are we to interpret the incorporation of Susan Barton, the revisions to Crusoe's narrative, and the roles of both Friday and Foe? Who has the power to speak, to write, and/or to represent others' experiences?

Foe was written and published in the mid-1980s, when South Africa still existed under conditions of apartheid, an institutionalized system of racial segregation implemented to ensure economic and popular control by the white population. How does this retelling of DeFoe's novel, most of which is set back in England, speak to or about the history of colonialism and apartheid?

We're nearing the end of the course, and you'll find *Foe* challenging in different ways you haven't seen before. Take heart that you'll surmount this challenge as you have all the others, and know that you'll become particularly au courant when we discuss the sources of this challenge in postmodernism.

Until tomorrow,
Prof. Dujardin

Student: Ellie Berry
TA: Tara Hilman
Assignment: Recitation (Fall)
Presentation notes:
- *Beowulf* lines 1537–56 (longer than necessary)
- Accurate recitation
- Dramatic intonation and movement
- Standing
- Strong enunciation
- Paid attention to clues in the structure (enjambment)
- Very engaging

Discussion notes:
Why this passage?
- Wanted a passage that depicts the relationship between Viking culture and Christianity
- Likes the action and battle within the passage, finds it fun and exciting
- Wanted something with a strong beginning and a strong end so that it fits together with a nice tight circle—is part of a larger story, but is also somewhat self-contained

What process did you use to approach this text?
- Practiced standing and body movement (mimicking battle)
- Wanted to stand because the section is dramatic
- Listened to audio
- Used techniques from drama for memorization
- Practiced sections in bits

What observations did you make about the text during this process?
- Beowulf and Grendel's mother are similar, and almost seem to be enjoying the battle
- The end (where Christianity was discussed) was harder to memorize—was almost out of tune with all or the rest. It is almost as if Christianity was tagged on as an afterthought

Comments:

Excellent work! Your recitation was accurate and incredibly engaging, and you explained the ways in which your insights impacted your presentation and were impacted by it. The choices that you made—for example, choosing an exciting and somewhat self-contained part of the text and standing and moving during your recitation—were strong and thoroughly explained. Moreover, the observations that this assignment led to were interesting and insightful.

5/5

Student: Ellie Berry
Assignment: Recitation (Winter)
TA: Tara Hilman

Presentation notes:

- J. M. Coetzee's *Foe* 1st full paragraph on pg 131
- Brilliant execution!
- Flawless memorization and excellent dramatic intonation.

Discussion notes:

Why this passage?

- It is a speech—it is declarative. She is speaking for herself
- It encapsulates the importance of storytelling—she wants her story told her way
- She is also confused about identity in the moment
- Freedom is highlighted here (Friday is free, but is she really? And she is free, but tied to Foe economically and Friday because she feels responsible for him)
- Love this book, because you need to think while you are reading it
- A great contrast to Robinson Crusoe

What process did you use to approach this text?

- Said things over and over until they stuck
- Lots of pacing and repetition
- Learned sections each day

What observations did you make about the text during this process?
- Noticed that she speaks in a formal way
- It was almost like Shakespeare—there are extra words that you wouldn't say otherwise
- She has a confidence in her voice, but simultaneously does not believe that she can tell her story
- She wants her story told, but she doesn't want to be reduced to a story
- Contrasts to *Crusoe*; all of the accounts are hers, rather than Crusoe's
- This novel portrays the story in a more "realistic" way—hers does not involve cannibals. You want to believe her despite the complications involved in the idea truth
- The novel forces you to ask what you actually believe about truth—can you really find truth?
- There is one bit right before this passage where she questions how she can tell who she is if she doesn't believe it. She is not just an empty receptacle
- "How can we live if we do not believe we know who we are, and who we have been?" ties into colonialism. How do you define yourself when everything that has been written about you is skewed—would have liked to do an even longer recitation, because she loves that passage

Comments:
Brilliant work! Your recitation was incredibly engaging; the level of emotion and energy that you brought to the text was remarkable. The depth of your critical reflections during our discussion of the text was also really impressive; your insights into the complicated nature of truth, storytelling, and the way in which these loaded conceptions interact in postcolonial discourse, were really thought provoking. Great job!
5/5

The Survey as Pedagogical Training and Academic Job Credential

TIM ROSENDALE, SOUTHERN METHODIST UNIVERSITY

The rumored and perhaps partially real demise of the literature survey has prompted a great deal of salutary reflection on what is lost with the decline of the survey model, and conversely on what surveys' real benefits are for undergraduates.[1] Less often considered, though, is the potential value of survey-teaching in graduate programs. In this essay, accordingly, I will describe a different kind of rethinking of the survey, on the axis of a different variable: not in terms of innovative undergraduate pedagogy, but in terms of fully realizing the value of survey-teaching for graduate programs and subsequent careers. Even conventionally conceived surveys—which are still often well-suited to the larger research institutions that offer PhDs, as well as to the many schools that lack the resources for more labor-intensive "active learning" models—can offer remarkable opportunities to powerfully reinject literary history, contextualized close reading, and above all *teaching* into graduate training. Since most hires in English literature value candidates with a record of successful teaching, and many jobs continue to involve traditional surveys or require other forms of range, making good use of such courses can be enormously beneficial to graduate students and programs alike.

Assuming that the three central tasks of doctoral education in English are to teach PhD students how to be (a) good scholars, (b) good teachers, and (c) *employed*, I will argue here that graduate experience in teaching survey courses contributes greatly to the second and third of these goals. It may contribute to the first as well: if/as we increasingly admit graduate students who are the products of decreasingly historical undergraduate curricula, we may well find (as I repeatedly have) that their own sense of historical context benefits quite directly from the experience of teaching a survey. Properly deployed, then, literature surveys can provide a uniquely effective way to remediate the discipline's drift away from history by producing better-informed students, scholars, and teachers, with jobs.

In 2010, I created a new course—a slightly crazy single-semester, wall-to-wall, introductory-level survey of British literature from *Beowulf* to Seamus Heaney—partly to offer broad historical context to undergraduates, partly to serve the university curriculum and attract new majors, and partly to provide pedagogical experience and training for our advanced PhD students in British literature. The vast scope and team-taught structure of this course, combined with its low curricular level and largely nonmajor population, have in interesting ways sharpened the challenges inherent in any survey course, and made this one a kind of pedagogical laboratory. In four iterations of it, I've learned a lot about how to tell an effective and flexible fifteen-century story that is cohesive without being oversimplified, usable without being constricting, and wide-ranging without being mystifying; how to effectively focus each week's readings, lectures, and discussions into a comprehensible and interconnected chapter of that story; and how to be purposeful and engaging without alienating or patronizing my nonspecialist students. And I have also—while becoming a better and more reflective teacher myself—learned a great deal about how to make these challenges deeply instructive and beneficial experiences for the graduate students who teach this course alongside me.[2] The remainder of this essay will be an analytical narrative of how I have tried to accomplish that goal, followed by a discussion of its relation to job placement.

Our doctoral program is relatively small and new (we admitted our first class of six PhD students in 2007), and we were determined from the start to handle graduate teaching more deliberately than the standard, minimally supervised, and sometimes abusive comp/TA model. When our second-year students begin teaching composition, they are closely mentored by a veteran teacher in weekly practicum meetings and class visits. After a few semesters of composition teaching, and as they embark on their dissertations, we typically begin transitioning them into low-level literature courses, but here too they are not thrown into a classroom and wished good luck; they work closely with experienced faculty to learn how to teach literature well. Those who have never taught literature before are often surprised at how *different* it is from teaching first-year writing, not just in material but in modes of instruction and thinking. I created the new survey (aka English 1385) in an effort to address these needs in structured, experiential, and productive ways.

At the outset, I established three constitutional principles for this course, all designed to maximize its pedagogical value. The first is that it would be comprehensively collaborative: while I was of course the executive and guiding member of the instructional staff, everyone was to be in on *everything*, from course design to the final exam, in a dynamic much more like co-teaching than the traditional professor/TA model. The second principle followed necessarily from the first: each time I teach the course, it is rebuilt from scratch, from the ground up. And from these two principles follows a third: we try not to proceed via assumption or instinct, but rather via direct thought and discussion. We really talk through everything, and it has been highly beneficial to me as well to think explicitly about—and be questioned about—principles and practices that experience has made almost automatic.

The process begins the preceding semester, when I round up three or four textbook possibilities and give them to the graduate students to assess with a set of guiding questions: What are the strengths and weaknesses of each? What possible course objectives does each make easier, or harder, to pursue? What desirable readings does each include and omit? How usable are they for undergraduates (this involves considerations from editorial apparatus to typeface and layout to cost to, sometimes, sheer physical weight)? Such questions get graduate students immediately into the mindset of thinking like teachers, both practically and intellectually, and prompt them from the first to consider basic questions regarding what we want to accomplish in a given course, and why, and how. (I suspect that many of us in this profession experienced a moment of youthful shock when we first realized that the syllabi our teachers gave us did not appear randomly or magically, but were rather the products of sustained prior thought about the course's purpose and content; for at least some of my mentees, this is such a moment.) So by the time we meet to discuss and democratically select a textbook, my co-teachers are deeply involved in core questions of course conception and design.

Those deeper questions are pursued and concretized in a subsequent syllabus meeting that typically takes an entire day which proceeds much like I imagine the 1787 Constitutional Convention did: everyone comes with different interests and ideas, many of them good, but many of them also incompatible with others, and things can get raucous as a result—but we have to end up with a workable and consensual document. I begin by explaining my basic course policies, and the principles and considerations involved in each; I then invite questions, comments, objections, and proposed modifications, all of which must be specifically grounded in principle or practicality. How (and why) should we handle attendance policy, reading quizzes, writing and rewriting assignments, grade weighting, undergraduates' persistent desire to focus on me as the "real" authority figure, and so forth? How are each of these nuts and bolts germane to effective teaching? We discuss all of these and their implications, and resolve disagreements via group vote (mostly; I do reserve the right, and have the obligation, to override a majority if I'm convinced it's really wrong about something important, but this happens very rarely), and we end up with course policies that are thought-through and agreed-upon.

Thankfully, the logic of the A-to-Z British historical survey course suggests an intuitive chronological structure, and we almost always agree on a distribution which, while no period gets as much as we'd like, is generally equitable: something on the order of three weeks on the Medieval period, five on 1500–1700, and two weeks on each remaining century. Philosophy gets really and immediately concrete, though, when we turn to the week-by-week schedule. The course's vast scope suggests vast readings, but its introductory curricular level demands very modest ones, and consequently there is never room for all of our good ideas and desires in a given week.[3] This laboratory-like pressure further entails that each day's reading must be intensely purposeful and productive, and this provokes a torrent of challenges and discussions. Only one Canterbury Tale? Where's my favorite specialty author? No novels? (No; no time.) We don't have room for both Shelley and Byron (or Margery Kempe and Julian of Norwich, or Conrad and Woolf, or Shakespeare and Marlowe, or . . .); how, and on what basis, do we choose? What are the course's macro- and micronarratives, and what does each require? How exactly should each week's readings, lectures, and discussions contribute to them, and fit together?

You can see why this takes all day, and ends at a bar: these are all valid, important questions that normal people have never thought about before, but English professors must. And none is more important than the last two, because they are what shapes the whole and each element included in it. The macronarrative is usually quite straightforward: a chronological survey of major writers and texts in the British tradition, contextualized in literary, intellectual, and sociopolitical history, and rendered into a story that involves sometimes-surprising combinations of continuity and change. It's the micronarratives, recurrently surfacing and submerging, that provide the particular texture and nuance of each iteration of the course.[4] Which (and how many) threads should we include—gender? religion? language? influence? literary form? some other persistent interest of the tradition? And how will these be woven together? Most of these are topics of general and fundamental importance, but every time we have rebuilt this course, the final product has been substantially strengthened by individual grad students' advocacy of thoughtful ways to weave their particular interests productively into the syllabus. On one occasion, for example, one of my co-teachers pressed for more persistent attention to gender; another, to religion; another, to intertextual and formal connections across time—and the course was significantly better as a result.

Many of the issues I've been walking through here will be unsurprising to experienced survey teachers, but again, to normal people who are not, they can be quite radically new. By the time the syllabus is framed out, grad students who come to my course without prior literature-teaching experience have engaged in many kinds of pedagogically crucial new thinking, both theoretical and practical. They know what we will be doing, and why, and what will be required of them. All that remains is the doing, and this, of course, entails its own challenges and discoveries—which are enhanced, strengthened, and deepened by the demands of this kind of survey course.

The challenge that looms largest to my mentees, I think, the thing they regard with various commixtures of excitement and dread, is lecturing.[5] Very few of them have any experience of standing in front of a crowd and speaking for fifty minutes, let alone of knowing how to do so in ways that are substantive, purposeful, interesting, and structured. So we work hard on this: they pre-plan, research (most of these lectures require some combination of contextual and textual content), outline, re-outline, and practice, conferring with me along the way. Some turn out to be naturally gifted lecturers, but most are not, and I assure them that this is both normal and remediable; most good lecturers had to work and practice to become so. To this end, I usually have each person lecture four times: twice in or near their own period of specialty, and twice far afield from it, so that an early modernist, for example, might lecture on the Sidneys and on Milton, but also on Chaucer and on Woolf. The goal, of course, is that they get some depth of experience lecturing in their own field, but also significant range, flexibility, and comfort well outside of it. They learn how to quickly self-educate on subjects outside their scholarly expertise, and how to effectively conceive, build, pitch, and deliver (with minimal notes) lectures that are both engaging and illuminating. Every single graduate student I've taught this course with has ended up, sooner or later, developing and giving really good lectures, and in many cases the growth of their confidence and skill has been exciting to watch.

Though lecturing is perhaps what makes my mentees most anxious, I have been surprised to observe how often they have struggled even more with leading productive literary discussions. When I reflect on this, it makes sense: when lecturing, one is largely in control of what happens, but discussion is a much more fluid situation and largely in the hands of others. Often, inexperienced teachers either bewilder their students with inaccessibly huge and abstract questions, or pepper them with rapid-fire volleys of overly specific or factual ones. So we work hard on this too, cultivating the art of opening up the texts via close, collaborative analysis, and then connecting that to larger issues and ideas. Our job in leading discussions, I tell them, is to demonstrate both the nature and the stakes of complex reading, to invite our students into the rewarding pleasures of such conversation and interactive rethinking, and to get them to think together about the historical relations and discontinuities sketched out in the course. Like lecturing, this does not come naturally for most. Knowing how and where to begin a good interpretive conversation is an art that most need to learn and practice, so we preplan with some basic questions and strategies to get things going.

- Identify one specific textual moment (or word or idea) that you think is especially interesting, and explain why.
- How does this text resonate or conflict with previous readings?
- What problems did you encounter in this text? At what points did you feel like something interesting was within reach, but you couldn't figure out how to get there?
- Good literature usually has bigger goals than just sounding pretty or being fun to read or making its author rich. Why do you think the author thought this text was worth writing? What is he or she asking of you? Are you being asked to accept an idea, or to think about some questions? How do they do this? What's at stake? Why does it matter?
- How does thinking about this text in historical context help us understand it more effectively?
- How and why do we disagree about this text? How can that disagreement be made useful and illuminating?

Once that conversation gets started, moving it productively forward in the midst of obstacles and distractions—quiet or unfocused or unprepared or disengaged students, fire drills, unexpected or irrelevant questions, student comments that need to be made into lemonade—can be a kind of knife-juggling group tightrope walk. Experienced teachers sometimes forget how difficult and complex a task it is to guide a conversation that is both improvisational and purposeful; new teachers have to learn it first, and I visit the discussion sections every week to assist with this. I expect my mentees to go into discussion with pedagogical goals, of course, and if those seem to have been inadequate or unachieved we'll talk about that afterward. But mostly we discuss how the discussion unfolded, what worked and what didn't, how it might have been better. Why were students excited to discuss poem A but not poem B? How might you have approached B differently? How might you have made better use of student comment C? Why do you think your question about rhyme, or your prewriting prompt, worked so well, and why were the small groups such a flop? These are questions that we should all be constantly asking ourselves, but I'll confess that I too often leave them for my unconscious dream work to sort out; in this area, as in so many others, I have found it enormously reinvigorating to my own teaching to be explicitly and actively recalled to the basics of what we do.

Of course, there are various courses in which one can get lecturing experience, and one will lead discussions in most imaginable literature courses; why is doing these things in this kind of survey especially valuable? In three words: range, depth, and flexibility. In its survey of all major periods and genres of British literary history, this course forces both its undergraduate students and its graduate co-teachers to think broadly and relationally. While the former group constitutes the course's putative end-users, the latter group is also presented with a remarkable growth opportunity. Both groups build their skills in thinking about texts, ideas, form, and so forth over the long term of history, better contextualizing their reading and deepening their understanding by extending it both laterally and vertically. What, for example, did Gerard Manley Hopkins reject of his immediate literary inheritance, and what did he reach back centuries to recover, and how did this affect subsequent poetic practice? In the general move away from the survey model, many English departments have attenuated their own ability to explicate or indeed even perceive these relationships. Cultivating that capacity in a wide-scale survey can give our graduate students significant advantages as teachers and scholars, and in so doing we also give them demonstrable and invaluable experiential range in thinking about their own specialization in relation to all other periods and genres.

Lecturing, discussion-leading, and much else is addressed in our weekly staff meetings. There, we do group analyses and critiques of the preceding week's lectures, including mine, offering each other feedback and suggestions for improvement. We discuss the week's discussions and what has gone well or poorly in them. We plan for the week to come. We develop essay prompts, and calibrate our grading by reading each other's graded essays. We compose and grade quizzes and exams together. We talk as a group about any problems or challenges that have arisen, and how one goes about figuring out or fixing them. We share successes and stories and advice with each other. We think about how the course might be improved. The weeklies, in short, are a shared scaffolding in which we can support and learn from one another, and as a result become better teachers individually.

The present essay is focused on the role of survey-teaching in graduate education, but it is only fair to ask how this has worked out for the undergraduate students who are, after all, the course's primary objects of instruction. Inevitably, the students of a novice teacher will suffer some consequences of their instructor's inexperience and trial-and-error learning process. But I recently reviewed all the anonymous student evaluations I could locate for these courses, and was struck by how few complaints they contained about the teaching setup. A few disliked it when the co-teachers disagreed about texts—so much for teaching the conflict!—and would have preferred a single authority figure. But most either didn't complain, or had very positive things to say. One self-identified senior wrote that "it was surprising and unusual to have three professors teaching. At first it seemed as though it might be overwhelming or create confusion . . . but it had the opposite effect. Each teacher brought a different voice that kept things interesting and fresh." Another said that "the rotation of the lecturers and their individual styles of presentation seemed to harmonize nicely with one another." Another wrote that "The instructors were very effective. Each instructor was extremely knowledgeable of the subject at hand and very effective in making sense of the subject. They stimulated interest in a course I would not usually have interest in." Admittedly, there were some complaints about course policy (turns out students would rather not have reading quizzes), and more significantly about some awkwardness and inutility in discussion sections. But given that every new literature teacher has to learn and make mistakes, it seems very likely to me that in comparison with grad students thrown into classes by themselves, the close instruction and supervision that mine receive both minimizes such problems and makes them more productive. The available evidence and logic suggests that the cost to undergraduates is minimal, and the benefits considerable, while the benefits to the graduate students are enormous.

Now all this work is aimed at a handful of closely related goals beyond educating a specific roomful of undergraduates. One is its own warrant: to train our doctoral students to be really good at teaching literature. Nearly inseparable from this is a second goal: to prepare them well for the various pedagogical demands of the profession. And this leads organically to a near-cognate third: to make them strong and successful job candidates.

I suspect, though I have no data to support this, that most of us in this profession initially pursued it not because we dreamed of research but because we dreamed of teaching. I can say with certainty that while I enjoy and value research, I first wanted to be an English professor because I loved literature, and was inspired by those who taught me to love and understand it more fully. The pressures of graduate school and professionalization, however, tend to generate distortion and amnesia: love is suppressed as naïveté, and replaced with the "real" work of analysis, research, and publication, while teaching is often regarded as an inconvenience if not a necessary evil. This is not done out of malice, I think, but is a predictable effect of the rarefied air of PhD-granting programs, which tend to be at research-intensive universities. Minimal teaching is a selling point of doctoral programs that can afford it; in those that can't, excessive teaching often hampers graduate students' progress toward completion. Too often, that is, graduate students are taught to devalue teaching, and to conceive of progress and professionalization in narrowly scholarly terms.[6]

Nona Fienberg noted this disjunction, and particularly its manifestations in hiring, twenty years ago. When her nonelite state college hires, she wrote, teaching considerations prevail decisively over research factors.

> We don't speak of "the most impressive mind," "a first-rate intellect," we don't talk about "major coups," "aggressive appointments," or even about "rising stars." . . . Our language is different. We talk about "a match." We talk about teaching English composition, about general education required courses, about contributing to our curriculum revision process, about adapting pedagogy to different learning styles, about group work, the writing process, contributing to grant proposals, working to train the best secondary school teachers we can. Yet we see—from the University of Wisconsin at Madison, from Miami University in Ohio, from all over the country—job candidates who have learned exclusively and narrowly the monolithic discourse of the research institution.[7]

Fienberg's experience was corroborated by a 2001 survey that sought to determine "what search committees want" in their hires.[8] In a pool of 368 surveys, the investigators found that teaching consistently outranked research in terms of desirability. In the initial screening of applications,

> General teaching experience and experience teaching the advertised specialties were both ranked highly, more highly than research specialties and the potential for future research. Farther down the list the same pattern holds: evidence of teaching ability outranks evidence of research ability. Specifically, course evaluations and teaching awards were cited as more important than the number and quality of the candidate's publications.[9]

Furthermore, 63 percent of respondents identified teaching ability, performance, or experience as a deciding factor in identifying a top choice among their finalists, compared to just 44 percent who pointed to research. The authors observe that in the response pool, research universities were heavily overrepresented while baccalaureate institutions and community colleges were underrepresented, so it is likely that this emphasis on teaching over research is even greater than indicated.

Combine this with the ballooning of nontenure-track staffing and concomitant shrinkage of regular faculties—the AAUP's most recent report observes that over the past four decades "the proportion of the academic labor force holding full-time tenured positions has declined by 26 percent and the share holding full-time tenure-track positions has dropped by an astonishing 50 percent"[10]—and the likely outcome is that literature-teaching resources will be ever more thinly stretched, thus requiring increasing range and flexibility from fewer regular faculty. All of this suggests that teaching is a much more valuable job credential than PhD programs typically seem to realize or allow, and that job candidates with notably broad experience and range like the kind that comes from having taught a wide-ranging survey are likely to be, and will likely increasingly become, especially desirable to hiring departments that need to cover more bases with fewer people.

My experience supports this hypothesis. *Every single one* of the people who have co-taught this wall-to-wall survey with me are currently in full-time teaching jobs—37.5 percent in elite secondary schools, 62.5 percent (and five of the six who completed their PhDs) in tenure-track collegiate positions. That is 100 percent full-time teaching employment. Given the ongoing miseries of the academic job market, that would be an admirable placement record just about anywhere; at a recently established program it is remarkable. Certainly I don't claim that co-teaching the survey with me was the sole or dominant factor in these hires; each candidate of course had many other virtues. But nor do I think that it was irrelevant, and here too both observation and sense suggest that this experience made significant contributions to their professional desirability.

To begin with, rumors of the survey's demise have been greatly exaggerated. At the 2013 MLA convention, a roundtable on teaching survey courses was extraordinarily well attended; my estimate at the time was that the crowd numbered 150–200. This is several times the size of most panel audiences, and compelling evidence that many professors teach surveys and are eager to talk about it. Surveys—often quite traditional ones—are still widely taught and taken, particularly at smaller and more teaching-oriented institutions, but also at places like Harvard and the University of Texas. The *Norton Anthology of*

English Literature continues to sell and be revised, and other publishers (Longman, Blackwell, Broadview, etc.) continue to invest in this segment of the market. Surveys, in short, maintain a rather robust existence in American higher education, and schools that teach and value them are likely to look favorably on candidates with successful experience teaching them.

More broadly, teaching a survey documentably cultivates a wide range of skills and experiences that is difficult to match in courses with less breadth. Whatever their individual resumés looked like at the start, each of my grad-student co-teachers left English 1385 with a remarkable set of essential experiences. They had read, researched, lectured, and led discussions on every period of British literary history, both within their field of specialization and far outside of it. They had taught poetry, prose, and drama, and had done so contextually. They had thoroughly and experientially understood the differences (and commonalities) between teaching composition and teaching literature. They had participated in a collaborative and vigorously productive group endeavor. They had co-designed, co-administered, co-taught, co-evaluated, and in almost every respect co-run a large and complex course. To what conceivable course or teaching job could these proficiencies not beneficially lend themselves? When I advise our grad students as they head into the job market, I tell them that one of their central goals should be to make hiring committees fantasize about how much this candidate could *do* in and for their department. Having survey-teaching experience like this on their CV provides convincing evidence for such competence and utility.

I keep in touch with my former co-teachers, and they have testified extensively to the value of this experience in their hiring and early careers. Several report that the committee and school that hired them were deeply and immediately interested in their survey-teaching experience; in some cases, the hirers returned to it repeatedly, wanting to know more, thinking aloud about its potential value. One tenure-track 1385 veteran reflects that

> teaching a survey course as a grad student—particularly one that covers earliest lit to modern—is essential for helping to get a teaching job, because one will need to show breadth in teaching and familiarity with a range of periods, since most teaching-heavy jobs will have faculty teaching out of their area of research and often teaching more courses out of their area than in it. For grad students who have not taught before, the long survey gives them two or even three courses . . . that they can talk enthusiastically about and for which they can present search committees with sample syllabi and assignments.

Another concurs that "Given the generalist direction that jobs in our field are necessarily taking, especially at small private liberal arts environments . . . this experience feels critical to success on the job market." Yet another points to how our course

> gave me both broad talking points and specific examples that allowed me to speak confidently and honestly during my interviews for teaching jobs. Interviewers wanted to know a) whether I had taught a survey course before, and b) how I approached certain pedagogical decisions and situations in the general education classroom. They also wanted to see syllabi for such a survey course, and they asked questions about why I included the specific texts I did. I had ready answers—and very specific examples—for each question they asked.

Once one has taken up a job, I am frequently told, the benefits continue to accrue. Both having and reflecting on the experience itself smooths the transition into professional teaching in obvious ways. It provides a useful repository of ideas, materials, assignments, skills, and wisdom. This in turn lessens the impact of going from a 1/1 teaching load to a 3/3 or 4/4 by providing a carefully developed foundation for the teaching to come. Several indicate that, as advertised, 1385 has made them more useful, more flexible, and just better colleagues, ready to take on a wide range of courses and other tasks (course development, textbook selection, team teaching, committee work, interdisciplinary lecturing, etc.). One alum condenses this nicely in telling me that from the start, her colleagues have "appreciated that I was prepared to teach across the curriculum because I had been taught how to prepare." No one experience can prepare one for everything they will do or encounter in a career, of course. But I like to think that this one gives our graduate students a richly compact and deeply experiential introduction to being a good literature teacher and colleague, in ways that make them better job candidates and junior professors. Other courses can certainly do that too, but a broad survey, for the reasons I've outlined above, offers an especially multifaceted opportunity to give our students a really compelling head start.

This essay has necessarily focused on what this course has done for our graduate students, but I'd like to close with a brief word about what it, and they, have done for me. One of this survey's great strengths is that every time it is offered, it has a largely new staff—one with different expertises, experiences, ideas, and interests than the one that preceded it. Graduate students take up this teaching assignment right after passing their doctoral exams, with several semesters of composition instruction experience, and as they are developing their dissertation prospectuses, so they are flush with knowledge and bursting with ideas. Without exception, they have taught me things: about texts, about history, about pedagogical techniques. Time and again they have taught me how to better understand and teach a historical period or literary text, to re-think my grading or course procedure, to deploy nifty lecturing or discussion moves. I now, thanks to them, am a better teacher who uses prewriting, small-group work, and online discussion boards to enhance the educational experience in my classes. And they have strengthened my conviction that literature surveys have crucial roles to play in higher education—more, perhaps, than we have recognized—now and in the future.

NOTES

1.   Jennifer Summit describes Stanford's English majors, in a distributionist curriculum that "collapse[s] the vista into the close-up," as "not liberated by such a tasting menu but longing for the historical scaffolding that could bring their disparate classes—however vibrant, challenging, and popular—into a coherent whole." Jennifer Summit, "Literary History and the Curriculum: How, What, and Why," *ADE Bulletin* no. 149 (2010): 50.

2.   I should at the outset name and thank them: Michael Anderson, Austin Johnson, Kayla Walker Edin, Jennifer Boulanger, Kristina Booker, Megan Schott, Bethany Williamson, and Charles Wuest. All were excellent colleagues from whom I learned, and all were a pleasure to work with.

3.   The course's initial iteration turned out to be overpacked, and indeed each subsequent version has been slimmer than its predecessor, in an ongoing effort to do more with fewer texts. This has been a wonderfully challenging and invigorating experience for all of us, and probably most of all for me.

4.   Summit describes Stanford's analogous (if less traditional) effort to rebuild their major's "historical literacy" by way of "models of literary history organized around both the threads of continuity across time and the breaks that create discontinuities in time, as these threads and breaks are registered in and through literary works." Summit, "Literary History and the Curriculum," 51.

5.   The structure of a typical week is a full lecture on Monday that contextualizes the week's readings, some combination of interpretive lecture and full-group discussion on Wednesday, and discussion-section breakouts on Friday to individually apply and deepen these connections in a more intimate setting.

6.   See Leonard Cassuto, "Changing the Ph.D.: A Tilt Toward Teaching," *Chronicle of Higher Education*, July 28, 2014, http://chronicle.com/article/Changing-the-PhD-a-Tilt/147897.

7.   Nona Fienberg, " 'The Most of It': Hiring at a Nonelite College," *ADE Bulletin* 112 (Winter 1995): 11–13, https://ade.mla.org/content/download/7384/225147/ade.112.11.pdf.

8.   Ibid.

9.   See Walter Broughton and William Conlogue, "What Search Committees Want," *Profession 2001* (New York: MLA, 2001), 39–51, https://www.mla.org/Resources/Career/Career-Resources The-Job-Search-Information-for-Job-Seekers-and-Hiring-DepartmentsProfession-Article-What-Search-Committees-Want.

10.   Steven Shulman et al. for the American Association of University Professors, "Higher Education at a Crossroads: The Annual Report on the Economic Status of the Profession, 2015–16," *Academe* (March–April 2016): 9–23, http://www.aaup.org/sites/default/files/2015-16 EconomicStatusReport.pdf.

BIBLIOGRAPHY

Broughton, Walter, and William Conlogue. "What Search Committees Want." *Profession 2001*, 39–51. New York: MLA, 2001. https://www.mla.org/Resources/Career/Career-Resources/The-Job-Search-Information-for-Job-Seekers-and-Hiring-Departments/Profession-Article-What-Search-Committees-Want.

Cassuto, Leonard. "Changing the Ph.D.: A Tilt Toward Teaching." *Chronicle of Higher Education*, July 28, 2014. http://chronicle.com/article/Changing-the-PhD-a-Tilt/147897.

Fienberg, Nona. "'The Most of It': Hiring at a Nonelite College." *ADE Bulletin* 112 (Winter 1995): 11–13. https://ade.mla.org/content/download/7384/225147/ade.112.11.pdf.

Modern Language Association, and Association of Departments of English. *Education in the Balance: A Report on the Academic Workforce in English*. 2008. https://www.mla.org/Resources/Research/Surveys-Reports-and-Other-Documents/Staffing-Salaries-and-Other-Professional-Issues/Education-in-the-Balance-A-Report-on-the-Academic-Workforce-in-English.

Shulman, Steven, et al. for the American Association of University Professors. "Higher Education at a Crossroads: The Annual Report on the Economic Status of the Profession, 2015–16." *Academe* (March–April 2016): 9–23. http://www.aaup.org/sites/default/files/2015-16EconomicStatusReport.pdf.

Summit, Jennifer. "Literary History and the Curriculum: How, What, and Why." *ADE Bulletin* 149 (2010): 46–52.

COURSE DOCUMENT: ROSENDALE

English 1385
Power, Passion, and Protest in British Literature

• • •

Spring 2012
MWF 11–12
306 Dallas Hall

• • •

Instructors	office	discussion room	office hours
Prof. T. Rosendale	DH254		W12–1, F10–11
Ms. K. Booker	DH24	Hyer 102	M9:30–10:45,
Th12–1:30			
Ms. M. Schott	DH17E	Hyer 204	M9–10, Th9–10

Required Text **(available at the SMU bookstore)**

Masters of British Literature, **Volumes A & B, ed. Damrosch et al.**
(Pearson/Longman)

Course Description

This course is a one-semester introductory overview of British
literature, from its Medieval beginnings to (almost) the present
day, with special attention to literature's role as an instrument of
various forms of desire and power. As we survey this history, we will
consider not just great literature, but also its relation to the social,
political, intellectual, and religious histories in which it was written.
We will also offer multiple opportunities for improving your writing
and the grades you get on it. After successfully completing this
course, students should be able to

207

- identify several formal elements in a work of literature;
- write an analysis of an interpretive problem in a work of literature;
- demonstrate knowledge of major periods, authors, genres, and texts of British literature;
- explain some of the relationships among these; and
- write an acceptable essay addressing a literary topic.

Grading. **The tentative grade breakdown is as follows:**

Essays (total)	30%
Midterm Exam	15%
Final Exam	25%
Quizzes (total)	10%
Attendance, participation, etc.	20%
	100%

• • •

Schedule of Assignments
(* denotes a scheduled quiz day; there will be at least 5 others)

Important Note: These may be changed or supplemented as the semester progresses. Read the introductory headnotes for all assigned authors, and assume that the whole text (and/or author) is assigned unless otherwise specified.

Important Note 2: All "Lecture" and "Lecture/Discussion" meetings and exams will meet in McCord auditorium (DH306). Friday "Discussion" meetings will meet in Hyer 102 (Booker section) and Hyer 204 (Schott section).

Important Note 3: Our readings are pretty short, but they should take some time. Read the texts and notes carefully, and think about what issues, conflicts, or problems they present us with. Note anything that is particularly interesting or difficult. Look up and learn the meaning[s] of any words you don't know.

January 18—Introduction

The Middle Ages

20—Reading: *The Dream of the Rood* (p. 110), *The Wanderer* (115), *Wulf and Eadwacer* and *The Wife's Lament* (118)
Lecture (Rosendale): Old English and ancient British history

Week 2

23—Reading: Marie de France, *Lais* (124–44)
Lecture (Schott): Bad Romance and Good Knights: Love in the Arthurian Tradition
*25—Reading: *Sir Gawain and the Green Knight*, part 1 (pp. 144–57)
Lecture/Discussion
27—Discussion

Week 3

30—Reading: General Prologue from Chaucer's *Canterbury Tales*, lines 1–271, 447–543, 625–744 (all between pp. 220–54, but note: this is a side-by-side version in Middle and modern English; feel free to use it [or the Harvard Chaucer page at http://www.courses.fas.harvard.edu/~chaucer/teachslf/gp-par.htm], but do read as much of the Middle English as you need to feel comfortable and be able to answer questions on it) and Chaucer's Retraction (pp. 326–27)
Lecture (Rosendale): Reading Chaucer: Irony, Critique, Humor
February* 1—Reading: *The Wife of Bath's Prologue and Tale* (pp. 277–305; this is the heaviest reading day of the semester, so leave yourself plenty of time. Under the same conditions as above, you may use http://www.courses.fas.harvard.edu/~chaucer/teachslf/wbt-par.htm)
Lecture (Booker): Unruly Women and "wikked wives": Gender and Power in the Middle Ages
3—Discussion

Week 4

6—Reading: Langland, from *Piers Plowman* (pp. 328–45); *The York Play of the Crucifixion* (8 pages, on Bb)

Lecture (Rosendale): Making sense in/of *Piers Plowman* and *YPC*
8—Reading: Margery Kempe, pp. 378–85; other selections on Bb
Lecture (Schott): Medieval English Mysticism
10—Discussion

Reformation, Renaissance, Restoration

Week 5

13—Reading: Wyatt (pp. 437–40), Surrey ("Love that doth reign" and
"Wyatt Resteth Here")
Lecture (Rosendale): Humanism and Reformation
15—Reading: Spenser, *The Faerie Queene* I.i (pp. 462–76); Queen
Elizabeth I, Tilbury and Golden speeches (683–85)
Lecture (Booker): Fairies, Queens, and English Renaissance Ideals
17—Discussion; *Essay 1 due*

Week 6

20—Reading: Spenser, *Amoretti* 65, 68, 75 (pp. 611–13); Sidney,
Astrophil & Stella 1, 45, 52, 63 (pp. 648–51); Shakespeare, Sonnets 1,
73, 87, 130, 138 (pp. 773–80);
Lecture (Rosendale): Desire, Failure, and the Renaissance Sonnet
22—Reading: Wroth, sonnets 1, 5, 16 (p. 900); Donne, *Holy Sonnets*
4, 5, 10 (pp. 895–97); Milton, "To the Lord General Cromwell" and
"When I Consider How My Light is Spent" (943–44)
Lecture/Discussion
24—Discussion

Week 7

27—Reading: Marlowe, *Doctor Faustus*, Acts 1, 2, and 5 (pp. 704–23,
746–53)
Lecture (Schott): Marlowe and Faustus
*29—Reading: Donne, "Song," "Love's Alchemy," "The Flea,"
"Valediction: Forbidding Mourning," Elegy 19, additional poems
on Bb
Lecture (Rosendale): Donne and Dirty Theology
March 2—Discussion

Week 8

5—Reading: Herbert, "Easter Wings," "Jordan 2," "The Collar," "The Altar"; Lanyer, pp. 696–701; Herrick, "To the Virgins," "Upon Julia's Clothes" (908–9); Marvell, "To His Coy Mistress" (922)
Lecture/Discussion
7—Discussion and Review
9—*Midterm Exam*
March 12–16: Spring Break

Week 9

*19—Reading: Milton, *Paradise Lost*, 1.1–375 and 522–end, Bb selections from Book 4
Lecture (Rosendale): Satanic Milton, or, Sympathy for the Devil
21—Reading: *Paradise Lost* 9.99–178, 455–895; Behn, "The Disappointment" (1071); Wilmot, "The Disabled Debauchee" (1082)
Lecture/Discussion
23—Discussion

The Eighteenth Century

Week 10

26—Reading: Johnson, Preface to the *Dictionary* (Bb); periodical essays (pp. 1184–88, 1190–92)
Lecture (Booker): Reason and Reading in the English Enlightenment
28—Reading: Swift, *A Modest Proposal* (1287–94); pp. 1194–99
Lecture/Discussion (Rosendale): Urbanity, Satire, and *South Park*
30—Discussion; *Essay 2 Due*

Week 11

April 2—Reading: Pope, *Rape of the Lock*
Lecture (Rosendale): Understanding Pope and mock epic
4—Reading: Swift & Montagu, pp. 1224–30
Lecture/Discussion
6—Good Friday—No Class

The Nineteenth Century
(switch to anthology Volume B!)

Week 12

9—Reading: Wordsworth, "Lines written a few miles above Tintern
Abbey," "The World is Too Much With Us," "London, 1802,"
"Nutting," and pp. B198–200; Coleridge, "Kubla Khan" and "This
Lime-Tree Bower My Prison"
Lecture (Rosendale): Romantic Anti-Rationalism
11—Reading: Byron, Dedication to Don Juan (pp. 409–15); Shelley, "To
Wordsworth," "Ozymandias," "Ode to the West Wind," "To a Sky-
Lark"; Keats, "La belle dame sans merci," "Ode on a Grecian Urn,"
"When I Have Fears that I May Cease to Be"
Lecture/Discussion: Romanticism 2.0
13—Discussion

Week 13

16—Reading:
Tennyson, "The Lady of Shalott," "Ulysses," *In Memoriam A.H.H.* 1–8,
54–57, 95
Arnold, "Dover Beach" (plus Hecht's "Dover Bitch")
Lecture (Booker): "Red in Tooth and Claw": Looking Backwards and
Forwards in the Victorian Era
*18—Reading: R. Browning, "My Last Duchess," "Porphyria's Lover"
C. Rossetti, "Goblin Market"
Hopkins, "God's Grandeur," "Pied Beauty," "No Worst, There is None"
Lecture/Discussion
20—Discussion

The Twentieth Century

Week 14

23—Reading:
Yeats, "Easter 1916," "The Second Coming," "Sailing to Byzantium,"
"Leda and the Swan"; Joyce, "Araby"; Eliot, "The Love Song of J.
Alfred Prufrock," "Journey of the Magi"
Lecture (Schott): Collapse and Rebuilding: Foundations of Modernism
25—Reading: Eliot, "Tradition and the Individual Talent"; Woolf, from
A Room of One's Own, pp. 1303–11
Lecture/Discussion
27—Discussion; *Essay 3 due*

Week 15

30—Reading: Auden, "Musee des Beaux Arts"
Thomas, "Fern Hill"
Beckett, video viewing of *Waiting for Godot*
Larkin, "Church Going"
Heaney, "Punishment"
Bennett, "Colonization in Reverse"
Walcott, "A Far Cry from Africa"
Boland, "Anorexic"
Lecture/Discussion
May 1 *(Tuesday, but Friday class schedule)*—Review and Conclusion

Re-Visioning the American Literature Survey for Teachers and Other Wide-Awake Humans

JOHN A. STAUNTON

The eye is the first circle;
the horizon which it forms is the second;
and throughout nature this primary figure is repeated without end.[1]

First Impressions, Loomings, and Circles of Inquiry

It is a cold January evening in 2016, and I am meeting for the first time with my graduate students in a survey course in American Renaissance Literature: 1830-1860. We are a small but eclectic group, occupying multiple spheres as teachers, students, professionals, and citizens of the world. In our overlapping circles, we are writing instructors, teacher educators, caregivers, physicians, and mathematicians; creative writers, future high school teachers, scholars, and parents. The students represent four different graduate programs in our department (Children's Literature, Creative Writing, English Education, Literature), and I represent two (Literature and English Education). We are eyeing each other a little warily, sizing up the situation, and wondering if we have made a dreadful mistake.

That's in part due to the fact that the announced shared texts we have for the day—sent by me over the semester break as a sort of holiday reading—have suddenly multiplied. The Etymologies, Extracts, and first several chapters of *Moby-Dick* up to Ishmael's own first meeting with Queequeg at The Spouter-Inn—roused from peaceful sleep by the late-night materialization of his cannibal roommate—are now joined by three new texts students haven't prepared for—an image, a short instrumental piece of music, and a brief excerpt from a philosophical essay. As we prepare to talk about our first encounters with *Moby-Dick*, and introduce ourselves to each other in our shared enterprise for the

214

semester, I display these new texts from three separate sign systems. These are *transmediations*, which have been selected to create a multimodal aesthetic experience connected to our shared work in the course.

The use of transmediations has been a long-standing practice of mine that derives from and adapts research in new literacies studies, multimodality, and aesthetic education to reimagine the work of literature pedagogy at secondary, postsecondary, and graduate levels. As Peggy Albers notes of English teacher education programs, designing curriculum around multimodal sign systems allows teachers and students to draw upon multiple "modes of communication . . . to interpret and represent meaning" and to underscore for users of new literacies that "meaning is not located within any one mode, but in how modes are interpreted in relation to each other."[2] When we allow students to both recognize and mobilize—to read and to create—multiple sign systems to get at their understanding of the textual, curricular, and social worlds around them, we engage them in both an aesthetic and metacognitive process, "looking through the lenses of various ways of knowing, seeing, and feeling in a conscious endeavor to change perspective on the world."[3]

These ways of knowing are not to be confused with the language of "learning styles," which may seek to essentialize or instrumentalize different instruction for different kinds of learners. Rather, as Jerome Harste argues, sign systems are best understood as affordances and social practices, and that "the use of multiple sign systems enhances everyone's learning as well as meaning making."[4] Nor should they be seen as areas of concern outside the domain of literature courses and their faculty, for any course that includes teacher candidates or that is required for licensing and certification programs per force becomes a course modeling pedagogy and literature pedagogy in particular. Or at the very least, I tell my students, any course that is taught by someone like myself who lives in both programs can't help but spend some time focusing on the *how* and *why* as well as the *what* of teaching American literature. My own practice of limiting transmediations to *image-music-text* risks privileging those modes over others like dance or mathematical equations, say, but as an attempt to draw upon the *at hand* literacies and sign systems teachers and students from diverse backgrounds confront every day, I have restricted my classes to just these three to make the most use of the generative possibilities of multimodal teaching and learning.

The transmediations I have selected for this first class[5] also model how I will invite students to use them on their own. Each time students will offer a transmediation of their own they will include a short written rationale to connect their text to our shared readings for the day. Thomas Cole's painting (*A View from Mt. Holyoke*, 1836) predates Melville's novel, and offers a visual thematization of some core course concepts about nature and the sublime; the short excerpt above from Emerson's essay "Circles" (1841), points toward the philosophical and nonfictional discourses that surround Melville and his readers, and connects to specific language from our readings (we will also read the essay in its entirety in the coming weeks). But transmediations need not be entirely historical or contemporaneous pieces—and in fact, usually are not—so the musical piece, "First Impressions" from Yo Yo Ma, Edgar Meyer, and Mark O'Connor's 1996 collaboration, *Appalachia Waltz*, is offered both as an example of connecting past and present discourses and as a way to talk about mood, tone, and compositional elements of repetition and rotation. Taken together with the shared text, they refigure the opening minutes of the class as a sort of improvised work of art, a one-time installation or makeshift "happening," calling for interpretation.

Unsettling Prospects and "Wide-Awake" Reading

Conversation is a game of circles. . . .
All that we have reckoned settled shakes and rattles;
and literature, cities, climates, religions,
leave their foundations, and dance before our eyes.[6]

While we look, listen, and read, I instruct the class to "notice what you notice" about these texts—including the shared readings from Melville—and to "notice what you notice about your *thinking* **now**" about these texts. They are directives common to aesthetic education and are designed to resist what Chris Higgins observes as the return of the instrumentalist approach to education that besets so much of twenty-first-century educational discourse.[7] My own notes during this opening engagement focus on Ishmael and Queequeg and how we go about forming impressions and knowledge of each other and our shared worlds. I find myself alternately positioning myself and my students as first Ishmael, then Queequeg, unsettled and amused by the notion of the literature classroom as a balance between friendship and cannibalism. My students proceed with equal caution, a few even punctuating their initial observations of the experience with the discursive escape clause: "if that is what you want us to be getting." I give a pedagogical shrug and allow the question to echo back to them: "Who else would like to share?" The conversation turns to a focus on the circular compositional components in Cole's painting—the loop of the ox-bow, the arc of birds in flight—and someone even stands to physically trace upon the projection screen the rippling path of the viewer's eye the painting invites, his hands making temporary shadows of our thinking.

Focusing on Cole's masterpiece leads us to Ishmael's own musings on the pull of water on the wandering or aesthetic mind, Melville clearly invoking a later work by Cole (*A View of the Mountain Pass Called the Notch of the White Mountains (Crawford Notch)* [1839]:

> But here is an artist. He desires to paint you the dreamiest, shadiest, quietest, most enchanting bit of romantic landscape. . . . What is the chief element he employs? There stand his trees . . . here sleeps his meadow. . . . But though the picture lies thus tranced . . . yet all were in vain unless the shepherd's eye were fixed upon the magic stream before him.[8]

But hold! another student calls; this aesthetic reverie comes with its own caution, pointing us to the rest of the passage in which Ishmael's thoughts eventually flow to Narcissus, "who because he could not grasp the tormenting, mild image he saw in the fountain, plunged into it and was drowned." Another student continues Melville's passage: "But that same image, we *ourselves* see in all rivers and oceans. It is the image of the ungraspable phantom of life; and *this* is the key to it all."[9] Teetering on the edge of the next turn in the conversation, we all stand silent for a bit wondering just what to do with this metaphor. Our former math major, now a first-year writing instructor and creative writer, offers some clarity to pull us back from our interpretive precipice: a circle is the perfect equation, he intones matter-of-factly; the remark perhaps a plea not to let ourselves get too serious, here. When pressed, he actually produces the general definition almost verbatim, a circle is "all the points (x,y) on a plane that are a fixed distance (r) from a center (a,b)." And just like that we are back to Emerson, the end of one series beginning a new series—eye, horizon, nature, art and perception, repeated, not exactly without end, but so long as our minds and bodies allow, tucked away into an interior, windowless classroom, held captive by stimulating conversation and pre-molded, industrial chair-desks.

The opening engagement for the course has certainly called us to new reckonings through these transmediations, but the question remains: What exactly have we unsettled for ourselves or the enterprise of teaching American literature? Beginning a class with intellectual improvisation and invention such as the image, music, text transmediations afford certainly creates risk for teacher and students embarking on a new semester, for there is no way to know for sure where the circuit of inquiry will lead. When students themselves become the co-curators of these engagements as they do later in the semester, the classroom generates what Fecho, Graham, and Hudson-Ross call a productive "wobble" in our pedagogy and curriculum, which can make visible the figured worlds we construct as teachers and learners.[10]

What my graduate students and I were pursuing through our weekly trans-mediations was just this sort of "wobble-y" stance to both curriculum and pedagogy that put student inquiry about their experiences with literary history at the fore of the course design. Or, to extend the metaphor offered through my student's equation, we allowed a presumed curricular center point to arc out beyond the teacherly fixed point (a,b) to take up position along the learners' (x,y) trajectories. This is not to say that I didn't have institutional expectations (MA Exam readings lists, catalog descriptions, for instance) or my own inquiries or interests shaping the course as well. In fact, Melville figured so centrally this first day only because I had finally committed myself after nearly twenty years of teaching American Literature to find a way to have students read *Moby-Dick* in a period survey class. It is a text I myself had not read in full since high school, and probably then leapfrogging entirely over the sections like the etymologies and extracts I've started with today.

Taking as our cue the stand-alone (likely promotional) publication of "The Town-Ho's Story" in *Harper's Monthly* (October 1851), we allowed the fifteen weeks of the semester to configure a serialized version of *Moby-Dick*, combining weekly chunks of Melville with an admixture of essays, sketches, histories, and fictions in the style of the mid-nineteenth-century American magazines.[11] Students would also read the novel with a partner, sharing a dialogue journal in which they posed questions to each other about the novel, their insights, and struggles. The successive novel chapters alternately served as thematic lead-in or typesetter's filler to our shared reading of Douglass, Emerson, Fuller, Kirkland, Howe, and others. The *student* transmediations, then, became the productive and generative links that bound those issues and themes together, allowing students' interests and questions to direct my weekly pedagogical work. By engaging what Sheridan Blau calls "cold readings" of simultaneous student transmedi-ations, I was able to make visible my own performative literacies of meaning making, transferring what I know about one text in the service of understanding a new text, and to suggest ways in which those understandings can extend to other, as yet unexperienced, contexts. As Blau argues, this sort of transfer is made possible through the metacognitive demands that reading complex texts—particularly literary texts—entails. Such intensive reading practices "typically defamiliarize commonplace experience and thereby demand intense, sustained, and wide-awake attention; a tolerance for ambiguity and paradox; and a capacity to endure feelings of confusion and failure that can be productively addressed through multiple-re-readings and a continuing dialogue with the text and other readers of it."[12] The transmediations can certainly create moments of confusion and failure, but they are also designed to be low-stakes moments of exploratory thinking, reminders to "stay woke" to the possibility of new discoveries.

Snap the Whip, But Don't Carry It All

The transition is a keen one,
I assure you, from a schoolmaster to a sailor,
and requires a strong decoction of Seneca
and the Stoics to enable you to grin and bear it.
But even this wears off in time.[13]

In Emerson's language, these transmediations revealed just some among the many intersecting circles of inquiry directing our paths through American literary history over the course of the semester. In the weeks that followed, students drew from their prior knowledge of literary, musical, artistic, and scientific texts to inflect our understanding of antebellum American literature. For instance, our reading of Caroline Kirkland's *A New Home, Who'll Follow?* (1839) was framed by student selections of Winslow Homer's *Snap the Whip* (1870), an excerpt from *Gilgamesh* (c. 1200 BCE), and The Decemberists' "Don't Carry It All" (2011), allowing us to consider the odd ways in which Kirkland's nascent realism troubles the nationalizing narratives of community, progress, and development. The selections also showed an intellectual dexterity among the students to push each other beyond their strict program, cultural, and generational comfort zones not by trying to figure out "what you want us to be getting" or simply asserting a position, but by staking a claim about their own experiences and understandings and trying to invite others into these previously limited domains they had perhaps kept to themselves. By the time we got to Julia Ward Howe's *The Hermaphrodite* (2004 [c. 1846/47]) a few weeks later, my retired physician's text transmediation on the medical history of intersex joined the future English teacher's contemporary piano and cello duet, and the children's literature student's selection from a contemporary French landscape photographer. Each student would potentially have had those associations at hand for individual understandings, but the transmediations helped make that private thinking visible and generated new opportunities for the rest of us to look, listen, and read again.

But while I was having this success thinking pedagogically about American literary history with the transmediations, I was also hearing grumblings about

Moby-Dick (particularly in regard to the long discursive chapters on whaling). For some, it was a six-hundred-page burden made bearable only by the sense of obligation to keep up with one's partner and not leave them adrift. The transmediations then also come out of and perhaps reveal traces of those parallel struggles and resistances: arcane mathematical number sets; murder ballads; and alabaster busts of blind students. And when they do, those transmediations force me to reckon with my own assumptions about "what it is I want them to be getting," another uncomfortable pedagogical "wobble" in which my serializing enterprise is refigured as Ahab's mad pursuit of the white whale. In our end-of-course reflections on both the paired reading and transmediations, however, several students found in the novel other passages and images that captured their more positive experience with distributing the burden of making meaning. They also linked back to a number of the student transmediations they had shared over the semester. Their prior academic experience may have reinforced their sense of being "*Isolatoes . . .* not acknowledging the common continent of men, but each *Isolato* living on a separate continent of his own,"[14] or if "federated" at all, only in the service of some professorial Ahab's grievances. But this experience of reading with strangers and making meaning from unfamiliar texts and practices likewise called them back to reading as a kind of friendship and communion with the texts and other readers, joined in an Ishmael-Queequeg encounter, in which the weight and touch of another's presence gives shape and contour to the patchwork text they share.

Reinventing the Survey for Teacher Candidates

Are you he who would assume a place to teach or be a poet here in the States? The place is august, the terms obdurate.[15]

At the 2013 National Conference of Teachers of English (NCTE) Convention, I chaired a panel with several of the current contributors to this volume, titled, Re-Inventing the Literature Survey for English/Education. Reinvention was the convention theme that year, and we thought it an apt way of describing the practices we had begun to employ across our respective classrooms and programs. When teacher candidates enter a survey class—whether graduate or undergraduate—that class per force becomes a site where students must navigate the confluence of content standards, literary studies, and pedagogical training. Acknowledging that we in fact have students on different program paths allows us to consider how the teaching of content fits within larger disciplinary and institutional structures.

Prior to the session, I presented the short excerpt from Whitman above to participants on the conference blog site with this invitation:

1. Consider what this question and observation mean for you in your own teaching context. What might they mean for your students?
2. Share that understanding in the comments by uploading a text, image, or short clip of music.

The responses in the comment thread from teachers and former students—now new teachers—was instructive, tapping into the often ambivalent and antagonistic relationship that exists between teachers and students. Matt, nearly finished with his student teaching semester, linked a "colorized" image of Whitman and U2's "Who's Gonna Ride Your Wild Horses" to help him get at what was so "august" and "obdurate" about his students.

> A few weeks ago, I had a student tell me to stop getting so *excited* when they contribute ideas to our discussion about literature because they know I'm not *actually* surprised or interested. I'm reminded of that animosity by both of these pieces, because who are we to assume that we belong in a classroom? That students should listen to us? That what we have to say is worthwhile? We see ourselves as "august" (inspiring awe) but maybe to our students we're "obdurate" (stubborn)—or maybe they're stubborn.[16]

The consistency of entrenched positions—on teaching, learning, curriculum—offers a certain comfort for us and our students in our classrooms, for if things remain as they have been, we always know where we stand. The American Literature survey—at whatever level—in particular has the capacity to ignore contemporary anxieties about who counts in today's schools by reinforcing dominant nationalizing narratives of the "true American."

My undergraduate American Literature survey syllabus offers another set of encounters that student transmediations help complicate for future teachers. An early semester pairing (following the Martin Luther King holiday) from Columbus's "Voyages" and Wheatley's "On Being Brought from Africa to America" was inflected by two additional student texts: a nineteenth-century engraving depicting the news of The Emancipation Proclamation in a plantation church with Emily Dickinson's contemporary poem, "Mine—by the Right of White Election!" The ensuing discussion alternately expanded and contracted on history, literary form, and their legacies, all the while maintaining a focus on what it meant to be teachers and future teachers in America. Our later reading of Pauline Hopkins's *Peculiar Sam: Or, The Underground Railroad*

(1879), a play written to be performed by the family minstrel troupe ("the Hopkins' Colored Troubadours") used the transmediations to reimagine the deafening silence of the musical and dance interludes bracketed in the stage directions of the modern reprint. Such interpretive forays among undergraduate English majors—especially those training to become English teachers—help students grow from information-gathering to understanding, for in the act of transmediation they move "mere" content knowledge toward connected content knowledge and eventually to an emergent content pedagogy.

Imagining the Future Student in a Teacherless Landscape

People wish to be settled;
only as far as they are unsettled is there any hope for them.[17]

In 2013 I was invited by the ADE to deliver a state of the field address on English Education. The unsettling news I had then has not changed much. Most English Education positions continue to be in comprehensive, regional, public universities like mine, which have sizable, but rarely residential, student populations. Administrative costs carve away at educational budgets, and faculty are literally asked to do more with less. They are positions that require working in partnership with schools in communities that run the spectrum of college and career readiness. Those public schools themselves are often underfunded, understaffed, and deeply suspicious of yet another quick-fix solution from state or university educators. They are similarly under fire by the sort of political and public discourse my students invoked above, a discourse that is demeaning and unsupportive of the work teachers do.

So, it's difficult to argue that simply inviting students to share an image, a piece of music, and a short text at the start of a survey class will radically alter the material conditions of our profession. In fact, there are powerful forces at work to change secondary and postsecondary education—their motives and even their identities not always transparent—but the likely effect of their agenda seems clear: less autonomy and protection for teachers, fewer opportunities to engage or produce texts meaningfully, more fragmentation, and less oversight and control of teaching and learning at local levels. That doesn't mean it is not worth doing or that innovative challenges to status quo teaching should simply cave to the pressures of management, caste, and comparison. As Harste notes, literacies are social practices, and as such carry social values that may be obstacles or opportunities; "regardless of the modalities we value, literacy cuts some people in while it cuts other people out."[18] Sometimes, and with all of these caveats and cautions in sight, it is exactly such a multitextual approach that our teaching and students need.

This fall my campus has been victim to multiple incidents of racist vandalism targeting African American students, epithets and threats spray-painted and hand-scrawled on the walls of classroom buildings, in several dorms, and on the elevators, including one a week before the November election: "N****** Go Home." At a faculty-student rally in a courtyard dedicated to Dr. Martin Luther King, outside the School of Art Building, which was the site of the most recent vandalism, an art student's comment underscored the difficulty students had feeling welcome in either the classrooms or curriculum when encounters with diversity too often fall into catchall courses or electives and when students and teachers both avoid talking about anything unsettling, falling lazily into the consistency of traditional course content. The result was a pedagogical silence from many faculty, and growing class absences by African American students, including my own.

In my own course later that day—a writing-intensive gateway course for majors introducing students to literary theory as a lens on literature and culture—I had a decision to make. Three students who were scheduled to make a presentation on Queer Studies and Feminism had asked for a last-minute postponement to the following week. So, cancel class? workshop upcoming papers? or review theoretical approaches? The previous class session I had just introduced feminist criticism with transmediations spinning off Rose Terry Cooke's 1886 poem "Arachne." And the next week students would initiate their final inquiry projects by starting with their own transmediations. I quickly assembled a new set of texts to capture something of the events that had been plaguing our campus all semester and my own multimodal response to the troubling sense that traditional pedagogy and curricular designs were failing to respond to real student need. I titled it "Incident, Lineage, Masks"[19] and invited students to choose an image—Charles McGee's *Lineage* (2008) or Kehinde Wiley's *Officer of the Hussars* (2007)—and text—Paul Laurence Dunbar's "We Wear the Mask" (1896) or Countee Cullen's "Incident" (1924)—to accompany their listening to the "Memphis Blues" (1972) performed by Phineas Newborn Jr. (1931–89) and written [1912] by W. C. Handy (1873–1958). The dates established a certain history and provenance of the works I wanted students to have available to them.

Before beginning, I let students know where I had just been and that I had assembled the transmediations as an invitation to them to think through their own experiences over the last several weeks in the class, on campus, and/or in the world. Their opening instructions were very similar to those I had giving my graduate students in January, simply to "look, listen, read, and then look again. Then consider your responses." I offered my undergraduates four ways to enter into conversation with these new texts, since the only shared text we had was the imperfect experience of life as Eastern Michigan students/faculty in Fall 2016: a connection to their lives or to other texts; a question about the texts; a surprise they encountered reading, viewing, listening; and an extension to teaching or literary study. Though students were actively engaged in the invitation and animated in small-group discussion, they were nonetheless reluctant to share with the whole class. So, I gave them some historical contexts for the work and began to explain my own four points.

McGee's *Lineage* is a significant late sculptural work by a major African American artist, who happened to have been a professor at Eastern for many years. It sits right outside the student center in the heart of campus, and yet despite passing it virtually every week, students either claimed to have never seen it or not to have bothered to look more closely. Indeed, the university's own stock image of the sculpture features a student walking by the artwork, back to the viewer, head down lost in other concerns. I shared my own responses, which included a story about institutional thresholds, racial profiling, and canons of American literature I've written about before. In sharing that story with my students, I described my own struggle to acknowledge the unseen access or privilege I have to notice (or not) other texts, traditions, and perspectives. But I also was aware of the student silence, and I acknowledged that as someone whose work involves training future English teachers, I had the obligation to notice (or not) what masks my students have to wear to get by. The time ran away from us, and the students preparing for the presentation on Queer Studies promised these issues of noticing who counts and how in literature and culture would inform their presentation. And then they left.

I'm not sure if what we did would warrant an equivalency to a course that dutifully moved from one theoretical school to the next or that moved from transcendentalism to realism, or if it would demonstrate how students possessed content knowledge of a range of literary genres and periods—all possible external or administrative assessments of what a survey might do. And I'm not sure it matters. I'd like to think that the experience was something that would let them enter their own figured worlds of American literature, literary study, teacher education, or other landscape beyond the horizon of my classroom. Armed with knowledge and understanding of how texts and their readers speak to each other, carry other texts and their readers within them, even when there is no longer some teacher to keep directing them, they are ready to make those worlds habitable and companionable places to pursue inquiry together, whether with friends or strangers.

NOTES

1. Ralph Waldo Emerson, "Circles," *The Complete Works of Ralph Waldo Emerson*, vol. 2, *Essays* (1841; Boston: Houghton Mifflin, 1882), http://www.rwe.org/x-circles/.

2. Peggy Albers, "Imagining the Possibilities in Multimodal Curriculum Design," *English Education* 38, no. 2 (2006): 77.

3. Peggy Albers and Jerome Harste, "The Arts, New Literacies, and Multimodality," *English Education* 40, no. 1 (2007): 9.

4. Jerome Harste, "Multimodality," in *Literacies, the Arts, and Multimodality*, ed. Peggy Albers and Jennifer Sanders (Urbana: NCTE, 2010), 30.

5. John Staunton, "First Impressions, Loomings, Circles," in *Teaching Literature/Inquiry in Community: Notes on Pedagogy, Literature, and Teacher Inquiry*, http://johnastaunton.blogspot.com/2016/02/first-impressions-loomings-and-circles.html.

6. Emerson, "Circles."

7. Chris Higgins, "Instrumentalism and the Clichés of Aesthetic Education," *Education and Culture* 24, no. 1 (2008): 6.

8. Herman Melville, *Moby-Dick, Or, The Whale* (1851; New York: Penguin, 2003), 4–5.

9. Ibid., 5; emphasis added.

10. Bob Fecho, Peg Graham, and Sally Hudson-Ross, "Appreciating the Wobble: Teacher Research, Professional Development, and Figured Worlds," *English Education* 37, no. 3 (2005): 175.

11. I drew upon a group assignment I use in my late-nineteenth-century American Realism and Naturalism class in which student teams read the serialized versions of short novels by Henry James, Sarah Orne Jewett, Julia Magruder, Mark Twain, as well as the literary, cultural, and political features and ephemera surrounding those serializations in *Harper's*, *The Atlantic*, and *The Century*.

12. Sheridan Blau, "Literary Competence and the Experience of Literature," *Style* 48 (2014): 44.

13. Melville, *Moby-Dick*, 6.

14. Ibid., 131.

15. Walt Whitman, "By Blue Ontario's Shore," Section 12, *The Walt Whitman Archive*, ed. Ed Folsom and Kenneth Price, Center for Digital Research in the Humanities, University of Nebraska–Lincoln, http://whitmanarchive.org/published/LG/1881/poems/197.

16. John Staunton, "Transmediating the Survey for Teacher Candidates—An Invitation for #NCTE13," in *Teaching Literature/Inquiry in Community*, http://johnastaunton.blogspot.com/2013/11/transmediating-survey-for-teacher.html.

17. Emerson, "Circles."

18. Harste, "Multimodality," 31.

19. John Staunton, "Incident, Lineage, Masks," in *Teaching Literature/Inquiry in Community*, http://johnastaunton.blogspot.com/2017/05/incidents-lineage-masks.html.

BIBLIOGRAPHY

Albers, Peggy. "Imagining the Possibilities in Multimodal Curriculum Design." *English Education* 38, no. 2 (2006): 75–101.

Albers, Peggy, and Jerome Harste. "The Arts, New Literacies, and Multimodality." *English Education* 40, no. 1 (2007): 6–20.

Albers, Peggy, and Jennifer Sanders, eds. *Literacies, The Arts, and Multimodality.* Urbana: NCTE, 2010.

Blau, Sheridan. "Literary Competence and the Experience of Literature." *Style* 48 (2014): 42–47.

Emerson, Ralph Waldo. "Circles." *The Complete Works of Ralph Waldo Emerson.* Vol. 2, *Essays.* 1841. Boston: Houghton Mifflin, 1882. http://www.rwe.org/x-circles/.

Fecho, Bob, Peg Graham, and Sally Hudson-Ross. "Appreciating the Wobble: Teacher Research, Professional Development, and Figured Worlds." *English Education* 37, no. 3 (2005): 174–99.

Harste, Jerome. "Multimodality." In *Literacies, The Arts, and Multimodality,* edited by Peggy Albers and Jennifer Sanders, 27–43. Urbana: NCTE, 2010.

Higgins, Chris. "Instrumentalism and the Clichés of Aesthetic Education." *Education and Culture* 24, no. 1 (2008): 6–19.

Melville, Herman. *Moby-Dick or, The Whale.* 1851. New York: Penguin, 2003.

Staunton, John. *Teaching Literature/Inquiry in Community: Notes on Pedagogy, Literature, and Teacher Inquiry.* http://johnastaunton.blogspot.com/.

Whitman, Walt. "By Blue Ontario's Shore." *The Walt Whitman Archive,* edited by Ed Folsom and Kenneth Price. Center for Digital Research in the Humanities, University of Nebraska–Lincoln. http://whitmanarchive.org/published/LG/1881/poems/197.

ENGAGEMENTS/INQUIRIES

1. Dialogue Journals/Shared Reading & Reflective Essay (150 pts)

At the beginning of the semester you will each find a partner to read *Moby-Dick* with you. Together you will read this text on your own (using the schedule I've established on the syllabus as a guide), keeping an ongoing reading response log of your experience. This log should take the form of a *dialogue journal* in which you write "response letters" to each other about your reading. These letters do not need to take a particular form, but they should be substantive and engage the text(s) and the other reader in conversation about the work(s) as well as make connections to relevant readings from the course (between 150 and 200 words per "letter" is a good range). You will be expected to exchange these journals at least every time we meet in class (though you may of course do so more frequently). You will write a reflective essay analyzing and evaluating the experience of reading the novel in this way and with this partner.

2. "Time-Travel" Reading (150 pts)

In addition to the semester-long dialogue journal reading described above, you and up to 3 other members of the class will choose to read (together) two consecutive issues of one of the four periodicals above (*The United States Democratic Review, The Dial, The Atlantic Monthly, Putnam's Monthly*). This reading will be conducted outside of our regular meeting times and will be coordinated by the members of each group according to particular reading roles. On the days designated on the schedule, your group will come to class prepared with a 300–500-word written brief, reporting on your selected journals, and an artifact(s) (can be edible) that will engage the rest of the class in some pertinent issue(s) or feature(s) of your periodical. You must bring copies of this brief for the rest of the class and be prepared to field questions about your report.

3. Image-Music-Text Artifacts/Transmediations (150 pts; 3 @ 50 pts each)

Starting the third week of the semester and continuing through the end of the semester, you will have the opportunity to demonstrate and share your understanding of the readings through an artifact or *transmediation* (from one of three different sign systems). NOTE: a transmediation is not simply a representation but offers an interpretation or critical perspective on the text. You are responsible for 3 such transmediations by the end of the semester, and each should be accompanied by a 1-page rationale/explanation linking your image, music, or text to the work we are reading. For **Image:** select period or contemporary artwork (original or reproductions), film slips, photography, or other visual texts (maps, sketches, charts, graphs, etc.) Pictures of the author are **not** valid image artifacts for this assignment. For **Music:** provide a short (1–3 minutes) sample of music that is contemporary to the text we are reading, that is more recent but which attempts to portray that era of the text, or that captures for you something of the themes or features of the text we are reading. For **Text:** provide a short work (no more than 2 pages) in either prose or poetry; again the artifact may be period or contemporary. Any transmediation may of course be an original work of your own that takes up similar themes or issues of the text(s) we are reading. Except for **music** transmediations, provide copies of your transmediations/ artifacts and rationales for everyone in class.

Contributor Biographies

Kevin Bourque is Assistant Professor of English at Elon University, where he teaches courses on the novel, LGBTQ studies, early British literature, and the long eighteenth century. His current research links celebrity culture, the early novel, and the development of fictionality.

Gwynn Dujardin is Assistant Professor of English at Queen's University in Kingston, ON, Canada, where she teaches courses on the History of Literature in English, Renaissance Poetry and Prose, Renaissance Magic, and Edmund Spenser's *The Faerie Queene*, among other subjects. Her research focuses on sixteenth- and seventeenth-century English pedagogy, poetics, and philology. She is a three-time recipient of the Fourth-Year Choice Teaching Award, given by the graduating class to the professor who has made the most significant contribution to their education.

Joan Varnum Ferretti teaches in the Liberal Studies Program of New York University. Her article "Religious Apostasy and Market Rebellion: The Early Republic's Crises of Authority in Catharine Maria Sedgwick's *A New-England Tale; or Sketches of New-England Character and Manners* (1822)" was published in the 2013 Annual Edition of *Literature in the Early American Republic*. Her article "Assimilation and Apostasy in Catharine Maria Sedgwick's 'The Catholic Iroquois'" was published in the Summer 2010 issue of *the Pennsylvania Literary Journal*. She earned both her PhD in English and American Literature, and her MA in Creative Writing-Fiction from New York University.

Desirée Henderson is Associate Professor of English at the University of Texas Arlington. She is the author of *Grief and Genre in American Literature, 1790–1870* (Ashgate, 2011) and *How to Read a Diary: Critical Contexts and Interpretive Strategies for 21st Century Readers* (Routledge, forthcoming). She has published essays in *Early American Literature, Studies in American Fiction*, and *The Walt Whitman Quarterly Review*, among other venues, and serves as the Features Editor for *Legacy: A Journal of American Women Writers*.

MELISSA J. JONES is an Associate Professor of English at Eastern Michigan University, Ypsilanti, MI. She teaches survey classes in Renaissance literature and Shakespeare, and special topics that incorporate her research interests in early modern bodies, affects, and identities; feminist methods and practice; and transhistoricism in the classroom. She has recently taken a break from her book project, *Early Modern Pornographies: For Her Pleasure*, to focus on questions of pedagogy and humor in early modern literary studies. She is also a lover of dogs and a novice breeder of children.

JAMES M. LANG is a Professor of English and the Director of the Center for Teaching Excellence at Assumption College in Worcester, MA. He is the author of five books, the most recent of which are *Small Teaching: Everyday Lessons from the Science of Learning* (Jossey-Bass, 2016) and *Cheating Lessons: Learning from Academic Dishonesty* (Harvard University Press, 2013). Lang writes a monthly column on teaching and learning for *The Chronicle of Higher Education*; his work has been appearing in the *Chronicle* since 1999. His book reviews and public scholarship on higher education have appeared in a wide variety of newspapers and magazines, including the *Boston Globe*, *Chicago Tribune*, and *Time*.

KRISTIN LUCAS is an Associate Professor in the Department of English Studies at Nipissing University. She teaches courses in early modern drama, tragedy, and graphic narrative, and coordinates Shakespeare After School, a theater workshop for children. She has published on early modern and contemporary drama.

SCOTT L. NEWSTOK is Professor of English at Rhodes College, where he directs the Pearce Shakespeare Endowment. At Rhodes, he received the 2012 Outstanding Faculty Award and the 2016 Clarence Day Award for Outstanding Teaching. Newstok joined the Rhodes faculty after teaching at Harvard, Oberlin, Amherst, Gustavus Adolphus, and Yale. He has published three books: a scholarly edition of Kenneth Burke's Shakespeare criticism; a collection of essays on *Macbeth* and race (coedited with Ayanna Thompson); and a monograph on early modern English epitaphs. A fourth book is under advance contract from Princeton University Press: *How to Think Like Shakespeare*.

JENNIFER PAGE is an Assistant Professor of English at Northwestern Oklahoma State University. In addition to the early British literature survey, she also teaches composition, Shakespeare, world literature, popular literature, and literary theory. Her current research is focused on adaptive strategies for developmental writing classes, but she is also interested in popular culture iterations of canonical works, especially supernatural appropriations of Shakespearean texts.

TIM ROSENDALE is an Associate Professor of English at Southern Methodist University in Dallas, where he divides his pedagogical time between the undergraduate, graduate, and honors programs, and is relieved to be a former director of undergraduate studies. He is the author of *Liturgy and Literature in the Making of Protestant England* (Cambridge, 2007) and various essays and articles on early modern literature, history, and theology. His second book project (*Theology and Agency in Early Modern Literature*) is forthcoming from Cambridge University Press.

AARON ROSENFELD is an Associate Professor of English at Iona College, where he teaches classes in twentieth-century poetry, modern literature, and composition. His current scholarship focuses on the question of what it means to teach literature to non-English majors and on appreciation as an educational goal. His essays have appeared in *Twentieth Century Literature, Critical Survey*, and *Doris Lessing Studies*; a recent essay on appreciation appeared in 2017 in *Pedagogy: Critical Approaches to Teaching Literature, Language, Composition, and Culture.*

JOHN A. STAUNTON is Professor of English Education and American Literature at Eastern Michigan University, where he has served both as Coordinator of English Education and Director of Graduate Studies in English. He is the author of *Deranging English/Education: Teacher Inquiry, Literary Studies, and Hybrid Visions of "English" for 21st-century Schools* (NCTE, 2008), and his work has also appeared in *Studies in American Literature, Religion and Literature* and the *Journal of Teaching Writing*. He is a Codirector of the Eastern Michigan Writing Project, a site of the National Writing Project, and has been involved with local and national teacher research networks for the past fifteen years, most recently to support site-based teacher research and teacher inquiry groups in southeast Michigan.

CHRIS WALSH is Interim Director of the College of Arts and Sciences Writing Program at Boston University. His work has appeared in *Civil War History, Foreign Affairs, The New Republic, The New York Times, Times Higher Education*, and *The Yale Review*, among other places. His book *Cowardice: A Brief History* was published in 2014 by Princeton University Press.

SARAH FIONA WINTERS is an Associate Professor in the Department of English Studies at Nipissing University. She teaches courses in Children's Literature, Religion and Literature, and Fandom Studies. She has published on J. K. Rowling, C. S. Lewis, Suzanne Collins, and Margaret Mahy and is currently writing a book on evil in postwar British children's fantasy.

Index

education (*continued*)
  forced assimilation in, 59
  general education classroom and,
    204
  of high school students, 110, 121
  humanist grammar schools and,
    185
  mastery goals in, 110, 180
  multiple-choice testing and,
    61n11
  National Council of Teachers of
    English and, 4
  panel Re-Inventing the Literature
    Survey for English/Education
    and, 220
  poetry and, 46
  problems with institutions and, 58,
    222
  professionals in, 214
  racism and, 59
  required courses and, 201
  research on teaching and learning
    and, 4, 8
  secondary and postsecondary
    education, 222
  secondary school teachers and, 201,
    202
  skills for English programs and, 6,
    133
  students of, 147n8, 154
  students' professional lives and,
    146–47n8
  surface learning, 2, 4, 8n1
  teaching outcomes and, 182n3
  younger university students and,
    171
  See also higher education; pedagogy

*Elephants Teach: Creative Writing
  Since 1880, The* (Myers), 32
Emerson, Ralph Waldo, 31, 50, 65, 117,
  216, 218
Equiano, Olaudah, 11, 20–21
Erasmus, 33, 34, 48, 93, 126, 129n16

Four Loves, The, 161
Franklin, Benjamin, 32, 57, 59, 65,
  116
Friendship in Literature (Winters),
  153, 157, 160–62, 163, 165,
  167–69

gender
  British tradition and, 178
  in *A Doll House* (Ibsen), 159
  female authorship and, 178
  female sexual autonomy and, 126
  gender identity and, 159
  gender inequality and, 58
  Hamlet and, 120
  in historical survey courses, 196,
    197
  and the masculine self, 124, 159
  Power in the Middle Ages and, 209
  in *Romeo and Juliet* (Shakespeare),
    159
  Shakespeare's sonnets and, 186
  in "The Knight's Tale," 21
  in "The White Heron" (Jewett), 56
  women's bodies and, 122–23
Gooblar, David, 105, 106–7, 109
Graff, Gerald, 72

Hawthorne, Nathaniel, 82, 91, 118
Hemingway, Ernest, 57, 66, 83, 158,
  166

Reacting to the Past (*continued*)
  inventor of, 90–91
  learning outcomes and, 95–96
  primary source documents and, 93
  Richard III and, 92
  role-immersive game play and, 92,
    93–95
  skills developed in games and,
    88–89, 93, 95, 96
  *Stages of Power: Marlowe and
    Shakespeare*, 1592 game and, 88,
    91–97, 98n20, 98n30, 100–101
  staging scenes from plays and, 92,
    93, 94, 95
  students' engagement and, 5–6, 93,
    95, 96
  *Threshold of Democracy: Athens in
    403 BCE* game and, 88
  *Trial of Anne Hutchinson: Liberty,
    Law, and Intolerance in Puritan
    New England* game and, 91
  website of, 91
religion
  in American literature, 115, 116
  Canterbury Tales (Chaucer) and,
    16
  Christian concept of God and, 174
  Christian history and, 14, 177
    table 2
  Christianity in *Beowulf*, 190
  Christian values and, 174
  Church's preeminence in Medieval
    period and, 14–15
  conversion and, 174
  Equiano the Christian and, 20–21
  God and, 16, 174
  historical survey courses and, 196,
    197

Holy Sonnets (Donne) and, 179,
    210
  Jewish history and, 24n28
  Old Testament and, 126
  pagan values and, 174
  Piers Plowman (Langland) and, 14
  poetry and, 108
  religious pluralism and, 58
  Restoration and, 22
  *Stages of Power: Marlowe and
    Shakespeare*, 1592 game and, 92,
    93, 96
  theology and, 210
  Viking culture and, 190
  York Crucifixion play and, 177
    table 2, 209
Road, The (McCarthy), 69, 76, 82
Romeo and Juliet (Shakespeare), 120,
    121–23, 128, 136, 159, 166

Seneca, 33, 45, 46–47, 48
sexuality
  anal eroticism and, 122, 123
  early modern sexual culture and,
    125, 129n7, 159
  female sexuality, 126, 138 fig. 9
  heterosexuality, 125, 159, 163
  Lars and the Real Girl (Gillespie)
    and, 159–60
  medical history of intersex and,
    219
  poetry and, 123–25
  queerness and, 160, 163, 223, 224
  Romeo and Juliet (Shakespeare)
    and, 121–23
  sexual assault and, 126
  sexual orientation and, 163
  See also gender

transmediations, 7, 215–19, 223, 224, 227–28

Understanding by Design (Wiggins and McTighe), 57–58

What the Best College Teachers Do (Bain), 172
Whitman, Walt, 52, 65, 69, 83

American literature and, 105, 106
Re-Inventing the Literature Survey for English/Education and, 221
"Song of Myself" and, 102, 103, 104, 106, 112, 117, 119
Woolf, Virginia, 69, 76, 81, 196, 197, 212
Wordsworth, William, 3, 16, 36, 40n11, 69, 75. *See also* poetry